The Navy
Lieutenant's Wife

The Navy Lieutenant's Wife

Passion, Murder and American Justice in 1892 Yokohama

ROGER DINGMAN

McFarland & Company, Inc., Publishers
Jefferson, North Carolina

ISBN (print) 978-1-4766-9522-8
ISBN (ebook) 978-1-4766-5456-0

Library of Congress cataloging data are available

Library of Congress Control Number 2024056644

© 2025 Roger Dingman. All rights reserved

No part of this book may be reproduced or transmitted in any form or by any means, electronic or mechanical, including photocopying or recording, or by any information storage and retrieval system, without permission in writing from the publisher.

Front cover image: an illustration of Bessie Hewes Hetherington created from contemporary sources (cover art created by Kaitlin Dingman).

Printed in the United States of America

*McFarland & Company, Inc., Publishers
Box 611, Jefferson, North Carolina 28640
www.mcfarlandpub.com*

For My Family
Linda and Our Children,
Grandchildren, and Great-Grandson

Table of Contents

Preface: Bessie's Coffee 1
1. Iowa Sailor 5
2. School of the Sea 13
3. Delaware Belle 24
4. Marriage in Crisis 32
5. Fateful Journeys 40
6. Propriety and Passion 52
7. Escalation 62
8. Death 73
9. Murder 81
10. Unquiet Rest 92
11. Celebrity 99
12. Opening Day 110
13. Guilty! 120
14. Innocent! 129
15. Shipmates 138
16. Friends and Accomplices 151
17. Servants' Tales 164
18. Suspicion 174
19. Rage and Remorse 179
20. Confessions 187
21. Summing Up 194

22. Verdicts	202
23. Departures	213
24. Reconciliation?	219
25. Afterlives	233
Chapter Notes	241
Bibliography	255
Index	261

Preface: Bessie's Coffee

On a beautiful late summer morning in Seattle in September 1923, Bessie McConnaughey lingered over her morning coffee. Her husband, J.W., had gone off to work as a bank auditor. She picked up the newspaper he had brought in earlier and glanced at its headline: "DEADLY EARTHQUAKE IN JAPAN!" Over the next few days, details of the disaster trickled in, splattering into still more horrifying headlines: "TOKYO RAVAGED! DEATH AND DESTRUCTION EVERYWHERE! YOKOHAMA DESTROYED!" The city where 30 years earlier Bessie's life had changed forever was gone. She probably was one of the few people on Earth glad to see it go.[1]

For a few months in 1892, she was the most famous navy wife in the world. Bessie Hewes Hetherington. Lieutenant James Henry Hetherington, United States Navy. George Gower Robinson. One woman, her husband, and her lover locked together in a love triangle in Yokohama, Japan. James sent her and their infant daughter there so that they could be together when his ship came into its home port on the Asiatic Station. Before he arrived, Bessie caught the eye of Gower, the city's most eligible bachelor. He seduced her, fell in love, and seized every opportunity to be near her. The foreign community was scandalized. James warned the Englishman repeatedly to stop paying undue attention to his wife, but Gower could not. He was love's prisoner, unable to give Bessie up. Her husband could not abide the thought of that—and shot and killed him. That set the stage for an unprecedented murder trial in the American consular court. What came to be known as "the tragedy in Yokohama" turned into a drama that unfolded before the eyes of newspaper readers around the globe. What happened to Bessie in Yokohama all but destroyed her marriage. Then another ten years passed before she realized that the love affair there made it impossible for her to continue as a navy wife.

She lived on for another decade after the earthquake, but the story of the tragedy in Yokohama all but died. It lay buried, the transcript of a long-ago murder trial, in the archives of Columbia University Law School. More than a century later, legal scholars found it, recognized its value as a textbook, and reprinted it in *Making of the Modern Law, Trials, 1600–1926*. I stumbled onto the text while working on a projected history of the United States Navy in Japan. Once I started reading it, I was hooked. Here was a compelling true story historians in America and Japan had completely missed. Perhaps every historian's dream was coming true for me. I could write what no one else could or would.

The more I read, the more convinced I became that I should do so. Why? First, because the evidence the trial transcript provided was extraordinary. Page after page detailed the social life of the Yokohama foreign community. More important still, revelations about Bessie's, James's, and Gower's feelings, emotions, and even their intimate relations with one another—the kinds of things normally kept hidden from public view—followed one after another.

Second, because my life experiences had paralleled, at least in part, those of James and Bessie Hetherington and given me empathy for them. I had once been a navy midshipman on a training cruise, excited and uncertain about whether I could measure up to the challenges that awaited me. Just like James had been long before me. The navy sent me to Japan as a junior officer just as it had him. Years later as a graduate language student, I returned to Japan, new bride in tow, as clueless about how she might fare there as James had been about what Bessie would experience in Yokohama. Perhaps, I thought, I could give readers a deeper understanding of who they were and why they acted as they did.

Third, because my career as an international and naval historian who wrote about the causes, conduct, and consequences of the Pacific War sent me to Yokohama many times over the years. I became familiar with the city, its historians and historical sites, and I enjoyed the privilege of teaching at Yokohama National University. I felt I had a feeling for the landscape and atmosphere of the city that could enrich readers' understanding of the place where fate had reshaped the lives of Bessie and James Hetherington.

Thus my life experiences prompted me to research and write this book. It tells a particular tale—one of love and lust, passion and adultery, retribution and death, and not least of justice pursued and delivered. But Bessie, James, and Gower's story also provides the opportunity to look beyond its particulars to aspects of the wider world in which it unfolded—life in the post–Civil War United States Navy; the social norms, temptations, and tensions of expatriate life in Japan's treaty ports in their mature form; the pursuit of justice in consular courts in capital murder cases; the transmission and transformation of news by the press in a world newly bound together by steamship, cable, and telegraphy; and, not least, the impact of a husband's naval profession on the life of his spouse. In short, the emergence of the modern navy wife.

My thanks go out to those who helped me in researching and writing this book. Professor Ōnishi Hiroshi of Ferris University in Yokohama; Mrs. Hori Nakatake Kanami and the staff of the Yokohama Archives of History (Kaikō Shiryōkan) in Japan; the archivists at the Old Military Records Branch, U.S. National Archives, and the Naval History and Heritage Command in Washington, D.C.; Dr. John Arnold of NICOR Inc. in Alexandria, Virginia; the staff at the Jefferson County Washington History Center; and Dr. Meg Vivers of Armindale, New South Wales, Australia. The late Professor Amakawa Akira, fellow historian, translator, and friend over many decades, introduced me to the history of Yokohama and the pleasures of living and teaching there.

Special thanks must go to executive editor Lisa Camp and her colleagues at McFarland, who transformed my manuscript into this book, and to my granddaughter Kaitlin Dingman, who designed its cover.

A word about sourcing, photographs, and names. The principal source for this book is *The Trial of Lieutenant Hetherington, U.S.N. for Shooting George Gower Robinson, Esq., Containing All the Testimony Verbatim from the Minutes of the Court Stenographer, the Speeches of Counsel in Full and the Letter Put in Evidence, Together with the Motions, Pleadings and Judgment* (Yokohama, Japan: "Box of Curios" Printing Office, 1892). This 331-page volume will be cited in the notes as *Trial Transcript*. Bernd Lepach's massive online biographical collection of foreign persons and firms active in Japan during the Meiji period (1868–1912), *Meiji Portraits*, proved an essential supplement to the trial record. No photographs of Bessie Hetherington or Gower Robinson are known to have survived, but two images of Lieutenant James Hetherington will be found in the text. Japanese names are presented in their usual Japanese form—this is surname first, followed by personal name.

This book would never have been finished without the love, understanding, and occasional goading of my wife of 59 years, Linda.

Now the story must begin. Not with navy wife Bessie, but with her husband, James—far from the sea, in Iowa.

1

Iowa Sailor

It all began with him—James Henry Hetherington. Born Friday, November 21, 1856, in Dubuque, Iowa, he was the firstborn son of Henry Samuel and Sarah Hill Hetherington. Like all parents, they held great hopes for his future. At that moment they could not possibly have imagined that the red-faced bawling infant would grow up to become a naval officer and a killer.

How did that happen?

Answering that question demands looking closely at the three major influences that shaped James Hetherington during the first two decades of his life: family, community, and career choice.

By the time James arrived, his parents had acquired the financial means and social status to give him a stable and mostly happy childhood. They were an aspiring middle-class couple living in the Midwest on the cusp of the Civil War. His father was a first-generation Irish American who had come to Iowa from Pennsylvania in 1843. He was trained as a mason, a skill that served him well for the first decade of his life in Dubuque. During that time, Iowa became the 29th state, Dubuque grew from a mere cluster of miners and Mississippi River boatmen into a small town, and Henry accumulated real estate worth $2,500. He courted and married Sarah Hill, fathered a daughter, and persuaded his younger brothers to join him in Dubuque. By the time James was born, he was working in the office of the surveyor general and making money on the side as a land speculator. In 1856, Henry built a handsome Federal-style brick home for his growing family at 1209 Prairie Avenue. The site marked the Hetheringtons' move up from the working-class riverfront to the fashionable Bluff neighborhood that overlooked the Mississippi.[1]

The move also symbolized the Hetherington family's position on the second tier of Dubuque's society, just below the families of the very first settlers. The Hetheringtons, thanks to Henry's growing wealth and civic involvement, belonged to the city's new middle class of merchants and

Hetherington family home, Dubuque, Iowa (courtesy Dr. Ronald and Maria Conti Condon).

lawyers, doctors and engineers, and educators and entrepreneurs. They had transformed Dubuque into a hub of economic growth and prosperity. By 1856, when James was born, the city boasted more than 900 arrivals and departures from its port, 13 churches, seven banks, four newspapers, 11 drugstores, and more than 60 grocery and dry goods stores. That same year, the Illinois Central railroad arrived, making it easy for still more new arrivals from the east—many of them German and Irish immigrants—to pour into the town. Filling these peoples' needs for housing, goods, and services generated jobs and wealth for those already there.[2]

James's father promoted Dubuque's growth and prosperity as well as his own. He became a city alderman, a property assessor, and a founding trustee of the city's first college for young men. He lobbied voters to approve loans for harbor dredging, fire department improvement, and waterfront property development. In 1858, they elected him mayor. After the Panic of 1857, he proved a shrewd observer of economic change, transforming himself from an advocate of publicly funded civic expansion into a guardian of civic budgetary responsibility.[3]

He nimbly changed his occupation at just the right moments. In 1858, he left real estate speculation and went into the grain and produce business. When the Civil War broke out, Dubuque shifted from delivering food from Iowa's farms to Eastern Seaboard cities to putting lead from nearby mines into bullets destined to kill Confederate soldiers. James's father became a lumber merchant providing the wood needed to build Union army camps, wagons, and coffins. In 1864, when Union soldiers occupied more of the South and disrupted its agricultural economy, he helped provide the food that they needed by going into the pork packing business. That move guaranteed him ever larger incomes well beyond the end of the fighting. By 1870, he owned real property worth $9,000 and had accumulated $10,000 in personal property. The next year, he joined what would become one of the nation's largest meat packing firms, George Rath & Company.[4]

Henry Hetherington's political and civic activities made his family members of Dubuque's elite. His business acumen guaranteed his son economic security throughout his early years. That meant James did not have to work to supplement the family's income when he finished elementary school. Instead, he became one of the relatively few students to go on to Dubuque High School and the dozen or so who graduated three years later. That achievement suggested that he was intelligent and hardworking. It also proved an essential prerequisite for his eventual career choice.[5]

James's early years were not free of emotional trauma, however. In 1865, he lost his two-year-old brother. In 1866, just before he turned 10, his mother died. That plunged his father into grief until he remarried in February 1869. Maria Soule, who was 16 years her new husband's junior, became James's stepmother. A year later, she was pregnant—a condition likely to render her feeling ill and emotionally volatile at times, as well as somewhat embarrassing to 14-year-old James. When his baby half sister, Clara, arrived in 1871, he suddenly had a very demanding competitor for his parents' time and affection.[6] That could have left James feeling emotionally isolated as he faced the self-doubts that came with adolescence and the challenges of his studies.

Despite the emotional difficulties he faced at home, James knew by the time he was 17 that he wanted to be a naval officer. Why the navy beckoned him in the early 1870s remains something of a mystery. The U.S. Navy, the largest in the world by the time the American Civil War ended in 1865, had shrunk dramatically. Ships were laid up or sold off. The number of cadet midshipmen entering the new Naval Academy dropped year after year. The lists of nongraduates grew to match, and at one point even exceed, those who went on to become commissioned officers. Prospects for promotion within the navy were slow. Officers pay paled in comparison with what could be earned in civilian life. And naval officers faced years of separation from family and service on distant overseas stations. The navy in and of itself was not a particularly desirable career choice.[7]

For James in 1873, however, it may have seemed more appealing than the alternatives. If he took up some occupation in Dubuque, he would be living in his father's shadow. If he stayed there, he might die without seeing much of the world beyond. The navy offered different possibilities. He would be his own man, not just his father's son. He would have opportunities for discovery and adventure in lands and seas far from Iowa. He might even have the chance to become a hero in battle.

On the other hand, if he, like so many other young American men in the 1870s, chose some more remunerative career such as railroad building or pioneering in the far West, he might fail miserably. That possibility might have seemed especially real to him because he finished high school in the midst of the Panic of 1873. That economic crisis hit the Midwest, particularly hard, already suffering from drought, a plague of locusts, and low farm prices, spawning bank failures, railroad collapses, and massive unemployment. Far worse than the last economic downturn, which had happened when James was just a baby, this "panic" would later be reckoned the most disastrous to date. The economic volatility he witnessed in the civilian world may have made young James see the stability, economic security, and social status that life as a naval officer promised as the real prize to be gained in his future.[8]

Whatever his reasons for doing so, James's choice of a naval career was the most important decision he would make in his early years. The navy, perhaps even more than his family or community, determined who he would be as an adult. To understand why that was so, it is necessary to look closely at the process by which James became a naval officer—first on land, then at sea.

In 1874, Iowa was not a breeding ground for future naval officers. Only eight young Iowans had graduated from the Naval Academy by the time James sought admission there.[9] How did he gain acceptance? There were three requirements: graduation from high school, nomination by the secretary of the navy or a member of Congress, and passage of an examination attesting to mastery of basic mathematical and linguistic skills. Young James met all three.

After graduating from high school in June 1873, he spent a year working and beefing up on subjects he knew academy applicants would be tested on. His father may have lobbied one or more of Iowa's eight Republican members of Congress, on his son's behalf. Perhaps Senator William B. Allison, a longtime Dubuque resident and attorney, nominated James. Having gained that honor, early in June 1874, he boarded an Illinois Central train bound for Chicago. A day and a half and two changes of train later, he arrived at Annapolis, Maryland, the "quaint but not ... attractive town" that was the state capital. Then one of the "boys," as African American males in Maryland were then called, guided him to the United States Naval Academy.

It sprawled, just outside the city limits, along the southern bank of the Severn River near where it flowed into Chesapeake Bay. Entering the school's gate, he passed into "another world" where tall trees "cast their shadows across the beautifully kept lawn [and] a little fountain sparkled and murmured." Looking beyond, James could see a "handsome brick building, painted grey, with a tall clock tower." It would be his home for the next four years.[10]

Over the next two days, he took two examinations. One was to see if he was physically fit to become a cadet midshipman. He easily measured up to the required standard: over five feet tall; possessed of strong sight, good hearing, and teeth; and "of good moral character." The other exam required him to convert Roman into Arabic numerals; add, subtract, multiply, and divide whole numbers and fractions; and comprehend ratios and proportions. It asked him to "write from dictation in a good hand, showing a ... good knowledge of spelling and punctuation." He had to know enough geography to be able to list the countries (and their capital cities) one would pass making a sea voyage from New York City to San Francisco. In an era when high school curricula were not yet standardized, Naval Academy faculty needed to find out if prospective students had mastered the prerequisites for success in the courses they would be taking. James passed both tests with flying colors. On June 9, he and 84 other young men were sworn into the navy as cadet midshipmen.[11]

Taking that oath marked the end of one phase of James's life and the beginning of another. Up to that point, his parents and family, friends, and community had exerted the greatest influence on who he was. From June 9, 1874, the United States Navy would shape his life. For the next four years, the academy would determine his everyday activities: when he got up, the clothes he put on, what he ate, what he studied, how he exercised, when he socialized with others outside academy grounds, and when he went to bed. Thereafter the navy would determine where he lived, whom his friends were, and what kind of work he would do. In short, on that June day James surrendered control over his life to the United States Navy.

But before that control became permanent, James had to meet the challenges that lay before him at the academy. The first were psychological. James in 1874 was not unlike any 17-year-old sent off to college today. Back home, he had a room of his own. Insofar as schoolwork and chores allowed, he was free to come and go from it at will. At the academy, he had to share a room with three other young men in a former army barracks that housed all of the more than 300 cadet midshipmen. Pictures and photographs could not be hung on its walls. He could bathe only once a week and would be marched to the bathhouse by seniors who made sure there was no talking or horseplay while he bathed.

Upperclassmen and instructors would determine when and where he could go from those spartan quarters. Saturday afternoon was his only time for leisure. He could play ball on the athletic field, row or sail a boat on the Severn, or go into town to spend pocket money on "nothing worse" than cake, candy, ice cream, or soda water.[12] James was not as free as he had been back home.

He also had to work to make new friends and live with those who sometimes treated him as if he were an enemy. There was only one other Iowan in his class, and he was not from Dubuque. Being somehow different, or thinking oneself different from others, was not something 17-year-olds then or now find easy. James eventually found a buddy, indeed a lifelong friend, in Alan P. Rogers, the only North Carolinian in the class of 1878.[13]

First-year classmen like James had to come to grips with the way upperclassmen treated them. Marines taught them the ritual movements of military drills on the training grounds outside. But inside their quarters, the newcomers were treated to all the meanness and hazing that their seniors could dish out. If one's uniform were disheveled or one forgot to salute properly or one broke some rule, a senior classman could chew one out. Hazing had been banned the year James arrived at the academy. But academy officials turned a blind eye to it so long as it did not inflict extreme physical harm on a cadet midshipman or interfere with his studies.[14] Accepting such control over even the small details of one's daily life was not easy for James. But doing so taught him the essentials of self-discipline that he would have to possess if he were ever to become a naval officer who exercised discipline over others.

Young James had only a few lapses along the way to mastering that self-control. Officials there carefully monitored behavior and awarded demerits for infractions of regulations. Those numbers, together with academic achievement, determined eventual class standing, the ranking that a naval officer carried with him to death and beyond. By the time he was ready to graduate in 1878, James had accumulated 122 demerits for the year, which was just about the median number for his classmates.[15]

Academics presented a second, different sort of challenge for him. A new superintendent, Rear Admiral Christopher Raymond Perry Rodgers, took charge of the academy just when James arrived. He came determined to modernize the school's curriculum. During James's first two years at Annapolis, professional classes outnumbered academic ones. In

1874–75, he studied only mathematics, English, history, and French. By his final year, Rodgers's reforms were in place. James was graded not just in seamanship, naval tactics, ordnance (gunnery), and infantry tactics, but also in astronomy, electricity, calculus and mechanics, English composition, and French and Spanish. That same year, the academy won a gold medal for excellence in academic instruction at the Paris International Exposition.[16]

James was not a stellar academic performer. He apparently had a flair for words, however, and usually ranked high in English composition. In other subjects he consistently fell behind his classmates, ending up at or near the bottom of the grading curve. But he was diligent, treated study as duty, and managed to get by. That was good enough for his superiors. The academy's mission was to produce naval officers, not scholars.[17]

Cadet midshipman Hetherington easily managed the physical and social challenges put before him at the Naval Academy. He played newly instituted intramural sports. Never having seen the ocean, he nevertheless survived sailing lessons on the broad reaches of the Severn River. He took to drills aboard the USS *Dale* like a duck to water—repelling boarders in mock skirmishes, running up rope ladders onto its yards, and loosening or furling sails with the best of his classmates. Every summer except his first, the last when he was allowed to visit home, he went on cruises north from Annapolis to Halifax, Nova Scotia, with brief port calls in small towns along the way. Those stops provided an opportunity to meet and socialize with proper young ladies.

Back on academy grounds, he learned how to socialize properly with others, both within and beyond the navy. As an upperclassman, he earned the nickname "Judge," perhaps because he hazed but did not harm or bully lowerclassmen. He survived fencing instruction unscathed and took readily to dancing class. And not least, he learned proper social behavior with women at the weekly Saturday evening "hops" and grand Christmas balls to which proper Annapolis young ladies were invited. James was training to become a gentleman, in the fullest sense of the word, as well as an officer.[18]

When graduation neared in 1878, 40 percent of those who had entered the academy with him four years earlier had failed or left for other reasons. James ranked near the bottom of his class.[19] But he had demonstrated that he had the grit and determination, the will to succeed, needed to meet the challenges the academy had put before him. He was a survivor. An achiever. He had every reason to feel proud on graduation day, May 15, 1878.

He had matured at Annapolis into the kind of person that post–Civil War navy leaders wanted up-and-coming officers to be. He was deeply, even passionately, dedicated to the United States Navy. He was willing to take on whatever duties it might impose upon him. He had shown that he could perform well under trying circumstances—something that life at sea was certain to demand of him. He could be counted on to follow orders from his superiors without question. He had become "an officer and a gentleman"— an honorable young man, possessed of solid professional and basic academic knowledge, and endowed with the discipline, social graces, and sense of propriety that would make him a respected member of society and a competent naval professional.

James Henry Hetherington, 1878 (Special Collections & Archives Department, Nimitz Library, U.S. Naval Academy).

But that was not enough. James still had to prove himself—at sea.

2

School of the Sea

In the early days of the republic, the ship was the school of the sea. Smooth-cheeked youths signed on aboard a navy ship, and if they learned the ropes of its sails, showed promise of mastering the art of navigation, and accepted its strict discipline, they might eventually become commissioned officers. By the 1840s, the founders of the U.S. Naval Academy realized that such on-the-job training was not enough. Prospective officers needed schooling ashore as well as practical experience at sea. That was why James was only a midshipman in 1878—an officer on probation. He needed to prove himself over the next two years, aboard a ship that would sail the open sea, not just northeastern coastal waters. He would have to keep a journal to record what he had studied and experienced. When his midshipman cruise came to an end, he had to pass an examination that proved he had mastered lessons that only the sea could teach. The ship was still the school of the sea.

The first days after they left the Naval Academy were a time of mixed emotions for James and his fellow cadet midshipmen. They swelled with pride when they returned home for the first time in three years but wondered anxiously about where and aboard what ship the navy might send them for the ultimate test of their suitability to become commissioned U.S. Navy officers. The Bureau of Navigation in Washington kept them waiting. Ninety days back home on half pay slipped away before James and nine of his classmates learned that they must report for duty aboard the USS *Richmond* on September 20, the first day of autumn. The ship was then in Boston, fitting out at the Charleston Naval Shipyard in preparation for a long overseas voyage.[1]

The *Richmond* was the perfect training vessel for officer candidates and ordinary sailors alike. Commissioned in 1860, the 2,600-ton ship normally carried 259 officers and enlisted men. It was a hybrid vessel—one that could move through the sea at speeds up to nine knots, powered by either its steam engine or its sails. James and his fellow midshipmen must have been impressed when they reported aboard—by the ship's gracious wooden hull, its towering three masts and 21 cannons, and, not least, by its service record. During the Civil War, the *Richmond* had contributed to the 1862 capture of New Orleans, the 1863 siege of Vicksburg, and the 1864 Battle of Mobile Bay. After the war, the ship had rescued American seamen held hostage in Cuba and gone on around the Horn to serve as flagship on the Pacific Station.[2]

When James reported aboard, the ship was technically out of commission, lying in drydock. Although piles of cannon balls and old unused lumber littered the Charlestown Navy Yard, its shabby gray machine shop and ropewalk buzzed with activity. Engineers installed a state-of-the-art ventilation system designed to keep lower decks from becoming fetid and germ-filled. The captain's cabin got new furniture, and carpenters and painters repaired ordinary sailors' spaces. In mid–November, 70 new sailors came aboard to fill out the ship's complement. Ten days later, nearly three months after James had arrived, the ship finally got underway, steaming past the outer islands of Massachusetts Bay and out to sea. On that day, everyone aboard, but especially the midshipmen, must have been excited.[3]

A shakedown voyage followed. The *Richmond* was to be the flagship

USS *Richmond*, midshipman cruise ship (NH 4495, Naval History and Heritage Command).

of the Asiatic Station, gone from the United States for at least two years. Before it left home waters, the captain had to be sure that everyone aboard knew his duties and that the ship performed as it should. That took a while, for the *Richmond* spent considerable time operating out of Norfolk, Virginia, before its final departure on January 11, 1879.[4]

During the long trans–Atlantic voyage that followed, James and his fellow midshipmen had to adapt to the traditional demands of life at sea aboard a naval vessel. They were, as the name of their rank suggested, midshipmen, not yet fully commissioned officers, but officer-learners who occupied a position in between enlisted men and officers. They ate, washed, and dressed in a steerage space that measured only 18 by 9 feet. They slept in hammocks, not in bunks in cabins like junior officers. The midshipmen did not eat in the wardroom with the *Richmond*'s officers. They had their own mess and chose one of their number to serve as its manager. He supervised the cooks who prepared their food and the servants who waited on them.

Early in their voyage, they ate very well. Warm soda biscuits, pancakes with maple syrup, hash, oatmeal, potatoes, and coffee and tea for breakfast. Lunch, or tiffin as they called it, consisted of canned meats, sardines, jelly, crackers and cross fresh bread, lobster salad, potato chips, and coffee or tea. Those same beverages rounded out dinners of canned soups, two kinds of meat and potatoes, canned fruits, and cookies, pies, or cake. But after weeks at sea, their meals might be reduced to "salt horse" (actually, salted beef or pork), rice and beans, and hard tack (unsalted hard crackers).

Midshipmen did not swab decks like ordinary seamen did, nor did they command them as officers did. But they supervised sailors and learned about the ship alongside them. With the exception of Sunday mornings, when divine services might be held on deck, their todays, yesterdays, and tomorrows were all the same. After getting up, washing, and breakfasting, James went to morning quarters, where the crew mustered on stations. He would then either report for duty on watch or shadow officers so as to learn more of their tasks and the ship's routines. Officers and crew normally stood four-hour watches, one of which was "dogged" or cut into two-hour segments, so that their time on watch rotated from daylight to evening to midnight hours. When not on watch, James would have taken noon "star-shots" with a sextant and completed calculations so as to determine the ship's position. He would have spent time with the ship's engineers, learning about the *Richmond*'s boilers and engines. On deck, James would have worked with the deck crew managing the sails. And if he was sent for duty on the bridge, James would have taken turns at the "conn," that is, giving directions to the helmsman at the wheel, so as to keep the ship on correct course. When evening quarters were called, he could be designated midshipman of a particular division, which meant taking charge of 25 men, some of whom might not even speak English.[5]

That was the routine of a normal midshipman training cruise.

This cruise, however, turned out to be anything but normal.

A single passenger not yet aboard when the *Richmond* left Norfolk transformed it, first into a 12,000-mile race, then into a spectacular diplomatic mission. Back in October 1878, Secretary of the Navy Richard Thompson wrote former president Ulysses S. Grant offering him free passage aboard the *Richmond* to Japan. Grant had been traveling in Europe as an unofficial ambassador, visiting with kings, prime ministers, and captains of industry. Crowds showered him with adulation, and President Rutherford B. Hayes recognized that his celebrity could be put to good purpose. He could show the world the strength of the reunited United States and promote its trade and commerce east of Suez and on beyond to Southeast and East Asia.[6]

Although Navy Secretary Thompson assured Grant that the *Richmond* was "in excellent condition" and would provide "a pleasant voyage" (at government expense), he hesitated to accept the offer. He was homesick and thought his wife might find such a long journey too taxing. But she surprised him by welcoming the prospect of visiting "the exotic East." Thompson reported that the *Richmond* ship hadn't left Norfolk yet and couldn't pick up the Grants on the French Riviera, which they planned to leave in mid–January. They could go ahead by commercial steamer to ports along the way east, however, and the *Richmond* would catch up with them. On Christmas Day 1878, Grant accepted the navy's offer of free transportation to Japan.[7]

What followed was a six-months-long chase to catch up with him. That didn't happen until June 1879 for two reasons: the *Richmond* was a "slow sailer," and the Grant party kept leaping ahead and leaving possible ports of rendezvous. James's ship took seven weeks to cross the Atlantic and tarried another week at Naples, where its captain, Andrew Benham, got orders to catch up with Grant as soon as possible. He tried in Ceylon, in Singapore, and again at Hong Kong, but Grant had already gone ahead—at first by commercial steamer, then by the gunboat USS *Ashuelot*. It took the former president up the China coast to the Taku Bar at the mouth of the Peiho River. Late in May, Grant went ashore there and on to Tientsin and Peking (Beijing) for talks with Chinese officials.

The *Richmond* did not reach Hong Kong until May 15, 1879, 155 days after leaving Norfolk. There Captain Benham got the alarming news that the *Ashuelot* had taken Grant north to the Taku Bar. That made it all the more urgent for his ship to race ahead, lest the ex-president suffer

2. School of the Sea

the humiliation of arriving in Japan aboard a small gunboat rather than the magnificent *Richmond*. Finally, on June 1, barely four days after Grant had arrived there, the *Richmond* anchored outside the Bar alongside the *Ashuelot*. Its captain told Benham that the two ships would have to wait until Grant returned from the Chinese capital.[8]

Seventeen days passed before he did so. That time must have been boring for James and everyone else aboard the *Richmond*. The ship lay three miles offshore, and there was no town at the mouth of the river. Tientsin was too far away for a day's visit, so no liberty for the crew. But the long chase to catch up with Grant came to a spectacular end. He arrived at the Bar escorted by the viceroy of Tientsin and his fleet of gunboats. The guns at the Taku Bar forts, the viceroy's vessels, and the two American ships awaiting the former president boomed 21-gun salutes. Another round of salutes followed when Grant and the viceroy came aboard the *Richmond*. At that moment, just after noon on June 17, 1879, James and every other *Richmond* officer, all in full-dress uniform, stood at attention on deck to honor the former president. At long last, the man they had chased halfway around the world was safely aboard. The race to catch him was finally over.

The day's festive ceremonies did not end, however, until nearly midnight. Captain Benham feted Grant and the viceroy with a magnificent dinner. The Chinese official toured the ship before departing under another halo of gunfire. Then James and the rest of the crew returned to duty to prepare for getting underway. Finally, at four the next morning, the *Richmond* weighed anchor with its precious presidential party aboard and headed out to sea.

The ship did not proceed directly to Japan but tarried in Chinese waters so its distinguished guests could sightsee. The Grants had not been able to visit the Great Wall from Peking and asked to go ashore briefly at Shanhaiguan, where it ended at the sea. Captain Benham obliged and let as many officers and men as possible go with them. James and his fellow cadet midshipmen probably looked on as a sailor dabbed China's most famous structure with white paint to commemorate their ship's visit there. Then the Grants wanted to stop again at Chefoo (today's Yantai) to shop for souvenirs. Captain Benham honored their request and gave his crew a day's liberty in the small treaty port city. Midshipman Hetherington got his first chance since Hong Kong to stroll through a Chinese city. He could not resist sampling savory hot foods and fresh fruits from the stalls that lined Chefoo's narrow side streets. That produced unfortunate gastrointestinal consequences later on.

From that point onward, the training cruise turned race and sightseeing tour became something even more special: a diplomatic mission. Grant would be paying a goodwill visit to Japan, and it was exciting for everyone aboard the *Richmond* to have him and the former first lady aboard, even if one caught only an occasional glimpse of the famous couple. They rated special treatment, of course. Captain Benham gave them his cabin. The *Ashuelot*, following along in the *Richmond*'s wake, provided extra protection for them. And even before land was sighted, a magnificent Japanese warship appeared on the horizon to guide them toward the Land of the Rising Sun. A sense of excitement about what awaited them in Japan swept over James Hetherington and everyone else on the USS *Richmond*.

On June 21, 1879, the ship entered Nagasaki harbor to the sound of 21-gun salutes fired in Grant's honor. His presence changed the nature of James's first experience of Japan. What would have been a brief coaling stop at Nagasaki became five days of ceremony, celebration, and sightseeing. The emperor sent a special jinrikisha from Tokyo to take the Grant party to receptions, dinners, and the city's famous sites. James and his fellow midshipmen got the chance to visit hillside temples; the bazaar on the tiny island of Deshima, once the only place non–Asian foreigners were permitted to live; and teahouses where "entertainments not always in strict accordance with European morals" were held.[9]

Rather than following the more direct ocean route from Nagasaki, the *Richmond* detoured through the beautiful Inland Sea en route to Yokohama. The ship reached its offshore anchorage there on July 3. One of the iconic diplomatic events in the history of American relations with Japan was about to begin. James would be not just an eyewitness but also a participant in it.[10]

Friday, July 4, 1879, marked two anniversaries: the 103rd of American independence and the 20th of Yokohama's opening to foreign trade and residence. Americans and Japanese were ready to celebrate. The *Richmond* glided into the inner harbor fully dressed with a rainbow of flags and pennants flying. The ship fired a 21-gun salute, answered by a cacophony of return salutes from all but one of the warships present. British guns remained silent, for the Royal Navy was not about to honor the loss of the American colonies. Then a parade of dignitaries came aboard the *Richmond*. First, Rear Admiral Thomas Harwood Patterson, commander in chief Asiatic Station, with all of his decorations.[11] Then the American minister (ambassador) to Japan and the Yokohama consul general in black frock coats. Finally, the Japanese party that included a prince, a full admiral, and a former Japanese minister to Washington, all resplendent in their formal attire. After lunch, the dignitaries boarded a barge headed for the Yokohama Admiralty pier while James and all the officers on deck and sailors manning the *Richmond*'s yards looked on. As the visitors approached land, bursts of fireworks and still more ceremonial gunfire burst in the air.

2. School of the Sea

From that point onward, Japanese officials took charge of the welcoming ceremonies. Their government had taken special pains to show the Americans how firmly it was committed to "modernization," that is the norms of international intercourse, the forms of European and American government, and even the acceptance of Western styles of dress. Japan, once closed to non–Asians, was now fully open and equal to the nations of the Western world. Two more princes and the emperor's special railway carriage waited at flag-bedecked Yokohama Station to take the Grants and "a numerous suite of naval officers" that may have included James and his fellow midshipmen to Tokyo. When their train arrived in the capital, the Imperial Guards band struck up *Hail Columbia*, then America's de facto national anthem. After a brief exchange of greetings, the Grant party, accompanied by the secretary of the American Legation and "several officers of the American navy," went to the Imperial Palace for an audience with the emperor and empress. On that occasion, His Majesty touched a foreigner for the very first time by shaking hands with Grant.

The festivities continued that evening at the Seiyōken restaurant in Ueno Park, which was festooned with thousands of red and white lanterns. Two hundred American and Japanese guests—including "a brilliant gathering of naval officers" from the *Richmond*—awaited the Grant party. When they arrived, the ship's band struck up its version of "Hail Columbia." A reception with more speech-making, dinner and toasts, and still more speeches rounded out the Independence Day celebrations. The Grants then retired to a renovated guesthouse for foreign visitors. Guests from Yokohama boarded another special train that did not get them to their homes and ships until two thirty the next morning.[12]

James Hetherington would certainly remember that Fourth of July. It was his first experience of "showing the flag" abroad, a primary mission of the post–Civil War navy. Doing so was meant to advertise America's strength, protect its citizens abroad, promote its trade, and advance international peace and goodwill. That was why the United States Navy kept a squadron of ships in Asiatic waters. Nothing that James experienced later in the *Richmond*'s stay in Japan matched the splendor of its beginning.

What followed immediately, however, proved very unpleasant for him. A week later, he was admitted to the U.S. Naval Hospital, a rambling wooden, gas-lit facility that sat atop the bluff overlooking Yokohama. He complained of severe stomach pains and chronic diarrhea that he suspected had come from eating street food in China. The doctor prescribed bed rest and a special diet that included shots of brandy and opium to reduce his pain. That worked—sort of. Discharged two weeks later, he returned to duty aboard the *Richmond* only to land back in the hospital barely a week later with the same intestinal problems. That meant 10 more days of confinement on bed rest and a limited diet.[13]

After that, James was glad to return to normal shipboard duty and eager to enjoy liberty ashore in Yokohama. What was the city like then? How did he and his fellow midshipmen experience it? What impact on his later life did this visit have on the young man of 22?

The city and country that he saw in 1879 had changed dramatically over the quarter century since Commodore Matthew Calbraith Perry had forced a reluctant Japanese government to sign the 1854 treaty that began the process of "opening" Japan. A second agreement four years later required the Japanese to build a new town and open it to foreign trade and residence in 1859. Yokohama was designed as much to control as to welcome foreigners. A canal was dredged that turned the peninsula where the town perched into a de facto island. Guards were posted at the bridges linking it to the mainland. To satisfy the foreigners, the government built new homes and shops, as well as the fabled Gankiro, a pleasure palace that provided food, music, dancing, and sexual services to the bachelor merchants and traders who made up most of the new town's population.

In the 1860s, Yokohama was a violent place "filled with hustlers … Western [and Japanese] cheaters" and wrongdoers who could simply run away. Violence at the hands of samurai opposed to the presence of foreigners "stalked in the shadows." Nineteen "incidents" targeted foreigners, 11 of whom died. Nonetheless, trade flourished. A few pioneer foreigners and Japanese entrepreneurs took great risks and struggled to make money.

All of that had changed by 1879. Eleven years earlier, a new government had come to power after a brief and nearly bloodless civil war. Its leaders welcomed foreigners as agents of change and bringers of prosperity. Developments overseas—silk blight in Europe and war and civil unrest in China—prompted traders to come to Japan for silk and tea. Yokohama became a magnet for Japanese entrepreneurs who capitalized on their demands and opened the door to prosperity for all the city's residents. They and their foreign counterparts made Yokohama Japan's principal and most prosperous port.[14]

Prosperity triggered a population boom that transformed the city. By 1879, some 1,300 foreigners—Britons, Americans, Europeans of various nationalities, and Chinese—lived and worked in Yokohama. They needed more room. The Japanese government obliged in 1877 by opening the beautiful bluff overlooking the original foreign settlement for their use. The foreigners, in turn, made the city look like the places they had come from. The Chinese created a warren of shops and residences at the heart of the original settlement. The Europeans and Americans built new structures and established institutions that gave the city the feel of "home." By 1879,

2. School of the Sea

Yokohama boasted all kinds of shops, five banks and hotels, three hospitals and taverns, 10 social and sporting clubs, and numerous churches and religious establishments. The expatriate community now was surrounded by a much larger Japanese town whose residents profited from the foreigners.[15]

What might a midshipman like James have done when he had liberty in Yokohama? Visit with friends and former classmates aboard the gunboats *Ashuelot* and *Monongahela*, then in port. Jump into one of the rickshaws that swarmed around him and his friends when they stepped ashore and go for a ride around town, first along the bund or waterfront, then to Motomachi for shopping or just browsing in curio stores, then up Nogeyama street for a stop at one of its many teahouses, where they got a taste of Japanese customs—taking off their shoes before they entered, sampling tea and sweets, and flirting as best they could across the language barrier with the beautiful kimono-clad hostess girls.

On other occasions, James and his friends might opt for less energetic activities—perhaps a meal at the Grand Hotel or a languid afternoon or evening at the Yokohama United Club, a British-style gentlemen's club, to which they were accorded honorary memberships. There they could catch up on the newspapers, play cards or billiards, socialize at the bar, and dine on Western-style food. A midshipman's time in Yokohama could be pretty tame.[16]

But was it so for James? What about sex? Most foreign men in the city were bachelors and needed it. The fabled Gankiro had burned down, but other such facilities had long since replaced it. The famous perfectly legal brothel Nectarine No. 9 Junpuro catered exclusively to the "better sort" of foreign gentlemen. One teahouse had a particularly friendly madam who specialized in welcoming foreign naval officers to the delights her girls provided. The opportunity for James to enjoy casual sex while he was in Yokohama was certainly there. His superiors would not have objected if he did so, so long as the encounter was discreet, did not harm his health, and did not keep him from performing his duty. In 1878, the chief medical officer for the Asiatic Station gave a green light for sex in Yokohama by reporting that venereal disease there "gives no trouble" because diseased women were immediately excluded and treated at lock hospitals. Sex could be safe.[17]

That did not mean, however, that midshipmen like James would seek it out. He may have abstained from it for religious reasons. Nineteenth-century Christians were taught that sex outside of marriage was a grievous sin. Or racism of a sort may have kept him celibate. As another midshipman put it, "the 'almond-eyed beauties of the East' were ugly"—not his style. Or he may have thought that going for sex in a

Japanese brothel was simply not proper behavior for an "officer and a gentleman"—on probation. Rudyard Kipling had yet to proclaim, "East was East and West was West." That is, that the rules for sexual behavior back home simply did not apply in Yokohama.[18]

How James behaved sexually in the summer of 1879 or during the *Richmond*'s subsequent port calls in Yokohama remains unknown. But one thing is certain about his first stay there: he came away from Japan with a favorable impression of the place. Nearly a dozen years later, he remembered Yokohama as pleasant, safe, and civilized enough for him to bring his wife and child there.[19]

The remainder of James's midshipman cruise took him the rest of the way around the globe. Late the next summer, the *Richmond* called for a last time at Yokohama and then headed east across the Pacific bound for Panama. During the nearly 6,000-mile voyage that followed, James had ample opportunity to demonstrate that he had learned what the "school of the sea" had to teach. When the *Richmond* reached Panama City (then in Columbia) in mid–May 1880, James left it for the last time. He and his fellow midshipmen likely departed with mixed feelings: glad to be heading home but sad to be leaving the ship that had taken them on such an extraordinary cruise to so many interesting ports—Yokohama foremost among them.

Three more weeks passed before James and his fellow midshipmen reached Annapolis, where their naval education had begun and where it would end. They sweated for two hot days on a train crossing the Isthmus of Panama. They waited still longer at the Caribbean port of Aspinwall for a ship to take them north. Ten days at sea followed before they reached Norfolk, Virginia. From there they headed north by rail to the academy at Annapolis.[20]

James took his last tests there: exams meant to prove that he was qualified to be promoted to full-commissioned-officer status. He and his fellow *Richmond* midshipmen passed those tests with flying colors. Graduation—the real, final graduation—from the Naval Academy and "the school of the sea" followed on May 31, 1880. Four days later, exactly six years after he entered the navy, James Henry Hetherington was commissioned a professional naval officer with the rank of passed midshipman.[21]

The document he received attesting to that fact was the most important he would ever receive. It signified that one phase of his life had come to an end. His education, on land and on sea, was over. He was no longer a student, trying to master the knowledge and skills he would need to succeed in life, to become what he wanted to be, but a professional, a full adult, a naval officer. He was what wanted to be. The commission James Hetherington received on that June day defined his profession, his rank in the navy, his status in society, and what he would be for the rest of his life: first, last, and always, a United States Navy officer.

That James was a naval officer made all the difference for everything else that followed.

3

Delaware Belle

By the time he was 29, James Hetherington had, to paraphrase the Book of Proverbs, flown like an eagle from his birthplace into the navy. He had basked in moments of enjoyment and adventure in ports around the world, like a serpent warming itself on a rock. He had learned how to sail a ship on the high seas. He may have experienced the way of a man with a maid in the flesh, but not with a woman he truly loved. The time had come for him to find his lifelong lover and companion, a wife.[1] He did not find her until long after he had embraced his mistress, the navy. Nine years passed between his commissioning as a naval officer and his marriage. During those years, the navy was his love and his life.

James's duty assignments were not glamorous or exciting, but they proved richly rewarding professionally and experientially. The first and largest was the elderly sloop of war USS *Kearsarge,* famous for having sunk the Confederate raider *Alabama* during the Civil War. By the time James came aboard, however, the ship was a beautiful anachronism. The secretary of the navy praised it as "a good ship in peace" but added that it was totally useless in war. Its primary mission was showing the flag.

That gave James 18 months of pleasant duty. He came aboard just as the ship was transferred to the European Station, which led to a leisurely cruise to the western Mediterranean complete with port calls in Spain and Morocco. Then the *Kearsarge* shifted stations and went on patrol in the Caribbean, calling at various islands in the West Indies before sailing north to New England resort harbors at the height of the summer tourist season. The *Kearsarge* added its full-sail beauty to celebrations in New York and Hampton Roads marking the centenary of the climactic battles of the Revolutionary War, then headed south for another winter in warm Caribbean climes.

This was not arduous duty. James spent four times as many days in port as at sea. In Spain and Morocco, he encountered foreign cultures and savored their foods. The same was true for New Orleans, a multiracial, multicultural city as foreign to him as any abroad. He gained promotion to ensign, junior grade and got a $50 annual pay raise. For a year and a half, James experienced precisely the mix of economic stability and adventure that figured in his decision to join the navy in the first place.[2]

Then his duties changed drastically. In June 1883, he was ordered to the lowly steam schooner *Thomas R. Gedney*.[3] It was not even a navy ship, only a Coast Survey vessel. For the next four years, he served on it or its sister ship, the *George S. Blake*. That may have seemed like a comedown, but in fact service on these two ships allowed Ensign Hetherington to develop new valuable specialized skills, carry out one of the navy's most enduring peacetime missions, and tighten his bonds with the navy itself. Although it certainly did not look like it, duty on smaller ships like these proved to be a good career-enhancing move. It also indirectly helped him find his future wife.

On these Coast Survey ships James became a hydrographer, a scientist of the sea who carried out another of the 19th-century navy's basic missions. His predecessors had gone from charting coastlines and harbors to compiling data on currents in and winds above the surface of the ocean. They plumbed and plotted the depths along America's eastern and southern coasts, finding "highways of the sea" that benefited commercial and naval mariners alike. While James studied at Annapolis, the navy's exploration of the seas shifted from the surface to the depths of the ocean. Naval hydrographers developed much more accurate techniques and tools for taking deep soundings. Working more closely with civilian scientists, including the famed Harvard geologist Louis Agassiz, in 1880–1881, they determined the depth and course of the Gulf Stream.[4]

Despite these innovations, however, the basic tasks of deep-water hydrography and bathymetry did not change for young officers like Ensign Hetherington. He spent "days in small open boats, exposed to the elements, heaving the sounding lead over and over, reading azimuths and other sextant angles" so as to produce accurate charts and achieve "precise quantification of the natural world." The work was hard, tiring, and monotonous. During the summer of 1885, James and others aboard the *Blake* took over 92,000 soundings in a 121-square-mile area. They worked so closely with warrant officers and ordinary sailors that the barriers between officers and enlisted men that prevailed aboard large navy ships broke down. In doing such precise scientific work, James had to cooperate with and learn from ordinary sailors, not just direct them.[5]

Duty aboard coast surveying ships was far from unpleasant, however. The work was seasonal, stretching from early spring to as late in fall as weather permitted. The ship would take on fresh provisions and coal during the winter and then head to warm and sunny Gulf Coast waters.

When summer neared, it would return up the coast from the Carolinas to Maine to resume surveying work there. That gave James and his fellow junior officers the opportunity to join in the pleasures of Atlantic summer seaside resorts. They honed their courting skills by dining and dancing with young ladies of marriageable age. And in the winter, when they spent months ashore in large cities like New York, Philadelphia, or Washington, D.C., they enjoyed the social elite's seasonal entertainments.[6]

The impact of this kind of duty on James was profound. He bonded more closely with a wider group of Naval Academy graduates. He achieved promotion and personal recognition. In 1884, the captain of the *Blake* went out of his way to commend James and four other ensigns for their "hearty and intelligent cooperation" in the ship's surveying operations. James became a full ensign.[7] He discovered that not all naval duty was as socially isolating as that aboard a large combatant vessel on a distant overseas station. That small-ship experience reaffirmed his affection for the sea service, his comradery with fellow officers, and his willingness to accept the navy's direction, indeed control, over his life.

Little wonder, then, that James embraced his mistress, the United States Navy. He understood that whatever else followed in his life, she would be with him. James loved her but knew she was not enough. By the time he neared the end of his 20s, he began his search for a wife.

James met Bessie Hewes early in September 1885 at Cape May, the southernmost of the New Jersey shore resorts. While fewer than 200 people lived there year-round, during the summer the town's population swelled to more than 4,000. People flocked there to escape the heat and humidity of Philadelphia and New York City. They could come from the City of Brotherly Love by train for only a dollar round trip or travel in style on a luxurious old side-wheel steamer. They frolicked in the waves, watched yachts racing offshore, admired the lighthouse, and dined heartily on fresh seafood.[8]

James knew the town well, for his ship, the U.S. Coast and Geodetic Survey *Thomas R. Gedney*, had spent the summer surveying the entrance to Delaware Bay and the shallow shores of southern New Jersey.[9] On the weekends, if he did not have duty aboard the ship, he and his brother ensigns would go to Cape May Point for a good meal at one of its luxurious hotels. If they were lucky, they might meet one of the many eligible young ladies who came there on vacation with their families. The town was the perfect place for boy to meet girl and romance to blossom.

That did not happen immediately for James. But he could not help being drawn toward a beautiful young woman he spotted. She was delicately built, with bright blonde, almost yellow hair. And when they came close to one another, he could see that she had sparkling, deep blue eyes.

3. Delaware Belle

Exactly how James met Bessie Hewes remains unclear. Perhaps they splashed out of the waves, clad from shoulders to ankles in the "bathing costume" of the day, close enough to strike up a conversation. Perhaps they first exchanged words between nearby tables in one of the hotel dining rooms. Or James may have screwed up his courage to leave the company of his fellow officers and go up to Bessie to ask for a dance at a hotel evening prom.

Theirs was not love at first sight, but there was a spark of attraction between them. Each saw something physically attractive about the other. She was, as James later put it, a young beauty just on the cusp of blossoming into full womanhood.[10] He was, in her eyes, a sturdy, sandy-haired young man with a broad, clean-shaven face deeply tanned by his work on open waters. When Bessie probed a bit to find out who he was, James told her he came from Iowa. She learned that he was a naval officer. That suggested to her that he was a man with desirable qualities. Graduates of the military and naval academies were reputed to be gentlemen who were physically superior, socially adept, and wonderful dancers. Although he was obviously older than she was, a man of that sort might be fun for Bessie to get to know.

When James asked about her background, she readily responded to his questions. Home was Wilmington, Delaware, where she lived with her parents and two younger sisters. Her father was a lumber merchant. He made enough money for them to live comfortably and for her to come, with family or friends, to Cape May almost every summer. At 17 going on 18, she would be going back to Vassar when classes resumed in a few weeks. Those last words gave James a clue to who Bessie was: a Delaware belle, beautiful, and with family, money, and intelligence enough to become, in time, a good wife.[11]

Shortly after that first meeting, Bessie left Wilmington for Poughkeepsie, New York, and her second year at the Vassar Preparatory School. That she was able to do so was a testament to the support her family and community had given her during a golden childhood and early adolescence. She was born to parents of good Quaker stock, Emlen and Mary Augusta Hewes, in February 1868 in Franklin, Pennsylvania, where her father helped build a new railroad. She grew up, however, in Wilmington, Delaware.[12] The state was still struggling then with the issues of Civil War and Reconstruction. Delaware had stayed in the Union, but its young men had fought wearing both Union blue and Confederate gray. Bessie's father put on neither, perhaps out of Quaker conviction that war was wrong, perhaps because he was making good money in the lumber business. When Bessie was born, about a tenth of Wilmington's residents were Black and Delaware had neither ratified the 13th Amendment nor formally abolished slavery.[13]

Bessie grew up at a time when a "new Wilmington" was emerging. Between her birth and her first meeting James, the town's population jumped from roughly 30,000 to nearly 50,000. Its citizens enjoyed, except for a brief moment during the Panic of 1873, remarkable prosperity. During the Civil War, they made gunpowder for the legendary Dupont arms manufacturers. After the war, the shipbuilding industry exploded on Wilmington's waterfront. Hundreds of men built wooden coastal freighters and fishing boats, ironclad steamers, and even yachts that triumphed in the coveted America's Cup races. By the time Bessie was 10, a Wilmington firm had become the largest producer of iron ships in the United States. The year she met James, two local companies had contracts with the navy, one manufacturing steel plates for gun turrets on the ships of "the new navy," the other building a floating dock destined for the New York Navy Yard.[14]

As its population and income levels swelled, Wilmington spread outward and upward from its watery creek and riverfronts. The Hewes family moved up to a new three-story brick home on tree-lined Delaware Avenue, the city's "principal showplace." It boasted granite and brick paving, gas streetlights, a new electric trolley line, and easy access to trains running to Baltimore and Philadelphia. The city fathers built a new courthouse and new schools and paved more and more streets. A new Trinity Episcopal Church was erected just around the corner from the Hewes family's home. Developers built new shops and businesses close by where Bessie, her mother, and sisters could browse and buy. They could walk to a beautiful new park along Brandywine Creek. And by the time Bessie reached her teens, there was a ballroom atop the Opera House where she went for dancing lessons.[15]

All of this change came without sharpening existing social class differences or creating new ones. To be sure, neither African Americans nor ordinary workers nor the descendants of pioneer Quaker families lived near Bessie's family. Public schools were racially segregated, but public entertainments such as concerts and baseball games were not. Shared prosperity and pride in their growing city bred an optimism that Wilmington residents took in with the air they breathed. That spirit, together with an unshakable determination to build a better future, made Wilmington an ideal place for Bessie Hewes to grow up in. In this environment, it would have been hard for her not to mature into a happy, free-spirited, and ambitious young woman.[16]

Wanting the best future for her, Bessie's parents decided to send her to something better than a ladies' finishing school. They heard about a college for women—Vassar, which was located in Poughkeepsie, about halfway between New York City and Albany. It was expensive—$300 annually, including room and board, plus extra fees for instruction in art and music. It was academically demanding and forward-looking; some of its alumnae went on to become pioneering medical doctors and college professors. But it seemed like the right kind of place for Bessie to develop her academic and social skills. She passed entrance exams in English grammar, geography, and American history but had not taken courses in other subjects required for admission. So she was admitted to Vassar's preparatory school. There she would have two years to make up her academic deficiencies and qualify for matriculation into Vassar Female College.[17]

Bessie left for her new school in the fall of 1884, when she was just 16. She arrived probably feeling anxious and excited about what lay ahead. She signed up for three courses that first semester and expected to do the same in the spring term. None looked easy. Over the next two years, she would have to complete five semesters of Latin, two of mathematics, two of rhetoric, one of physical geography, one of ancient history, and three semesters of French or German or two terms of Greek. But there would be fun, too. Bessie would find new friends and join in the college's musical, dramatic, and literary activities. There would be parties and dances like those she had enjoyed at Cape May. Social events with handsome young army cadets at West Point just across the Hudson or at the college promised to be particularly special occasions for the Vassar girls.[18]

Bessie survived her first year at Vassar, but her second did not go as well as she and her parents might have hoped. For reasons that remain unclear, she left the preparatory school in June of 1886, never to return. Perhaps she found higher mathematics or "dead" Latin and Greek too difficult. She may have chafed at, or even violated, the school's restrictions on her behavior and social activities. Perhaps she sensed that her lively personality just didn't fit in with the more serious demeanor of other Vassar students. Bessie at age 17 may have been more interested in boys than in books.

She was interested enough in James to come with a group of friends to visit him aboard the *Gedney*. He and his fellow bachelor officers must have shown them a good time, for over the next 15 months, James and Bessie met whenever they could. He remembered their visiting one another at Cape May, New York City, and Philadelphia, where he was sent for duty at the Branch Hydrographic Office after leaving the *Gedney* in December 1886. By that time their relationship had developed to the point that she invited him to her family home in Wilmington for Christmas. Bessie's parents liked what they saw in Ensign Hetherington: a handsome 30-year-old settled in a profession with a respectable income likely to grow over the years. He was polite, respectful, and an officer and a gentleman in every sense of the term. He could be a suitable son-in-law—when the time was right.

However, 1886 was too soon. James respected the fact that Bessie was not yet 21—that is to say, legally an adult. He—and she—likely felt they needed to get to know each other better. And her parents may have had qualms about their daughter's navy suitor. He was, after all, nearly a dozen years her senior. After that holiday visit, Bessie stayed on in Wilmington, and James likely came for visits when his duties in nearby Philadelphia permitted. But he was not her only suitor. She socialized freely with other young men, moving "in the best society ... [where she] was the acknowledged belle of her set."[19]

In May 1887, Ensign Hetherington was detached from the *Gedney* and ordered to report to the USS *Michigan*. The ship was the navy's first iron-hulled warship, an ancient paddle-wheeled steamer launched in 1843. It had patrolled the Great Lakes looking for Confederate raiders during the Civil War, but now just cruised the Great Lakes in summer, stopping at various ports in search of fresh recruits. In winter, when ice clogged the lakes, it remained homeported at Erie, Pennsylvania. Those bitterly cold months must have been especially lonely for James, and he likely wrote to Bessie and visited her when his duties allowed. Finally, on May 2, 1889, when she was 21 and he was 32, James asked Bessie to marry him. She accepted his proposal, and her father gave his consent to the marriage. That brought their long, quite proper courtship to an end.[20]

The next six months were a flurry of prenuptial activities for James and Bessie. They had first to pick a window of time for the wedding. December seemed best, for the *Michigan* would likely be in port rather than out on ice-strewn Lake Erie. Then there was the question of when Wilmington's Trinity Episcopal Church might be available for the ceremony. Tuesday, December 10, proved open. Bride and groom had to ask their possible attendants if they would be available. Bessie chose her younger sister, Helen, and longtime friend Minnie Carpenter, the county tax collector's daughter, to be bridesmaids. James asked James Henry Thomas to be his best man. Another navy friend, George Leroy Conroy, and five other men, including Philadelphia assistant district attorney Thomas D. Finletter, would serve as ushers. Last but not least, Bessie, doubtless with the help of her mother and sisters, had to pick out her wedding gown, with its accompanying long train and veil.[21]

If newspaper accounts in their usual breathless style are to be believed, the wedding was a "brilliant affair, attended by guests from New York, Boston, Washington, and Philadelphia" as well as James's family and friends from Iowa. At seven o'clock, Emlen Hewes proudly escorted his daughter, "a well known and very beautiful society lady," down the aisle to the front of Trinity Episcopal Church, where James, resplendent in his finest dark blue winter uniform, awaited her. Her attendants then straightened her long train and stepped forward to lift the veil from her face. The couple turned and faced the minister, who began the ceremony in the traditional ritual of the Episcopal Church in America. Did anyone know of any reason why James and Bessie should not be joined in holy matrimony? he asked. No one spoke. Then he reminded the couple of the sacred character of marriage, a bond that they both must be willing to enter freely and voluntarily. James responded, "I do," when the reverend asked if he would take Bessie as his wife, "forsaking all others," "to love, honor, and cherish" all the days of his life. The minister then asked Bessie if she would "love, honor, and obey" James, "forsaking all others" to be her husband all the days of her life. She replied, "I do." His best man then handed James the wedding ring, and he slipped it onto Bessie's finger. The minister pronounced the two man and wife as James kissed his bride. Amid smiles all around, the newlyweds then walked down the aisle to the church door, where they stopped to greet family members, friends, and guests.

When they stepped outside, James and Bessie were pelted with rice and good wishes for the future. They climbed into a waiting carriage, and the wedding party and guests followed them to the Hewes family home nearby. Bessie's parents had laid out sumptuous reception fare for them there. When the feasting and merriment neared its end, Bessie and James thanked everyone and retired for the evening. The guests left for their homes, hoping that a long and happy life together lay before the newlyweds. The bride and groom would depart the next morning for their honeymoon at West Point, New York.[22]

On that happy day, in the joy of the moment, no one probably pondered two sobering truths about marriage. It is the formal acknowledgment of a bond of love between two individuals. But love, as poets, priests, and philosophers have reminded us, can be fickle. It does not always prove enduring. Marriage is also a contractual bond, recognized by witnesses at a ceremony on behalf of the wider society, in which the two parties promise to abide by the terms of that contract. But contracts can be broken.[23]

No one, on that happy wedding day in December 1889, could possibly have imagined the shocking way in which the marriage contract between James and Bessie would be broken.

◈ 4 ◈

Marriage in Crisis

The first year of marriage can be a blissful but difficult time. Two people who have been living separate lives have promised to live one loving life together. That is not always an easy adjustment to make. A couple can find that they do not know as much about one another as they thought they did. Previously unknown or unexplored aspects of their personalities can reveal themselves in irritating as well as pleasant ways. They must learn to give as well as take if their marriage is to endure. And to cope with the challenges that life can put before them.

For James and Bessie, that first year of marriage was complicated by a third partner in their relationship: the United States Navy. Bessie discovered that James's mistress could be kind or cruel—a demanding and painful intruder into her new life with him. She came to realize that that mistress could not be given up or driven away.

During the first months of their marriage, nature ran its course for the Hetheringtons. A honeymoon and the Christmas and New Year's holidays came and went, and then Bessie moved with James to Erie, Pennsylvania, where his ship, the USS *Michigan*, was stationed. His duties aboard the old iron-hulled sidewheel steamer resembled service ashore more than sea duty. At least until spring thawed the ice on Lake Erie, his days were like those of a working civilian. He kissed Bessie goodbye, left the hotel where they lived for the ship, and spent the day with the friends and coworkers he had come to know over the past two years. Then he came home for dinner with Bessie. In the early evening they talked, or read, or perhaps played cards. And then they went to bed. There they discovered the joys of sex, over and over again. Repeated physical intimacy suffused with love that burned fresh and bright. Utter joy.

When morning dawned and they awoke, it was as if a dream had suddenly ended. James went off to his duties aboard the *Michigan*. Bessie stayed at home. Her days were lonely. She missed the companionship of her sisters. Life as a young bride in Erie was unlike anything she had

4. *Marriage in Crisis*

known. The city was not like Wilmington, but smaller, a railroad hub, and busier. She lived at its heart, near Perry Square, named for the naval hero of the War of 1812, not in a quasi-suburban village as she had back home. Erie was not a comfortable place—at least during the winter when the lake effect lashed the streets and filled the sky with snow such as she had never seen. No friendly neighbors lived in houses nearby. There was no circle of young navy wives for her to join, for most of James's fellow officers were bachelors.[1]

One morning, early in March, just as the first signs of spring began to show, everything changed for Bessie. She woke up feeling nauseous. When that kept on happening, she realized that she was pregnant, no longer alone but with a child growing within her. She was so excited that she could hardly contain herself until James came home. When she told him the happy news, he was overjoyed. Perhaps he gave her something just slightly less than a bear hug—not too tight lest he harm their child to be.

At that moment James and Bessie likely experienced a sense of complete happiness such as they had never known. They were going to be parents. And months of anticipation, of every day having something wonderful to look forward to, of talking about whether their first child would be a boy or a girl, of considering names for him or her, and for the birth itself spread out before them. Amazing! That news was so exciting for Bessie that she wanted to go back home to tell her parents and her sisters about it. James agreed that she could go to Wilmington for a short visit.

That sense of euphoria, of complete and all-encompassing happiness that James and Bessie experienced, effervesced a few days later when he received new orders. The navy intruded upon their married lives for a second time. The first time, only weeks after their wedding, that intrusion turned out to be brief and benign. He was ordered to report to the USS *Alliance*, destined for duty with the East Asian Squadron. That provoked anxiety for the newlyweds, for it portended years of separation. Five days later, those orders were cancelled.[2] Relief—great relief—followed. James returned to daytime duty on the *Michigan* and marital bliss with Bessie at night.

The second call from Washington proved more demanding and distressing. Ensign Hetherington was to report to the USS *Essex*, then undergoing repairs at the Brooklyn Navy Yard in New York City.[3] That was not bad news for James professionally. Every new assignment was a chance to improve oneself in the eyes of one's superiors. On a small ship with a small crew, a junior officer could do that by demonstrating sound judgment and individual command skills. On a large vessel, where one worked under a more senior officer, adaptability and accountability counted for more. But the *Essex* assignment was terrible personally. James knew that deployment to distant seas usually followed refitting. That meant separation from Bessie at the worst possible time for her—separation now during her pregnancy when she particularly needed his presence and emotional support; separation when the baby arrived; and then separation for years. The prospect of separation loomed over James and Bessie like a dark cloud moving ominously toward them.

When James reported aboard the *Essex* on April 22, 1890, he learned the ship was destined for two years of patrol on the South Atlantic Station, which stretched from the Caribbean to the southernmost tip of South America. James knew he had to give Bessie that news in person, so he telegraphed her to join him in New York City as soon as possible. She came immediately, and he told her the unhappy news. Then James and Bessie did what any recently married, newly pregnant couple would have done. They stayed together as long as they could—first in another hotel, then in rented quarters on a tree-shaded street not far from the navy yard. The move promised pleasant summer evenings together.

Not many happened. Bessie was suffering the pangs of pregnancy, feeling more uncomfortable with each passing day in the heat and humidity of a New York City summer. She wanted to go home to Wilmington, and James let her. He left on the *Essex* for sea trials and Fourth of July celebrations in Portland, Maine. When the ship returned to the Brooklyn Navy Yard, Bessie came back. Barely a week later, James was due to go to Washington for pre-promotion examinations for lieutenant. He felt very ill at ease about that, fell sick, and doubted he could pass the tests looming ahead. At this point, James and Bessie were miserable, pained by the very thought of being apart when their baby would be born. The situation would be even worse if James had sailed on the *Essex* and was gone for years. They agreed that under the circumstances, Bessie had best return to her family's home and stay there until their child was born.

That left James alone to face the question: What to do?[4]

Finding an answer did not come easily. James was pulled in different directions by his strong sense of duty. On the one hand, he felt he had to answer the navy's call and go to sea. On the other, he felt he should stay with Bessie, fulfilling his responsibilities as husband and father-to-be. "Judge" had been his nickname at the Naval Academy, and he still liked to be addressed that way. But he couldn't quickly decide what to do. He searched for one solution after another to his dilemma. The year 1890 had nearly ended before he found what he thought was the right thing to do.

At first he tried to have it both ways. He asked his superiors for a transfer from the *Essex* to a ship on the North Atlantic Station. That way he would go to sea but visit ports close to home where he could visit his wife and child. Washington turned him down. When he went to the capital

4. Marriage in Crisis

for pre-promotion exams, he tried to buy time before deciding. Could he have a year's leave before resigning from the navy? Asking such a question, deserting his mistress temporarily before leaving her permanently, must have pained James deeply. Commodore Francis Munroe Ramsay, the crusty old head of the Bureau of Navigation, explained that doing so would mean giving up his pending promotion and the additional income it would provide. James couldn't agree to that.

He returned to New York, where the *Essex* was in the last stages of preparation for its long overseas deployment, still uncertain about what to do. How could he leave the navy after 16 years of service? It had been his life. It gave him his friends. He expected to serve in it for the rest of his working life. But could he leave Bessie pregnant now, miss the birth of his child, and not see her and the baby for two years? That was unthinkable.

On August 14, two days before the *Essex* was due to depart, James got a telegram from Wilmington. Bessie asked him to resign from the navy. Her father offered to "see him through," that is provide financial support or temporary work in his lumber and hardware business until he could find a permanent civilian job. That message tipped the balance for James. Suddenly he knew what he had to do. He telegraphed his offer of resignation to the Navy Department. Hours later, he got a reply. If he would submit "a written, unconditional resignation," the commandant of the navy yard was authorized to detach him, effective immediately, from the *Essex*. He would be granted a year's leave with the resignation to take effect at its end.

James grabbed that lifeline. On Friday, August 15, 1890, he submitted his resignation, packed up his personal belongings, and bade his fellow officers goodbye. After saluting the flag as he left the quarterdeck, he walked down the brow to the pier and headed to the station for trains that would take him to Bessie in Wilmington. At that moment, he probably had tears in his eyes—tears of sorrow at leaving his mistress, the navy, and tears of joy at returning to Bessie, the love of his life. The next day, the USS *Essex* sailed out of New York harbor, bound for Brazil.[5]

James got a warm welcome when he walked through the front door of the Hewes home in Wilmington. At that moment, he was delighted to be with Bessie again. But the days and weeks that followed proved bittersweet. While he shared in the excitement that everyone felt while awaiting the birth of Bessie's baby, he found days of unsuccessful job hunting and inactivity trying. That changed, briefly, on Wednesday, October 15, when the postman delivered a puzzling letter from the Navy Department. James had been promoted to lieutenant, junior grade. How could that be, if, as he had been told, resignation precluded promotion?

That question remained unanswered for two weeks. Then a letter came from the secretary of the navy asking him to reconsider his resignation. The navy wanted him back, and that felt good. But he didn't answer the letter right away. The next day, Wednesday, October 29, 1890, while he waited outside, Bessie delivered their baby. She was exhausted, then so happy when she first held the infant, then proud as could be when James came into the room and she showed him their daughter. They named her Gladys. Days of happiness for everyone in the Hewes-Hetherington household followed.

James's joy, however, was tempered by the awful thought that submitting his resignation from the navy had been a mistake. That is a terrible, terrible feeling, as anyone who has ever made a big decision only to realize later that it was the wrong choice can attest. James loved his life in the navy, but he also loved Bessie, and now baby Gladys, every bit as much. Once again, he faced the question of what to do. Sensing that he just couldn't decide right away, he wrote to the secretary of the navy asking for "a little more time to consider the matter."

This time James took more time to decide than he had back in August. He wanted to ensure he would be certain his choice was right. He pondered the question, knowing that not just his own but also Bessie's and now baby Gladys's future was at stake. Once Bessie began to feel better after giving birth, he decided to talk with her about it. They talked about what he should do over and over again. Gradually his goal changed from finding some new answer to that question to persuading her to accept the choice he knew he wanted to make. He had to stay in the navy. They could live together as man and wife, as a family, as much as his duties would permit. She could manage those times when she would be, in effect, a single parent. They could enjoy a happy and secure future as a family—wherever the navy might send them.

It took time and many a talk, but eventually Bessie agreed to what he thought they should and must do. On Thursday, November 20, 1890, just a week before Thanksgiving Day, James wrote to the secretary of the navy giving his answer—the answer this time he knew was right. If the department was willing, he would like to withdraw his resignation and report himself ready for service at sea.

His superiors did not respond immediately, and anxious days for James and Bessie followed one after another as November faded into December. Finally, just 10 days before Christmas, another letter came from the Navy Department. James was allowed to withdraw his resignation "preparatory to going to sea." He could remain at home on leave until receiving orders that would reveal when and where that would happen.[6] That was the best early Christmas present the Hetherington family could have gotten. Their long-term future was decided.

So, too, was the state of their marriage. It would always have three partners: James, Bessie, and the U.S. Navy.

Four months passed before James, now a lieutenant, junior grade, learned when and where he was to report for sea duty. That time did not prove easy for the Hetherington family. Bessie found the first days of motherhood difficult. She may have found breastfeeding the baby painful or felt inadequate about how much milk she could give her. Baby Gladys did not thrive and worried her parents with sickliness for five weeks. Bessie slipped into unhappiness that lingered day after day.

Today new parents and their doctors would recognize that condition as the "postpartum blues." A physician would prescribe something for the new mother to ease her passage through that difficult time. In 1890, however, no one in the Hewes-Hetherington household knew what was wrong and what to do about it. James was particularly clueless. His Naval Academy education had been particularly deficient in the life sciences. James never had a class in biology at Annapolis because none was offered.[7] Neither there nor in school back in Dubuque was he taught anything about human biology, psychology, and sexuality. All he could do was fall back on a folk remedy. Perhaps a change of air would do Bessie good.

He took her and baby Gladys to Fortress Monroe, near Hampton Roads, Virginia, where Chesapeake Bay flowed into the Atlantic. Maybe the sea air would do her good. They stayed in one of the big old hotels that lined the shore there. James hired a nurse for Bessie and the baby. She regained her appetite, and they enjoyed fine food in the hotel dining room. Bessie's strength returned and she found mothering the baby easier. After 12 days, everyone was well enough, bodies better and spirits restored, to return to Wilmington. James still did not find the days there easy. He, a man used to action, found himself on leave with nothing to do. He was in the house most of the day, and that bred boredom. Uncertainly about his own and his family's immediate future lingered on—for months.

Finally, on Saturday, April 25, 1891, his new orders arrived. He was to report for duty to the USS *Marion*, a third-rate screw steamer then undergoing repairs at Mare Island Naval Shipyard, California.[8] The ship would be joining the Asian Squadron in the far Pacific where ships normally deployed for two or more years. Once again, prolonged separation from his family loomed before James. This time he was determined not to let that happen. While ships of the squadron patrolled from Singapore to Siberia, their longest and most frequent port calls came in Japan, particularly at Yokohama. James remembered the city from his visits there as a cadet midshipman a dozen years earlier. It had been safe and pleasant enough with Western-style shops and restaurants and hotels. Bessie and baby Gladys could live there while he had to be at sea. They all could enjoy happy times together when he returned. He made those points to Bessie, trying to persuade her to accept his decision about their immediate future. While they would have to separate for time, they could reunite in Yokohama.

The plan seemed logical. Better to be separated only some of the time rather than all the time during what was certain to be years of service on the Asian Station. James felt it balanced his obligations to his wife and his mistress. It grew out of his deep love for them both. But was it well thought out? Practical? Something that would be as good for Bessie and Gladys as it seemed to be to James?

In a word, no. He remembered Yokohama from his bachelor days, when he lived aboard the *Richmond*. He had no reason then to think about the costs of living in the city. Now, in April 1891, even with the modest pay increase that came with his promotion, would he have enough to cover his family's living expenses in Yokohama? An admiral or captain who earned far more than a mere lieutenant and brought his family to the city had no need to ask that question. And James had never met another married junior officer who had taken his family to Yokohama and could have told him about those costs.

No one could tell him, either, how wives in Yokohama fared while their husbands were away at sea. Officers on ships of the European Station had taken their wives and children to the Mediterranean for decades. Only recently had senior officers ventured to bring them to Japan. James also wasn't thinking about the social situation he would be putting Bessie in. She had been lonely in Erie. How much more so would she be in Yokohama, a strange city in a country she knew little or nothing about, so far away from home, and without friends of her own age and circumstance?

In James's mind, however, the plan was quite practical. The family would go to Dubuque together, and then he would go on to the *Marion* in California. Bessie and Gladys could stay with his father in Iowa. And then sometime in the fall, when his ship would arrive in Japan, they could reunite in Yokohama. That is what he told Bessie.

While she disliked having to separate in the short term, she "brightened up" at the prospect of their living together at least part-time. Nonetheless, the plan was daunting for her. Japan was so far away and so different from everything she had known in Wilmington. Traveling across two-thirds of the continent and then on across the Pacific with an infant would be difficult. But did she really have a choice to do anything other than agree to James's proposal? She had promised to obey him on their wedding day, and now she must do what he wanted. Bessie agreed to his plan—and started packing. The Hetheringtons' marriage had survived yet another crisis.

4. Marriage in Crisis

Three days later, after parting hugs and kisses from the Hewes family, James, Bessie, and baby Gladys left Wilmington. A day and a half later, they arrived in Dubuque, where his father, stepmother, and sister, Clara, greeted them warmly. Forty-eight hours of pleasant family time followed. Bessie got to know her in-laws. They in turn doted on her and their new grandchild. It was a brief happy time. Tears of parting flowed at the station when James boarded a train, bound for California.[9]

Little did James and Bessie imagine then how any days, weeks, and months would pass before their dream of reunion in Yokohama became true.

5

Fateful Journeys

James and Bessie parted on May 2, 1891. Six months passed before they reunited in Yokohama. Their journeys to Japan proved very different—geographically and experientially. For him, the journey marked a return to the familiar—but with a dash of the unexpected. For her, the trip was something entirely new—a great adventure that ended in a way she could never have imagined. The two journeys, no less than their ending in Yokohama, proved fateful for James, Bessie, and their marriage.

When James reported for duty aboard the USS *Marion* on May 7, 1891, one of the first things he did was ask about the ship's schedule. He was told it would arrive in Japan, at Yokohama, early in the fall. That seemed definite enough for him to go to the Pacific Mail Steamship office in San Francisco and book passage for Bessie and Gladys to join him there. They would sail on September 26 aboard the luxurious SS *China* and reach Japan about three weeks later—roughly the same time as the *Marion*. Hoping to reassure Bessie about the long journey ahead, he picked up a pamphlet about the ship that depicted the first-class stateroom she would have and mailed it to her. For weeks thereafter, as long as mail could be sent and received from the ship, James wrote Bessie daily and she responded. The Hetheringtons were together, if only vicariously, while they had to be apart.[1]

That ended on July 5, when the *Marion* sailed out through the Golden Gate and turned north, still bound for Japan, but now by way of Alaska and beyond into the Bering Sea.[2] That detour spelled delay and disappointment for James. The reunion with his wife and baby he dreamt of would have to wait far longer than expected, thanks to orders from his mistress, the navy.

The *Marion*'s new route resulted from Washington's determination to protect America's maritime natural resources and prevail in a diplomatic dispute. Specifically, to protect fur seals that bred on the Pribilof Islands north and west of the Alaskan mainland and swam as far south as the Aleutian Islands. In 1891, these mammals were threatened by

5. Fateful Journeys

USS *Marion* (NH 46404, Naval History and Heritage Command).

money-hungry American, British, and Canadian killers. These men made their living by selling sealskins to processors and manufacturers who in turn made fortunes by transforming them into protection for humans against winter's cold. Sealskin was in high demand and at the height of fashion in Europe and America at this time.

The United States and Great Britain had squabbled over how best to protect and profit from the fur seal fishery for years. Washington claimed it had exclusive jurisdiction over the land and waters the pelagic seals frequented. The Russians had proclaimed the same right back in 1821, and the Americans insisted it came to them with the purchase of Alaska in 1867. The British insisted that the Americans had no such policing authority beyond Alaskan territorial waters and disputed American experts' report that the North Pacific fur seal population was declining at an alarming rate. In 1890, London proposed arbitration to settle the dispute and rushed four formidable naval vessels from Asian to Canadian waters to back up their position. The U.S. Navy dispatched but one ship, smaller than the *Marion*, in response. Both sides wanted to avoid a clash and talks continued over the next year.

Finally, in June 1891, the two countries agreed on a temporary solution—a modus vivendi—that banned sealing on the high seas for a year and limited the number of seals that could be killed on land. Neither side, however, thought the other really sought a permanent solution to the dispute. That prompted the secretary of the navy to order the *Marion* and three other ships to Alaskan waters. Their mission was to enforce the terms of the modus vivendi by warning, seizing, or driving away ships that violated its terms. American officials hoped that would nudge the British into agreeing on arbitration procedures that would lead to a treaty regulating and protecting fur sealing in the northeastern Pacific. Thus the *Marion* was sent north to serve as a pawn on the diplomatic chessboard and to enforce the temporary sealing rules.[3]

The ship first called at Port Townsend, Washington, at the northwest tip of Puget Sound, where it took on provisions for the long journey that lay ahead. Then it stopped, just across the Strait of Juan de Fuca, in Victoria, British Columbia, to gather intelligence. By paying courtesy calls aboard Royal Navy warships in nearby Esquimalt Harbour, Commander John Russell Bartlett, the *Marion*'s captain, hoped to size up the capabilities of potential adversaries. He could also get charts and weather information about the waters his ship was about to traverse.[4]

The *Marion* took nearly two weeks to reach the Bering Sea. During that time, James bonded with his fellow officers. He already knew Captain Bartlett personally and by reputation. Alan Rogers, his fellow lieutenant, junior grade, was a classmate and his oldest friend in the navy. He had previously served with John Jacob Hunker, the ship's executive officer (second-in-command). He got better acquainted with Lieutenant C. Marrast Perkins, commander of the ship's small marine guard, the ship's two ensigns and engineers, and the two staff officers aboard—Paymaster Henry Colby and the ship's surgeon, Dr. Frank Bates Stephenson.[5]

Little did James know that these men would become his defenders when he went on trial for his life.

Working with them on the cold windswept waters of the northern Pacific was not entirely unpleasant. To be sure, there were storms and fogs that made duty aboard the *Marion* cold and wet. But there were also days of brilliant sunshine that poured light down on breaking seas and islands' shores. The days' actions varied—some alone peacefully, others action-filled in pursuit of sealers who killed their prey in violation of the terms of the modus vivendi. At the end of the day, James could enjoy conversation with his fellow officers over dinner in the wardroom. Then he could retire to a comfortable bunk in his cabin. Lying on it, he could look across to his desk and see the picture of Bessie and baby Gladys he kept there. Perhaps that triggered dreams of reunion with them in Yokohama.

When the fur sealing season ended in September, the *Marion* turned south, bound for Japan by way of Hawaii. It crawled along, not reaching Honolulu, capital of the then-independent kingdom of Hawaii, until the 26th of the month—the very same day Bessie and Gladys were scheduled

5. Fateful Journeys

to leave San Francisco for Yokohama aboard the SS *China*. A week later, on October 3, the *Marion* left Diamond Head in its wake and pointed its bow northwestward toward Japan. A moment of joy, certainly, for James, because it meant he would see Bessie and Gladys soon. That moment of happiness was followed by days of frustration and disappointment. The *Marion* was plagued with mechanical breakdowns, one after another, that slowed its progress to a crawl. Twenty-nine days passed before it dropped anchor off Yokohama late the afternoon of November 2, 1891.[6]

For James and Bessie that delay proved disastrous.

She had no idea her separation from James back in May would stretch on until November. Her journey to Japan, like his, did not go as planned. Neither direct nor predictable, it turned out to be a great adventure and a liberating experience. Perhaps too liberating for a navy wife.

James had tried to make Bessie's journey across the continent as easy as possible. He wanted her to begin it as relaxed and refreshed possible by staying with his family in Dubuque. She would not have it that way. After only a few weeks, not the months he had planned for her to remain in Iowa, Bessie decided to go back to her family in Wilmington.

Precisely why she did so remains unclear. Perhaps she felt ill at ease living with her in-laws. Perhaps they found having an infant in the house to be a burden. Perhaps she just wanted to spend time with her parents and sisters before spending nearly two years in Japan. If later newspaper reports are to be believed, she enjoyed herself, joining her mother and sisters for part of the summer at the fashionable Marine Villa at Cape May.[7]

Whatever her reason, leaving Dubuque lengthened Bessie's journey and made it more challenging. It took a day and a half to get back to Wilmington. When she finally headed west from there, it took as long again to reach Chicago, and then more than another day to reach Omaha, where she and Gladys boarded a Central Pacific/Union Pacific train bound for California. Nearly 2,900 miles, traveling day and night, passed before she reached San Francisco. All told Bessie, spent more than a week crossing the continent.

The Central Pacific advertised that the journey along the Great American Over-Land Route westward from Omaha would be made in "Speed! Comfort! And Safety." Trains pulled by modern locomotives would travel on steel rails and be halted by the newest Westinghouse brakes. Black porters would attend to passengers' every need, and the travelers could dine, even in the middle of the Nevada desert, at a restaurant that served "the finest delicacies of the season" for only 75 cents in coin or a paper dollar.[8]

The reality was rather more difficult. Sleeping car rooms were tiny and beds uncomfortable. One traveler described spending a night in one like lying on a mattress squeezed onto the bottom shelf of one's cupboard with the door shut. As the night wore on, the room became stifling because windows were locked. In the morning when they could be opened, a person was likely to get a face full of soot and smoke blowing from the locomotive. He or she would then have to go down to the far end of the car and wait in line to use the washbasin to clean up before returning to one's room to dress before breakfast.[9]

Such a long journey with Gladys must have been very difficult for Bessie. The transcontinental trip was the first time she had been alone with the child for any length of time. She had to meet the baby's every need—feeding her, comforting her, changing and cleaning her diapers, and getting her to sleep—all by herself. She was in the minority aboard the trains, for far fewer women than men traveled on them, and the fewer still of them with children had a husband along to help. She had to negotiate the crowds that swarmed into stations and restaurants along the way as well as those that queued up on the dock at Oakland while waiting for the ferry that would take them to San Francisco. That was wearing, to say the least. Bessie must have felt exhausted as well as relieved when she stepped ashore there.

From that point onward, however, things brightened up. She rested for a few days at a fine hotel while waiting for her ship to arrive. There she dined and conversed with other guests, including gentlemen who remembered her beauty and conviviality months later. Finally the day came—September 26, 1891—when she and Gladys boarded the SS *China*.

Seeing it for the first time must have been exciting. The ship was huge, stretching more than 400 feet from stem to stern. Its two funnels and four masts jutted skyward from the uppermost of its five decks. One hundred twenty first-class passengers could be accommodated in its staterooms, and up to 3,000 more could be squeezed belowdecks in steerage. Bessie and Gladys had their own stateroom on one of its upper decks.[10]

The moment was exciting for Bessie in another way. She had had little contact with people of color—few, if any, other than the porters and pullman stewards on the train. Now she was on a dock crowded with Asians—300 Chinese returning home plus a crew of baggage handlers, room boys, and waiters. These were the people who would cater to her needs aboard the *China*.[11]

Late that afternoon, the ship passed through the Golden Gate and out into the open ocean. Bessie, who had never been beyond the relatively sheltered waters of Delaware Bay, likely suffered a moment of anxiety. Giant swells rocked the ship, making it difficult to keep one's footing. Was she going to get seasick, or worse still, do so when baby Gladys was ill? Would the seas on the 4,800-mile sea voyage that lay ahead be this rough? Would she be able to endure three weeks at sea before reaching Japan?

5. Fateful Journeys

Life at sea could be boring. Breakfast, tiffin (lunch), and dinner followed one day after another in unchanging order. The view from one's room or on deck from bow or stern varied little. The color of the endless waters stretching to an empty horizon shifted only slightly from shades of blue to gray, depending on whether the sky was clear or shrouded by clouds and fog. The Pacific Mail Steamship Company tried to break the monotony with special meals, talks, concerts, and even dancing in the evening for its guests.

Bessie readily joined in those activities—sometimes with, sometimes without baby Gladys, whom she could leave temporarily with ship stewards. Most of her fellow passengers were men, but there were young women her own age, couples—well-to-do tourists—and a few missionary families with children. She made friends with people, conversed with them over dinner, and afterward joined them in the evening's entertainments. She socialized as freely with fellow passengers as if they were girlfriends or prospective beaus met when vacationing at Cape May.

Finally, after nearly three weeks at sea, the day everyone aboard was waiting for came: Tuesday, October 13, 1891. Someone spied land on the horizon. Japan at last! Mount Fuji jutting into the sky! The SS *China* slowed and took on a pilot, who guided the ship into Tokyo Bay, and headed on to Yokohama, where it dropped anchor about a quarter of a mile offshore. The ship arrived at a perfect time—*akibare*, the season of clear and cool autumn days. A swarm of sampans carrying hawkers for the various hotels in the city surrounded the ship. As soon as the captain allowed, passengers began debarking, climbing into the tiny vessels bobbing up and down in the waves. One of them took on Bessie, Glady, and their baggage. Fifteen minutes later, they were helped onto the *hatoba* (broad pier) and took their first steps on Japanese soil.

A rickshaw waited to take them to the Grand Hotel—Yokohama's finest. Bessie likely was impressed from the first moment she stepped inside. The hotel boasted cuisine prepared by a "first class French chef," a dining room that could seat 300 guests, "lofty and spacious reading and billiard rooms," and "baths with the latest sanitary improvements." After she registered, a clerk showed Bessie and her baby to their suite of two rooms. They were on the second floor of the rambling structure, at one end of the older section of the building, far from the hustle and bustle of the hotel's public areas. The second room would be needed for the *amah* (nanny) who would help take care of Gladys.

Bessie was delighted to learn that the woman, Shiraishi Tome, spoke some English, had previously worked for other foreigners, and came cheap—only $12 a month. While she normally returned home in the evening, she could stay overnight, if need be. That would allow Bessie to take

Grand Hotel, Yokohama, Japan, site of love and murder (71006-004 Kjeld Duits Collection, Tokyo).

her evening meal in the hotel dining room or go to one of the many entertainments in the city, even if they ended late at night. After having to care alone for baby Gladys on her long journey, Bessie would have help. Perhaps she felt suddenly liberated.[12]

Free she was until James would arrive. That turned out to be much longer—more than three weeks—than expected. Bessie had no time to be bored or lonely. Her introduction to Yokohama proved very different from his dozen years earlier. Then he had been a mere midshipman, a bachelor who had little chance and no particular desire to join in the social life of Yokohama's expatriate community. She, by contrast, was more outgoing than he, and her status as an American navy wife gave her easy entrée to the elite of Yokohama's 800-person English-speaking community. They recognized that she was different from the wealthy tourists who stopped only briefly in the city, using it as a jumping-off place for their further travels in and beyond. Her stay would be long and presumably pleasant, so she should be regarded as a new neighbor. So "the better sort" of Yokohama's English-speaking community readily welcomed Mrs. Lieutenant James Henry Hetherington, U.S. Navy, into their fellowship.[13]

She plunged into what one Tokyo-based American bachelor disparaged as "social life structured around middle-class femininity."[14] Bessie enjoyed herself thoroughly. She befriended the kinds of people she could never have dreamed of meeting back in Wilmington or, God forbid,

Dubuque. She became especially close friends with two couples. The first of them, John Frederick and Julia Lowder, became almost foster parents to her. They prided themselves on being among the oldest foreign residents of Yokohama. He had come to Japan in 1860 at 17 as an apprentice British diplomat and sometime soldier who defended Yokohama's resident foreigners from attacks by samurai opposed to their presence. He met and married Julia, the daughter of a pioneering American missionary. Over the following years, after serving in various diplomatic posts, he became one of Yokohama's most prominent and respected barristers. She was a devout Christian who promoted education for Japanese women and was regarded as the grande dame of the Yokohama expatriate social world.[15]

Julia may well have introduced Bessie to the second couple, two genuine aristocrats: Prince Anatoli Grigorievitch Lobanov-Rostovsky, the Russian consul, and his wife, Charikalia. Bessie especially enjoyed going out for walks with the princess. She and her diplomat husband had three children, and a fourth was on the way when Bessie met them. The American navy wife, the princess, and their children presented a pretty picture strolling along the *bund* (sidewalk) that fronted Yokohama's harbor.[16]

As a member of Yokohama's elite, Bessie was expected to behave properly. The English outnumbered Americans in Yokohama, and their sense of class and social norms governed the expatriate elite's behavior. She could dine alone, if she chose to do so, and she could accept invitations to a special dinner, a musical evening, and even the dances—some formal, others just informal Saturday evening "hops"—at the Grand Hotel. But she was expected to appear in male company. Since her husband had yet to arrive, that meant either as part of a group of friends or with a man to whom she had been properly introduced. Introductions here were formal—not casual as they had been back at Cape May when she first met James.

Most foreign men living in Yokohama in the early 1890s were bachelors. Single non–Japanese women were scarce, and ones like Bessie, blessed as she was with strikingly good looks, were rarer still. Her blonde hair and bright blue eyes naturally commanded the attention of men, young and old. One evening, about a week after she arrived, when she was dining with one of her fellow passengers from the *China*, an older gentleman who knew him came over to their table. He was introduced to her and joined in the conversation. After a bit, he asked if he might introduce a friend to her. She agreed. That was how Bessie met George Gower Robinson—the man who would become her lover, her husband's nemesis, and the victim he would kill.[17]

Who was George Gower Robinson?

His fellow expatriates knew him as a popular, well-respected, and successful English broker. Robinson was a partner in the firm of Bill and Bullion Brokers, located at #30, not far from the Grand Hotel. Gower, as he preferred to be called, was like many other young men who came to Japan to make their fortunes in the late-19th century. He arrived in Yokohama in 1880 as an assistant accountant for the Hong Kong and Shanghai Banking Corporation. He had trained for the position in Hong Kong, where he been born in 1856. His goal was to eventually head his own brokerage firm. That dream became reality in 1890, barely a year before Bessie and James Hetherington came to Yokohama.[18]

Gower, however, was by no means a run-of-the-mill fortune seeker. He was the scion of two distinguished British expatriate families. His paternal grandfather had prospered in Malta and then moved to Livorno (Leghorn) in northern Italy. His father, John, was born there, but when revolutionary unrest in northern Italy disrupted commerce, he decided to seek his fortune in East Asia. John S. Robinson came out to Japan in the early 1860s, but for reasons unknown decided to relocate to Hong Kong. There he met and married Gower's mother, Adaliza Letitia Gower. She had been born into another long-established British expatriate family in Livorno. In due course, the couple produced George Gower Robinson and his younger sister, Gwendoline. They spent their earliest years in a handsome home that their father had built for his family. It sat halfway up the mountain overlooking Hong Kong.[19]

When the children reached school age, they were, as British expatriate family custom dictated, sent "home" to England to get a proper education. They lived under the care of their aunt Rosina in Dulwich, located in what is now south London. Her house eventually became home to nine children, three of whom were each other's cousins. Gower attended the local Dulwich school, but eventually he and his sister completed their education elsewhere. She attended a finishing school in Geneva, and before being sent out to Hong Kong, he traveled elsewhere on the Continent.[20]

Gower Robinson came to Yokohama in 1880 as an ambitious 24-year-old bachelor. From the moment of his arrival, he stood out as someone different from his coworkers at the Hong Kong and Shanghai Bank and his peers in the broader expatriate community. His olive complexion, inherited from his Italian grandmother, and his black eyes, hair, and moustache, gave him an exotic look. He dressed "in rather a gorgeous way [favoring] velvet waistcoats and highly colored neckties." He was adventurous. One of his regular customers at the bank remembered meeting him at Jigokudani (The Valley of Hell) at Miyanoshita, near Mount Fuji, where he "bounded up the rocks of a steaming volcanic ridge like an antelope." He also had a beautiful baritone voice and sang at concerts in various languages.[21]

5. Fateful Journeys

Gower slipped easily into Yokohama's expatriate society. He frequented the United Club, where he dined and drank and played billiards with fellow bachelors. In time he acquired a handsome home—#172—at the far end of the bluff that overlooked the city. It came with two servants—a houseboy who cooked and cleaned and a *bettō*, or groom and stableman who cared for his horse and carriage. Gower was a generous host. He welcomed local couples to dinners and invited bachelor friends and associates, including British and American junior naval officers, to spend evenings or stay overnight at his home. He also attended services at Christ Church and joined in various community social events such as family evening musicals, dances at the Grand Hotel, and most certainly race days at the Yokohama Racing Club.[22]

In October 1891, when Bessie arrived, Gower was one of the most popular and well-liked men in the Yokohama foreign community. At age 35, still handsome, secure in his profession, and well-to-do, he was the city's most eligible bachelor. Women of all ages were drawn to him. He, in turn, had an eye for the most beautiful among them. That number included Mrs. Bessie Hetherington. He first saw her in the Grand Hotel dining room on the evening of her arrival. From that moment, he knew he had to meet and be properly introduced to her.

That happened a week later, on October 20, thanks to a Captain Gamble, who had been in Japan for some time and was waiting for the next ship bound for North America. Gower counted him as a friend and asked him for an introduction to the beautiful Mrs. Hetherington. She was dining that evening with Chicago railroad magnate Columbus R. Cummings, the uncle of one of her best friends from the *China*. The ship's other visiting passengers had gone off to Nikko, a beautiful mountain resort that featured the mausolea of the first and third Tokugawa shoguns, a shimmering lake, and numerous waterfalls. When Captain Gamble came to their table, he asked if he might introduce his friend, George Gower Robinson. Mr. Cummings nodded, and Bessie agreed. Then the handsome Englishman took her hand, looked into her eyes, and told her who he was. She smiled back at him, saying she was pleased to make his acquaintance.[23]

At that moment, Bessie likely thought their meeting was of no particular consequence.

Three days later, on Friday, October 23, she joined a group of acquaintances going to a concert in Tokyo. They left Yokohama late in the afternoon, dined at the Imperial Hotel, Tokyo's finest, and then listened to Herr Friedenthal, the famous German lieder singer, perform. His program ran longer than expected, so the concertgoers ended up taking the last train back to Yokohama. Their first-class car was configured British style, that is with outside doors that opened into compartments that seated only four people. Bessie found herself sitting with three men, one of whom was Gower Robinson. When the train reached Yokohama Station shortly after midnight, the passengers chatted together as they walked toward its entrance where rickshaws waited to take them to their hotels or homes. Gower Robinson came up to Bessie and offered her a ride. His *bettō* and trap[24] were waiting outside, he said, and riding with him might be more comfortable than taking a rickshaw. Without hesitation, Bessie accepted his offer.

Her response demonstrated how independent she had become since parting with James. Up until that time, she had always lived under a man's eye—her father's, the Vassar president's, her husband's, or her father-in-law's. On her journey to Japan, however, she had done extraordinary things on her own. She traveled across America and sailed across the Pacific, all the while caring for baby Gladys. She made her own way into Yokohama's expatriate community. All had all gone well, and her self-confidence had blossomed. She knew she could take care of herself.

So she had no qualms about accepting Gower Robinson's offer. Taking his hand, she climbed up onto the seat of the waiting trap. He walked around to its opposite side and took the reins from his *bettō*. The groomsman scurried around to the back of the trap and climbed up onto its rear-facing seat. The gallant Englishman then clicked his tongue and tapped the reins on the horse as a signal to start walking. They headed for the Grand Hotel, no more than 10 minutes away.

But Robinson did not stop at its front entrance. He continued on, rounded the hotel's farthest corner, turned left over a bridge, left once more, and then right onto Camp Hill Road. Gower slapped the reins on the horse's back once more to make it pull them up the road until they reached the top of the bluff. Then they proceeded down its winding lane, turned left once more, and stopped at #172—Robinson's house, which sat on a secluded site on the far side of the bluff. There Gower helped Bessie down and took her inside.[25]

She did not leave the house until the last hour of darkness, just after five the next morning—Saturday, October 24. The *bettō* drove her to the rear entrance of the Grand Hotel. Heavily veiled so no one might recognize her, Bessie went inside, climbed the stairs, and walked directly to her room. She was tired and went to bed, leaving it to *amah* Tome to care for Gladys that morning.[26]

One can only imagine what ran through her mind when she awoke. What had happened to her? Had she been abducted by a sexual predator and fallen victim to his advances or willingly accepted them? Was she innocent? Guilty? An unfaithful wife? An adulteress who had broken her marriage vows? Or had she just given in to natural desire, seeking sexual fulfillment after months of celibacy? Was what had happened "just one of those things," as songwriter Cole Porter later put it—or the beginning of something else? A delight—or a disaster?

We cannot know the answer to those questions.

But one thing is clear. Bessie Hewes Hetherington's long journey was fateful. It came to an end that neither she nor her husband, James, could have imagined. What happened on the night of October 23–24, 1891, would change their lives forever.

6

Propriety and Passion

Late in the afternoon of Tuesday, November 2, 1891, the USS *Marion* dropped anchor off Yokohama. After nearly six months apart from them, James could hardly wait to be reunited with Bessie and baby Gladys. He had missed them terribly. Every night he gazed at their photograph alongside his bunk before dropping off to sleep. Now the day he had been waiting for so long had finally come.[1]

About 15 minutes after the ship stopped moving, a boat came alongside. Someone in it handed up a newspaper that listed Bessie as a guest at the Grand Hotel. James read it and then hurried ashore as soon as his duties permitted. He went directly to her room, hoping to find his wife and daughter there, but they were gone. He waited for a good half hour. And then Bessie, *amah* Tome with Gladys, and another woman came in. Three of them left the room, leaving James alone with Bessie, eager to begin the reunion he had dreamed of for so long.

When he hugged and kissed her, she was not as warmly responsive as he had hoped. They talked for a while, freshened up, and went downstairs for dinner. Then they retired to their room for the night. At that point, as James later remembered it, Bessie seemed different—distant and even cold.[2] Afterward, he lay awake trying to explain to himself what might be wrong. Perhaps he had arrived at a bad time of the month for Bessie, when "the woman's curse" had struck her. Perhaps the dinner they had just eaten did not sit well with her. Maybe she was feeling the lingering strain of her long journey with the baby all the way from Wilmington to Yokohama.

James could not possibly have imagined what was probably troubling Bessie: mixed feelings about the night of October 23–24—the night she had spent with Gower Robinson. If she enjoyed whatever she did then, should she feel guilty about it now? And what would she do if her husband found out about it? Bessie certainly was not about to tell him. Pleasure, guilt, and anxiety warred in her mind. Little wonder she was not so responsive that evening to James's amorous advances.

6. Propriety and Passion 53

His presence in Yokohama changed everything—for him, for Bessie, and for Gower Robinson. Change struck James from the first moment he stepped ashore. The landscape. Yokohama in 1891 looked different from the city he had visited in 1879. Bigger. Its population, both foreign and Japanese, had nearly doubled. The number of Americans in the foreign community was about the same, but a third again as many Britons had arrived in the last dozen years. Yet the English he heard on the streets was definitely American—a dialect, Rudyard Kipling quipped, that bore more resemblance to Patagonian than to the Queen's English.[3] More up-to-date. A massive breakwater that would allow ships to anchor much closer to shore was under construction.

A new customs house boasting a handsome tower had just been built. The streets in the foreign settlement had been paved, curbed, and drained. A new enlarged waterworks promised safe drinking water, dispelling the fears of cholera that had swept over the city back in 1879. Some of the buildings that fronted the harbor, the recently remodeled and enlarged Grand Hotel foremost among them, now had electric light. The Yokohama foreign settlement that James saw had become an island of modernity, surrounded by a sea of Japanese.

The British controlled the foreign settlement's economic and social institutions, however. They dominated banking, shipping, and insurance firms and brought in more imports than any other nationality. Britons headed the United Club, the Chamber of Commerce, the Cricket and Athletic Club, and most of the ladies' clubs and associations that had proliferated as more foreign women and children came to the city. The greater size and firepower of Royal Navy ships that frequented Yokohama symbolized British socioeconomic dominance.

The greatest change for James, however, came in his professional and social status. That became obvious to him the morning after he arrived. In 1879, as a mere midshipman, he came to the city for personal reasons, seeking rest and recreation. Now as an officer of rank and responsibility, he was expected to participate fully in the diplomatic events as well as the social life of the foreign community.[4] That morning, he and Bessie had to rush to get ready to go to the emperor's birthday party in Tokyo that afternoon. They and the *Marion*'s other officers and their spouses would be joining the cream of Japan's foreign residents—diplomats, missionaries, businessmen and merchants—and the empire's ennobled entourage to honor the sovereign on his 39th birthday.

The event, originally meant to demonstrate how far Japan had come on the road from its isolated past to present-day modernity, demanded sartorial splendor. His Majesty and the empress would greet guests in their finest Western garb—he in a beribboned military uniform, she in a

Parisian-styled gown. Guests were expected to arrive in their best formal attire. James had to ready his full-dress dark blue uniform and clean his sword and scabbard. Bessie donned her formal gown and put on her finest jewelry for what promised to be a fairy-tale-like affair. A troublesome presence would darken it for her. That afternoon, when she and James boarded the train for Tokyo, there was Gower Robinson headed for the imperial birthday celebration.

The festivities continued until late in the evening. First a formal reception at the Hama Imperial Detached Palace, then dinner and dancing at a grand ball at the Imperial Hotel, Tokyo's finest Western hostelry. When James and Bessie retired to their room at the Grand Hotel, they saw something missing: a telephone.

The next day they went sightseeing in Tokyo, following the well-established route for foreign tourists. They strolled through Shiba Park, visiting the massive Zojoji Temple and shrines that housed the mausolea of the Tokugawa shoguns. They sampled Japanese food at two of the teahouses nearby. They walked through Hibiya Park to see the cherry blossom gate (Sakuradamon), once the entrance to the shogun's castle, reflected in the moat surrounding the Imperial Palace. A visit to the popular Asakusa quarter followed. It swarmed with people praying for good luck at a famous temple, buying food and trinkets of all kinds, and generally enjoying themselves. That was the closest they got to the place every foreigner had heard about but none dared visit: "the celebrated Yoshiwara, the abode of frail beauties" whose sexual charms were reserved for Japanese men.

After an early dinner, the Hetheringtons boarded an eight-o'clock train for Yokohama. Their visit to Japan's fabled capital, their first diplomatic event together, may well have warmed Bessie's and James's feelings toward one another. Perhaps it even figured in their dreams that night.[5]

Bessie awoke the next morning to a sobering reality: James's presence defined her place in Yokohama's expatriate society, and it would shape her social, as well as her personal, life. Until his arrival, even though she was introduced to people at the Grand Hotel as a wife awaiting him, her days continued much as they had at sea. She chatted and dined with her fellow *China* passengers as freely and without regard to wealth or position as she had aboard the ship. Freed from domestic duties and child care, she dined frequently with Gower Robinson. That was no more. No longer that free-spirited independent person she had been, she was now Mrs. Lieutenant James Henry Hetherington, an American navy officer's wife. She was expected to behave in accordance with the constraints of naval tradition and propriety that his rank imposed.

Bessie had to join the American navy wives' semiofficial club. Within that group, rank, appearance, and behavior truly mattered. Frances Belknap, wife of the admiral commanding the Asiatic Squadron, outranked all the other navy spouses. Jeanie Bartlett, as the *Marion*'s captain's spouse, took precedence over Bessie and other junior officers' wives. The navy wives group's most important community function was determining who should—or should not—be invited to American navy–sponsored social events such as formal balls and Saturday evening "hops" (dances) at the Grand Hotel. The more senior women also cast a sharp eye on the younger wives' behavior. They were expected to observe all of the naval service's traditions, showing deference to their seniors, presenting calling cards when required, and following their husbands' lead at social events.[6] In short, Bessie at age 23 suddenly was burdened with greater expectations and behavioral constraints than she had ever known.

Could she meet these obligations with the grace and dignity expected of a navy wife? Could she find her way in Yokohama's diverse, multinational expatriate community? In a society that presented temptations as well as previously unimagined opportunities? Could Bessie strike a balance between the propriety that her status demanded and the passions she felt within? Only time, her husband, James, and her sometime-lover, Gower, would tell.

James Hetherington's presence in Yokohama circumscribed Gower Robinson's social life as never before. His previous liaisons with visiting women had posed no threat to his reputation as a proper English gentleman, successful businessman, and the city's most eligible bachelor. Those women left. Bessie would stay. Her husband's presence limited what he could do in her presence. Single men were expected to keep their distance from married women. If chance circumstance or community social events brought them together, Gower would have to behave with the utmost propriety toward Mrs. Hetherington. If he did not ... what might others in the community think? And what might her husband do? Gower sensed that an element of danger such as he had never known had entered his life. Could he behave properly in the social whirl Yokohama sucked its foreign residents into? Could he hide or at least restrain his strong feelings, nay his passion, for Bessie with James present?

The Yokohama foreign community's crowded social calendar over the next month put James, Bessie, and Gower to the test. James passed it easily, for he had long since accepted the limitations on his life that the navy imposed. Duty came first, family needs second, and proper social behavior followed behind. He knew who he was and how he must behave in society, wherever he might be. Bessie found the test more difficult. She wanted to be a proper navy wife and to behave as "the better sort" of people in Yokohama expected. But she was younger, more vivacious, and used to socializing freely with men and women alike as she had back home in Wilmington and at sea. And Gower, whose company she had shared in public and in private, seemed to pop up everywhere.

That was no accident. The Englishman seized every opportunity the social calendar provided to get close to Bessie, with or without James. A week after the emperor's birthday celebration, the three of them went to an imperial garden party in Tokyo. That same evening, November 10, he sang at a benefit concert for Christ Church in Yokohama. Bessie attended but James did not. On November 19, the Hetheringtons and two other couples joined Gower for dinner at his elegant home on the bluff. Ten days later, he invited Bessie and James to go on a Sunday stroll along its winding main street, take tea at his home, and then be his guests for dinner at the United Club. When James and Bessie joined "the better sort" for a formal Saint Andrew's Day ball at the Grand Hotel, Gower was there. Four days later, he skated next to Bessie at a party that marked the beginning of the Christmas and New Year's holiday season.[7]

At each and every one of these events, Gower pushed the boundaries of acceptable behavior toward Bessie. He just couldn't resist trying to talk alone with her, walk with her, drink with her, and owerwise reveal his passion for her. His feelings for her burst into full public view at that November 10 benefit concert for Christ Church. James had duty aboard ship that evening and arranged for an officer from the USS *Charleston* to escort Bessie to the concert. When they arrived, Gower took a seat next to her and chatted amiably until the time came for him to perform.

Then, his voice quavering with emotion and his eyes casting longing glances toward her, he sang *Call Me Back*.

> If as you wander where of old we met,
> You hear a voice amid the sleeping flowers,
> It is my heart that cannot e'er forget
> Those hours with thee, those golden hours.

When the applause died down, Gower's face flushed. He returned to his seat and sat down again next to Bessie. Did she blush? Others in the audience thought she did.[8]

Gower's behavior that evening might seem innocent enough to 21st-century observers, but in 1891 it shocked everyone who observed it. Tongues started wagging about what might be going on between Gower and Bessie. By the end of November, she realized that she had to silence them—and stop him. She wrote Gower a letter, telling him that his overly familiar behavior toward her in public must stop. The closeness they had known since the October night they had spent together at his home could not continue. As a wife and a mother, her obligations to James and Gladys

6. Propriety and Passion

must triumph over whatever feelings she had for him. Bessie knew where her priorities must lie.[9]

So, too, did James. His suspicions about Gower's behavior toward Bessie had been growing. On the night of December 3, when the Englishman kept skating close and talking to her, they reached the point where he could no longer contain them. The next morning, he penned a letter to Gower directing him to "cease all attentions" to his wife. The letter contained an implicit threat. If Robinson did not do so, James wrote, anything more than "a formal recognition" would be considered "a personal matter." He did not spell out just what that meant.

Gower replied haughtily with a self-exculpatory letter. He assured James that "nothing wrong" had occurred between Bessie and himself. He meant no harm but had been led on, or possibly deceived by, her "frank and open manner." He begged to be allowed to speak to her in open society so as to disarm any suspicions of wrongdoing that others might harbor. James agreed to that and wrote back calmly, saying he hoped that that would put an end to the matter.

It did not.

The following week, the *Marion* was scheduled to go to sea for target practice. One morning before it left, James went to his commanding officer, Commander John Russell Bartlett,[10] and told him he had asked Robinson to keep away from his wife. He hoped the Bartletts would not invite him to their home, especially when Bessie might be visiting there. The captain agreed not to do so. But James wanted to know for certain what, if anything, might happen while he was at sea. So he hired Japanese detectives to shadow Bessie and Gower.

When the *Marion* returned to Yokohama, James went straight to their office to find out what had happened in his absence. What he heard proved reassuring but troubling. The official report, read to him in translation from the Japanese-language original, contained "nothing serious." It said that while Gower had "seemed very desirous" to see Bessie, she had shown "no desire and no inclination to see him." Later, however, two detectives came to James's hotel room and told him that Gower had sent a letter to Bessie in his absence. She had read it, crumpled it up, and thrown it in the fire in her room. That was very reassuring. Bessie, as James later put it, "was trying the best to do right." But Gower? He was not—"decidedly not."

That prompted James to send him a second, more threatening letter. He alleged that Gower had not kept his promise as a gentleman to stay away from his wife. If he "even attempted to pay any more attention to her," he, James Henry Hetherington, "would take it out of his miserable hide." The threat was clear. There was no need for Robinson to reply, James wrote. He wanted nothing whatsoever to do with him.

But Gower could not keep away from Bessie. A week before Christmas, an informal "leap year" dance was held at the Grand Hotel. When James and Bessie went down from their room to the ballroom, Robinson was already there dancing. At the next dance he came up to Bessie and asked her to dance. Someone in the room had suggested that he do so lest "it would look queer," he explained. James would have none of that. Four evenings later, the Hetheringtons went to a Christmas party at the home of Herbert Maurice Bevis, the manager of the Hong Kong and Shanghai Bank branch in Yokohama. He had been Gower's boss for years, and Robinson was certain to be there. Sure enough, he was. He spoke casually to Bessie as she was coming downstairs from dropping off her coat in an upper room. When he caught sight of James following just behind her, he snuck quickly into another room. That triggered James's suspicion of Robinson's intentions toward his wife. But somehow he managed to set it aside for Christmas. That evening he and Bessie enjoyed a traditional English holiday dinner at the home of John Frederick and Julia Lowder. Lowder was Gower Robinson's attorney.[11]

The next day, Boxing Day in British tradition, suspicion rekindled in James's mind. Sometime earlier, Bessie had shown him a picture of her that she had had taken before his arrival in Yokohama. She asked him if he liked it. Rather than saying something noncommittal, such as "It's nice" or "It captures you well," James replied that he didn't like it. Not wise words for a husband to speak to his wife. And a hint of the questions swirling in his mind at the moment. Why had she had the picture taken? He already had a nice one of her. Who might it be for? Bessie said nothing at the time, but her feelings were hurt. Sometime later, she removed the photograph from their room. When James went to look for it the day after Christmas, he couldn't find it.

So he went to Farsari's photography studio where the picture had been taken.[12] When he asked about it, the clerk showed him a locket containing photos of Bessie and baby Gladys. He said the locket had not been paid for. Hoping to find out who had ordered it and where it had been made, James went to a Japanese jeweler Bessie might have patronized. But the man there said he knew nothing about the locket.

James could only wonder who had ordered the photographs and the locket. The more he thought about that, the angrier he became. It had to have been Robinson. The next morning, even before getting dressed, he went to the armoire in their room, opened its doors, and took out a valise. When he dumped out its contents, formal notes, visiting cards, a photograph, and a race book tumbled to the floor. James spotted an envelope addressed to Bessie in handwriting he did not recognize. Opening it, he found a letter from Gower Robinson.

6. Propriety and Passion

The letter confirmed James's worst suspicion: the Englishman and his wife had been having an affair. Wanting to end it, Bessie had written begging Gower, "Don't ask me to meet you again. I mean to be a better wife, and good night and good bye." He wrote an impassioned reply, pleading, "Good God, darling, you don't mean you are going to throw me over after all that has passed!" Didn't she realize that she had made him "Love you, worship you?" And now she was saying "I have had enough" and bidding him goodbye? "Have you no heart?" he asked. He couldn't believe she meant to do that.

"Those great big blue loving eyes" could not have lied when they looked into his. When he saw her earlier smiling down from her hotel room window, her lips had said "I love you." He begged her as "My love, my love, see me once more.... I swear as a man and a gentleman that I won't ask you to meet me again.... But let me kiss those lips and eyes once more and then ... forget if I possibly can." Quoting from the song he had sung to her at the Christ Church concert—"those golden hours I passed with them"—Gower burst out, "I love you, my darling, and am crazy after you.... Meet me once more ere we part for good."

The words of that letter sent James into a paroxysm of fury and grief, shame and confusion. He was so angry with Bessie that he overlooked the fact that she had told Gower their affair must end. He was sad beyond life to think that she might have broken their marriage vows. Was his life as a married man, his life as protector of his family over? He was shamed, as shamed as any man who had just learned he might be a cuckhold would be. He wondered if he had somehow been an inadequate lover for Bessie. Not least, James was confused about what to do next.

When he confronted Bessie with the letter, she knew exactly what to do. She listened quietly to his first thought: He should send her home—get her away from Robinson and all of Yokohama's temptations—on the very next steamer. He would show their friends Robinson's letter so they would understand why she was leaving. She didn't want him to do that, and he didn't want her to take baby Gladys with her when she left. She pleaded with him to let her go but not be publicly shamed. She agreed to go home to Wilmington and leave the baby behind with him in Yokohama.

At that point, Bessie and James stopped talking. He got dressed, went downstairs, and left the hotel determined to put into effect his plan to end the affair between Robinson and his wife. Storming out the hotel back door, he hurried across the ride over the creek and started hiking up the road to the bluff. Once he reached the top, he headed toward the convent of the Sisters of St. Maur, who ran an orphanage and school. James thought the nuns would be willing to take Gladys in. But by that time it was a dark and rainy Sunday afternoon, and he couldn't find their place.

So he turned to Captain and Mrs. Bartlett for help. When he knocked on their door, Jeanie Bartlett answered and let him in. He poured out his heart to her, explaining what had happened. He had to send his wife home. Would she care for Gladys temporarily, until he found a permanent place for the child? She declined at first, saying that Bessie was "the proper guardian" for her baby. Then she relented and agreed to do as he had asked if her husband approved. James thanked her and left, relieved that he had found a way out of the terrible situation that Gower Robinson—and Bessie—had put him in.

When he returned to the Grand Hotel, the clerk told him that Bessie had come down looking for him—twice. When he went back to their room, she asked him to go to one of the Japanese stores—the only ones open on a Sunday—and get some food for Gladys. But before he left, he blurted out that he knew about the photograph and the locket that he supposed were for Robinson. He told her he had gotten detectives to watch her and the Englishman while he had been at sea. Furious, James spat out his words with a passion that Bessie had never seen in him before. The temperate spouse who liked to be called "Judge" had vanished. In his place, a raging bull of a man shouted at her.

Bessie begged him to stop and listen for a moment. She said she had changed her mind. She couldn't go back home and leave their baby in Yokohama with him. Not replying with so much as a word, James stomped out of their room to go and get food for Gladys. While he was out, he thought better of sending Bessie back to her parents' home. When he returned to their room, Bessie looked at him and burst into tears. She said she had written a letter to her mother saying that she was going to kill herself because he had "thrown her off." She had gotten dressed to go out and had taken off her jewelry—but not her wedding ring, James noticed. They argued on and on and on. Finally, James's heart softened, and he relented. He would not send her back to America. She could stay and care for their baby as a mother should. At that, he walked out of their room, turned, and locked the door behind him. Bessie was not going to go anywhere—at least for now.

He went downstairs, intending to go right outside. But he saw Captain Bartlett waiting for him in the lobby. The two men went on a long walk that lasted until nearly dark. They talked. James told his captain everything that had happened that day: finding the locket; discovering Robinson's letter to Bessie; arguing with Bessie and planning to send her home; and then deciding to let her stay. Bartlett assured James that he had done the right thing in giving Bessie—and their marriage—a second chance to succeed. That helped James calm down. When he returned to the hotel, he climbed the stairs, walked down the hall to his and Bessie's room, quietly opened the door, came in, and went straight to bed.[13]

6. Propriety and Passion

With that, Sunday, December 27, 1891—a day that had proved so awful for James and Bessie Hetherington—came to its end. But the dilemma they and Gower Robinson faced remained unresolved. Their heads told them they should do what was proper: Gower would leave Bessie alone. She would go back to being a faithful navy wife. And James? He would set aside his hurt and anger so as to save his marriage. But their hearts pushed them in a different direction. They had to follow where love might lead them, whether or not that was proper in the eyes of their society.

What would they choose to do?

~ 7 ~

Escalation

New Year's Day 1892 dawned cold but clear. The winter winds that blow down from Siberia through Manchuria, cross the Sea of Japan, and tumble over the mountainous spine of Honshu to bring rain or snow to Pacific coastal Japan had driven all the clouds out to sea. The day was a big holiday for everyone in Yokohama. Japanese wives had been busy for weeks, preparing special foods to be eaten over the next four days. Their husbands, who had seen to it that all debts were paid before the new year dawned, looked forward to happy days ahead. Parents dressed in their finest and most formal clothes took their children to visit temples and Shinto shrines in the city. They prayed for prosperity and good luck in the new year and feasted on tasty offerings from food vendors' booths set up around the sacred structures.

Americans in Yokohama were tired but busy. Many of them, including James and Bessie, had stayed up late at the New Year's Eve party surgeon Franklin Rogers had hosted at the U.S. Naval Hospital. They got up late, dressed in their finest, and then went out, or waited, to exchange visits and calling cards with their friends and acquaintances. Everyone expected to dine on the finest foods—beef, ham, oysters, and perhaps turtle soup as well—and wash it all down with many a glass of wine or ale.

It was not, however, a day of peace, happiness, and joy for Gower, Bessie, and James. Anything but. Their troubled relationship was escalating to new levels of emotional intensity that threatened to boil over into violence.

Despite his letter to Bessie promising to end their affair—the one James had discovered—Gower's passion for her burned as fiercely as ever. On the morning of Sunday, December 27, the same day that James had threatened to send Bessie home alone and that she had threatened to kill herself rather than leave without baby Gladys, Gower was consumed with passion and anxiety. His American friend Chandler Gibbens, a 32-year-old Bostonian employed by the legendary Jardine, Matheson, & Co. firm, had stayed overnight at his home. When Gibbens came down for breakfast,

7. Escalation

he found his host torn between calm and alarm. Gower showed him letters and notes from Bessie as well as James's threatening letters demanding that he stop seeing her. They decided to seek counsel from two close friends: Albert Carter Read, a British silk merchant who lived with his family nearby, and later that afternoon, Caspar Andreas Valdemar Blad, the Dane who had become Gower's partner in 1890. The three men might then give Gower good advice about what to do.[1]

Before that happened, two notes from Bessie arrived. The first blurted out that James had found out everything and was going to send her home by the next steamer. The second said he had relented and she would stay. The same question was implicit in both: What should Gower do next?

It took all day for Robinson and his friends to develop an answer—a complex and deceptive scheme. Gower would write Bessie a letter, meant for James's eyes too, declaring that their affair was over once and for all. He wrote as if he were Bessie's contrite and chivalrous admirer. Tongues were wagging with rumors about their behavior, so he would let it be known that bad news from England might force him to take the next steamer bound for Europe on January 9. He would be gone "ostensibly"—underlined—for only a few months.

Gower then took the blame for what had happened between them. "If through my carelessness or worse I have done you any serious damage as regards your relations with your husband, and socially here, I humbly beg your pardon," he wrote. He would prove his contrition "by leaving my business, my home, and my numerous friends, trusting to time ... to allow everything to be forgotten in Yokohama." His too-open admiration for her, he told Bessie, had "worked to my ruin, perhaps." But if so, "I deserve it."

Gower concluded by saying he was sorry "(more than I can write or express) for your sake and ours that we ever met." He wished that she would "not to think too badly" of him, for he was trying to do everything "to shield your fair name."

"Believe me, dear Mrs. Hetherington," he pleaded. He signed the letter "Yours sincerely, Gower Robinson" and sent it on to Bessie.

His second letter to her, meant for her eyes alone, was very different. He proposed that they both run away from Yokohama. He would go to Europe. She was to take Gladys and go to America—specifically to Denver, Colorado. His sister Gwendoline lived there with her Irish engineer husband, Tom Waters. They could take Bessie and Gladys in while she filed for a divorce from James. Once it was granted, Gower would come and marry her, and they would live happily ever after. To make all this happen, he would send her money to cover her travel and living expenses.[2]

That letter betrayed Gower's real, and still obviously very passionate, feelings for Bessie. But even as he wrote it, he was afraid, fearing what her husband might do if he found out about the plot. The crazy, jilted American might even kill him. If that, God forbid, were to happen and James was imprisoned or executed for the crime, he wanted Bessie to go on living comfortably. Therefore he wrote out a will leaving all of his money and property to Bessie. His friends Chandler Gibbons and Albert Carter Read witnessed it, and Valdemar Blad would be its executor. His partner would take it to Mr. Bevis, at the Hong Kong and Shanghai Bank, the next day.[3]

That morning, Gower met another friend, Brooke Pearson, on the street near the Hong Kong and Shanghai Bank. He asked Pearson, a fellow Englishman who had come to Yokohama five years earlier and worked in a tea trading firm, if he would be willing to deliver a note to Bessie at the Grand Hotel. Pearson agreed to do so. When he knocked on her room door, the *amah*, Tome, answered. He asked to speak to Mrs. Hetherington, and when she came to the door he told her he had a note for her. At that moment, the hotel manager, Louis Eppinger, passed by. Bessie whispered, "Don't give it now!" Then, when the manager had gone by, she took it.[4]

One can only imagine what Bessie must have felt when she read Gower's second note. What was he doing? One moment he sent her a letter promising to discreetly break off their relationship so as to scotch rumors and save her reputation. The next he was asking her to run away, divorce James, and marry him. Was he crazy? Confused? Serious? She didn't know what he really wanted.

The next evening, Bessie found out. She and James had just finished their meal in the hotel dining room. They stepped out into a waiting area, and James went to the hotel office to take care of some business. While he was gone, Brooke Pearson came up to Bessie and asked if he could sit down and speak to her. She agreed. Then he handed her an envelope with another note—and $500 in cash—from Gower. It was money to cover her expenses in running off to Denver as he had proposed. Did she pale in shock at that moment? Without reading it, Bessie stuffed the letter and the money into her purse just before James returned. He exchanged friendly greetings with Pearson, and Gower's messenger left.[5]

When the Hetheringtons retired to their room, Bessie took advantage of a few minutes when James was in the bathroom to bury the note and the cash in the bottom of her trunk. When he reappeared without having seen what she had done, she must have breathed a sigh of relief. Then they lay down together on the bed to go to sleep for the night. One suspects she did not fall asleep quickly or easily.

The next day, Bessie showed Gower's first letter to James. As he read its apologetic words for his "too open admiration" for her, his expression of regret at their ever having met, and his "Goodbye!" James would

7. Escalation

presumably conclude, as Gower intended, that the Englishman would stop pursuing his wife.

But James was not reassured. He told Captain Bartlett about the letter, and the captain volunteered to give Robinson a stern talking-to about his behavior. When he did so, Gower groveled before him and promised to stay away from the Hetheringtons. Bartlett believed him, but James doubted the Englishman could be taken at his word. He brooded for the next two days while on duty aboard the *Marion*. When he returned to their rooms at the hotel, he found Bessie "very irritable." She wouldn't eat much and was obviously unhappy. James couldn't figure out what was wrong. Did she feel torn between him and the Englishman? Was she just angry at him? She wouldn't say.

James stalked angrily out of the room thinking Gower must be the source of her misery—and his. He felt words alone would not keep the Englishman away from his wife. The time had come to do what he had threatened to do before. Hailing a rikisha on the street, he set out for the Japanese section of town, where he bought a rawhide whip. Then he headed for Robinson's office, determined to slash his wife's suitor's handsome face. That didn't happen because, as he was told, Mr. Robinson was out until later in the day. James turned back to the hotel, where he found Bessie and showed her the whip. He made clear his intention to punish the man who had caused them both so much trouble. She somehow managed to calm him down and persuaded him to leave the whip behind when they went to a New Year's Eve party later that evening.[6]

On New Year's Day afternoon, James left the hotel to pay holiday compliments to friends. He met the Lowders and invited Julia to visit Bessie in her room, which she did. He saw his best friend and shipmate, Alan Rogers, and invited him to come and see baby Gladys. Lieutenant Rogers did not. Nor did any of the other *Marion* officers. James took that as an insult, inflicted on him and Bessie because she had "lost caste" as a consequence of what others saw as her inappropriate behavior with Gower Robinson.

That perceived slight was kindling laid for the fire of emotions that exploded within James later that afternoon. Around five o'clock, Bessie called him to come and look out the window, saying "Come here. Here is our friend." When he did so, he saw Gower riding slowly by on his horse-drawn trap. Robinson paused, looked up at the window where Bessie was standing, and did not so much as tip his hat in greeting. Incensed by that perceived slight, James opened the window, shook his fist at Robinson, and shouted out that he was "a damned blackguard."

That incident became the spark that ignited the emotional tinder in James. It flared up into a fire of uncontrollable anger. Grabbing his hat and the horsewhip he had put on top of the armoire in their room, he ran downstairs, determined to give the villain the punishment he was due. Bessie called him to come back—to no avail. On the way out to the street, he found Alan Rogers and asked him to come along. Seeing his friend so enraged and carrying a horsewhip, Rogers tried to stop James. He couldn't.

Instead, the two men hurried to the United Club, where James found Gower in its billiard room. Snarling "I have got you now" and brandishing the horsewhip, he demanded that Robinson come outside. At that point, Rogers and Gower's friend Chandler Gibbens stepped between the two men. They tried to convince James, as an officer and a gentleman, not to behave in such a way at a gentlemen's club. Rogers talked with Gower, who agreed to come outside only if accompanied by friends and armed with a stick. The lieutenant managed to calm James down by saying that his honor would not be impugned if he left the club without whipping Robinson. Although James wasn't so sure of that, he agreed to go back to the hotel. Rogers promised to get Captain Bartlett to affirm that James's honor was still intact even though he had not carried out his threat to attack Robinson. Walking on the Bund on his way back to the hotel, James threw the horsewhip into the harbor.

Forty-five minutes later, Alan Rogers knocked on the Hetheringtons' hotel room door. When he entered, he found James lying on the bed, emotionally distraught. He tried to comfort him by reporting that Captain Bartlett agreed that James had done right by not attacking Gower Robinson. He added that his fellow officers had meant no harm by not calling earlier with formal New Year's greetings. Bessie tried to soothe James still further by saying that she was glad things hadn't gone further, because she knew Gower carried a revolver. James's attempt to strike back at him ended without violence.[7]

For the next three weeks, James tried to behave normally, whether alone with Bessie or when they were out in public. He acted lovingly toward her and enjoyed seeing her play with baby Gladys. He realized how lucky he was not to have destroyed his family and possibly his career by attacking Robinson. Hugging Bessie, he poured out his feelings. He must have been somehow responsible, he said, for her receptivity to the Englishman's unacceptable advances. Taking her in his arms, he asked her how he had fallen short or left undone what a husband should have been doing. If she would just tell him, he pleaded, he would do better.

Overwhelmed with guilt, Bessie realized that the Judge, as he liked her to call him, was the innocent party. She responded by saying he was the one who had suffered as a consequence of her actions. She promised never to write another letter to Gower Robinson or receive one he might send.[8] At that moment of shared affection and confession, James and Bessie both hoped that their lives would return to normal.

7. Escalation

That did not happen—for them or for Gower. As the days passed in January, James grew more and more worried because the *Marion* was scheduled to go to sea for 10 days later in the month. What might Robinson—or Bessie—do in his absence? Bessie recognized that she was caught between two men, both of whom were passionate about her. She wanted to remain faithful to James but could not simply cut Gower off. And the Englishman? His longing for Bessie did not diminish even as he tried to find some way of avoiding James's threats.

The day after New Year's, at breakfast, Gower hastily scrawled a note to Captain Bartlett asking him to call at his office later in the day. When the captain did so, he was shown into the outer parlor. A few minutes later, when Gower came in and the captain tried to shake his hand, the Englishman would not. Then he said angrily, "This thing has got to stop." He insisted he had done his "best to screen this woman and save her reputation in Yokohama." But her husband had "come forward and made a mess of it [by coming] to horse-whip me for something I never did." Furthermore, he alleged, he had meant no disrespect toward Bessie on New Year's Day when he passed her room without greeting her.

Captain Bartlett responded that he took Robinson's word as a gentleman that he was innocent of any wrongdoing. Then Gower spat out a litany of promises. He would not go to any of the Saturday night "hops" when Bessie was one of the hostesses. He repeated those words over and over again, prompting Bartlett to think that things had been smoothed over. Yet when he got up to leave the office, Robinson was "not cordial." Nor did he live up to his promises to stay away from Bessie.[9]

Over the next two weeks, Gower acted as if he had never made them. On Friday the eighth, he sent Bessie a note via Henry Blanchard. She refused to take it. The next day he tried again with Blanchard as the carrier. That afternoon at a tea aboard HMS *Alliance*, Bessie chatted with Blanchard. Surmising that James might be looking on from the *Marion* nearby, Blanchard suggested that she drop her handkerchief. He would stoop down, stuff a note into it, pick it up, and hand it back to her. Anyone observing them would conclude that it was just a courteous gesture on his part. Bessie took the note from Blanchard.

That evening there was a "hop" at the Grand Hotel. As one of the sponsors—all the women residing in the hotel were official hostesses—Bessie was expected to go to the dance. She would be alone because James had duty aboard the *Marion* that night. When Gower showed up around 11, she and Blanchard were just finishing a dance. She sat down to wait out the next one, and Gower came up to her. They talked for about a half an hour, and then he went out into the hall where Henry Blanchard was waiting. Gower asked him to leave the dance and accompany him up the hotel's front stairs so that anyone who saw them would think nothing of it. By the time they got to the second floor, Bessie, who had left by the back stairs, was already in her room. When Gower knocked on her door, Blanchard excused himself and left. That was about 11:30 that Saturday night.

Gower went into Bessie's room and did not leave until after midnight on Sunday morning.[10] To this day no one can be sure what happened during that time. Did the two just talk? Did he try to persuade her to agree to the plan of running away separately and then reuniting in Denver? Or was this another sexual encounter like their first back in October? We do not know. But Gower's behavior that night left no doubt that his passion for Bessie burned as strong as ever. And when he made advances, did she resist?

Over the next week, James heard rumors about Bessie being seen alone with a man during his absence. He surmised that man must have been Gower. When he saw Henry Blanchard, he asked him to speak to Robinson so as to "stop such talk!" He also told him "to be more careful"—a not-so-subtle hint that his fellow American should stop taking Gower's letters to Bessie. Blanchard, who already felt "some trepidation" about meeting James, left feeling that things were "getting too bad." He should no longer risk being seen as a courier between the two suspected lovers.[11]

On Saturday, January 23, events played out much as they had on the night of January 9. James had duty and would be staying aboard ship all day and on into the evening. Seizing the opportunity to meet Bessie alone, Gower signaled his desire to do so by buying and having Henry Blanchard deliver two tickets for an early-evening concert to her. He knew that after dinner she would go on to the Saturday night "hop" at the Grand Hotel. When she came into the hall for dancing, Gower was already there, waiting and watching her movements. That prompted Dr. Frank Stephenson, the *Marion*'s senior surgeon, to express his concern to Captain Bartlett about what might happen next.

His concern was well-taken. While Bessie was dancing, Gower sat down near her chair, leaned over, and picked up her dance card. He wrote something on it, then put it back in place. When Bessie returned, she picked it up and appeared to read it. Then first Gower, then Bessie left the dancing hall. Jeanie Bartlett saw what happened and told her husband about it. A breach of etiquette that belied Robinson's previous promises to keep away from Bessie and then the two of them leaving early to do God knows what! That made Captain Bartlett very angry.

When he stepped out of the dancing hall to go home, he saw Robinson's friend Chandler Gibbens and accosted him. Telling him what his wife had seen Gower doing, he said loudly, "This sort of nonsense has

7. Escalation

got to stop!" He was going to inform Lieutenant Hetherington what had happened. "This thing shall be stopped once and for all!" he demanded. Gibbens replied that he couldn't believe his friend Gower had done such a thing. Just then, Brooke Pearson came into the room. When he heard what the captain said about Robinson's behavior, he, too, said he could not believe his friend could have committed such a breach of etiquette.[12]

Captain and Mrs. Bartlett left to go home. Gibbens and Pearson stayed behind to talk about the allegations against their friend Gower. By that time he had already gone upstairs—to Bessie Hetherington's room.[13]

Gower Robinson awoke on Sunday morning, January 24, pleased, perhaps, by what he had experienced there the night before. But his happiness vanished once Chandler Gibbens arrived. Gibbens said he felt "very taxed" about Gower's having written on Bessie's dance card and his own encounter with Captain Bartlett afterward. Furthermore, he worried that the captain would tell James what had happened and that the two men would come and confront Gower. That got Gower excited, and Gibbens left for a time. Still worried, he returned at tiffin time to find Henry Blanchard and F.S. Morse, an American who worked in the Canadian Pacific Steamship Company office, lunching with Gower.

What followed was "a most terrible day" for the four men. Gower admitted that he was "crazy about this woman"—Bessie. He cried and threatened to kill himself. His friends realized they had to do something to keep him from harming himself or encountering James Hetherington bent on vengeance. They came up with a plan that Gower reluctantly agreed to. They would put him on the first ship available bound for Kobe or Shanghai. Then they would spread the word that he was away and would not return to Yokohama as long as the Hetheringtons remained there. That would provide time for everyone to cool down and prevent some kind of violent collision between Gower and Hetherington.

That same Sunday, while James was still aboard ship, Captain Bartlett sent his card up to Bessie in her room asking her to meet him downstairs in the ladies' parlor. When she arrived, several other women were there, so he asked her to walk in the hall so they could talk in private. Bartlett told Bessie he knew what had happened the previous night at the hop. He asked her to tell James what Gower had done. Then he left. Later he went to see Chandler Gibbens, who explained that Robinson was afraid that he and Hetherington were going to come to his house to attack him.

Bartlett insisted that would not happen. "There is going to be no shooting, no horse-whipping in this affair, done by any officer of my ship or in the service, if I can help it." But then he added an ominous proviso. Hetherington would not attack Robinson, "unless it is absolutely necessary." But if it had to be, he would go with his lieutenant to see that

Robinson got what he deserved. Gibbens told the captain that Gower had agreed to leave Yokohama and promised that his friends would get him "off," that is out of town, no later than the coming Tuesday, January 26.

Gower did indeed board a ship bound for Kobe at noon that day. Earlier that morning, however, James had gone to see Captain Bartlett, seeking his advice about what to do about a very troubling letter from Bessie to Gower that he had found. The captain asked him if he had told his wife about discovering it. James said he had not.

What was in that letter?

Bessie had written it the day before in response to Gower's note saying that he would be going to Kobe. She wrote him determined that nothing more about their encounter at the previous Saturday's hop be found out. She had scratched off what he had written on her dance card—and burned it. She pleaded with him not to be angry at her and asked him to stay away for several weeks. She had had to "suffer a great deal" because of their relationship, but it looked as if he was "getting the most of it" in the Yokohama rumor mill because theirs was "only one of his many flirtations." Those last words must have stung Gower when he read them.

What followed was even worse—from his point of view. Bessie announced that she had made up her mind not to go to any more dances without her husband—after the navy farewell to Admiral George Belknap, the outgoing commander of the Asiatic Station. It was already scheduled for the coming Friday, January 29. She insisted she wouldn't go alone to such events even "if I have to stay in all the remainder of the winter."

Then she turned defiant. People had been talking about her frequent visits to the Lobanovs. Some had even suggested that she and the prince were involved in more than a friendship. The princess had naturally been angry about that. But when Bessie told her about what people were saying about her public behavior with Gower Robinson, the two of them just laughed it off. The Lobanovs were her true friends, and she was glad to have at least two people "who simply laugh when they hear the *on dit* (gossip) of this miserable town."

Bessie closed her letter by reassuring—and warning—Gower. He shouldn't worry about James, she wrote, for he would not come and threaten him again. "He won't, I can assure you," she insisted. Gower should try to have a good time while he was away—and "take my advice, stay away as long as it is possible." The warning came in her postscript. "Gower, I know better than you what people are saying about us—about you." His enemies were doing everything they could "to have you put out of all society"; and Captain Bartlett had told her that some were even trying to exclude both of them from future social events. He told her that she was partly to blame for that but added that he, Gower, was "a thousand

7. Escalation

times more to blame." The Englishman had been "running around doing harm for years, and now it was going to be stopped," he snapped.

"Be careful, for God's sake, Gower," she concluded.[14]

That letter incensed James and prompted Captain Bartlett to recommend that he send Bessie home on the next steamer bound for America. James protested that it was due to leave the very next day, too soon for him to arrange her departure. The captain retorted that it was not and asked if James had the money to pay Bessie's fare. When he replied that he did not, Bartlett wrote out a check for the necessary sum and gave it to him.

That prompted a huge, daylong argument between James and Bessie. He told her he was going to send her home. She objected. He added that she could take baby Gladys with her. She could go either to her parents' or his father's house, and he would continue to support her. That would put an end to the nasty rumors about her that were circulating in Yokohama. She would simply disappear, and the world of gossiping expatriates "would not know that anything had happened." That would get her away from Robinson's advances and to a place where "she would be among proper friends." End of problem.

A message from the *Marion* interrupted the Hetheringtons' argument. Ensign William Crose had fallen ill. James had to replace him on the midnight watch. Bessie seized on that news to try to force James to change his mind about sending her away. She cried, on again, off again, all day long after he said she was to go "home." She would have none of that, even if he would let her take their baby. When he started getting ready to leave, she objected to the proposal all the more vehemently. He couldn't leave her to go to the ship before he promised she and their baby could stay with him in Yokohama.

Bessie triumphed. The next morning, when Captain Bartlett came aboard the *Marion*, James returned the check to him. He protested that he just couldn't send Bessie home and tried to explain why that was so. The captain cut him off. "Don't tell me anything more," he insisted. "I have heard more than I ought to, and I don't want anything more to do" with it. "Fight your own battles," he advised James—"until it is necessary for me to go along with you to...." His voice dropped off at that point. James knew what he meant: to do whatever was necessary to keep Gower Robinson away from his wife.[15]

That might have ended the troubles arising from Gower's and Bessie's behavior at the January 23 hop—but it did not. The ball in honor of Admiral Belknap was just a few days away, and, as was the custom for a navy-sponsored social event, the American naval officers in Yokohama and their wives had to vote on whom to invite. Doing so proved contentious. *Marion* officers and their wives, with the exception of James and

Captain Bartlett, voted to invite Robinson. Whatever they may or may not have known about his behavior toward Bessie, they may have surmised that excluding him would raise more eyebrows than including him. When Paymaster Ray's wife said Bessie Hetherington should be excluded, too, Captain Bartlett quickly squashed that suggestion by saying that voting for or against inviting Robinson didn't matter because he would be in Kobe on the night of the ball, Friday the 29th.

It went off without incident. James and Bessie attended and danced together like any other married couple. No eyebrows were raised. No tongues were set to wagging about what had happened in the past or about Gower Robinson's absence. The ball proved the harbinger of a much-needed weekend of calm in the Yokohama foreign community.

The situation looked peaceful. James and Bessie had reconciled, and she had extracted from him a promise not to harm Gower. His friends had persuaded him to leave Yokohama, for the time being. Bessie had told Gower that their relationship was at an end, once and for all, and extracted from James a promise not to harm her sometime lover. For the moment, Bessie felt that she could somehow manage the situation so as to avoid a spasm of violence between the two men who loved her.

But appearances can be deceiving—especially when matters of the heart are at their strongest in telling people what they must—or must not—do.

8

Death

James Hetherington could not get over it. As February 1892 dawned, everything seemed to be going wrong. His marriage was not following the path he thought it should: loving within, proper without. What he knew about Bessie's affair with Gower Robinson left him feeling wounded to the core. He feared for his status in the community. He might not be seen as he should be: a naval officer and a gentleman, a loving husband and father, and a model American deserving the respect of all. Whether true or not, he felt that his shipmates, his fellow officers, and even his best friend, Alan Rogers, were distancing themselves from him and his wife. Was what had happened in Yokohama going to wreck his friendships? His career? His relationship with his mistress, the United States Navy? James could not bear the thought of that.

Despite the efforts of his and Robinson's friends, and those of his wife, to return things to normal, James may well have felt that he was teetering on the brink of disaster. What had occurred over the last 60 days left an indelible mark upon him—on his body, his innermost being, his soul. He feared something much worse might happen—today, tomorrow, any day soon if he laid eyes on Gower Robinson. The villain had gone away, but he could come back.

James tried to prevent that by getting first Alan Rogers and then Robinson's friends to help him. Late on Tuesday afternoon, February 2, he met Rogers in the Grand Hotel's billiard room and asked him to walk with him to the United Club. His shipmate didn't want to do that, but James pressed him to come along, saying that he understood Robinson was coming back to Yokohama. Rogers said he thought James was mistaken about that. James replied that he hoped Rogers was right about that but added if the man came back, he "was certainly going to whip him." Then he asked Rogers to go to the club and tell Robinson's friends to keep him away from Yokohama. They should warn the Englishman of "what to expect if he did come back": James "was certainly going to whip him."

Alan Rogers tried to prevent James from doing anything rash. He should at least "wait again and think it over" until he was sure Robinson was going to come back. Wasn't there some way other than whipping the man to satisfy his honor and keep him away from Bessie? James then replied in desperation: "What can I do? Is there any way other than whipping Robinson?" Rogers allowed that he couldn't see one. James then blurted out exactly how he was going to horsewhip the man who had seduced his wife.

The two men went to the club to talk to Gower's friends. While James waited outside, Rogers went in, found Albert Carter Read, and asked him to warn Robinson to stay away. If he did not, there would "be trouble." He wanted the man to know "what to expect if he came back." Read rebuffed Rogers's request, saying that he had washed his hands of the whole Robinson-Hetherington affair. Rogers should talk instead with Chandler Gibbens.

Just then, Gibbens entered the room. Rogers repeated his message: warn Robinson not to return to Yokohama. Gibbens said he was "very sorry he was mixed up in the affair" and wanted to do what he could to prevent any more trouble. Rogers said that was exactly how he felt. The best way to do so was "to keep Robinson away from here." At that, Gibbens agreed to telegraph a "wait letter" to him in Kobe. The two men parted amicably. Gibbens then wrote Robinson to reinforce the point, saying that if he returned to Yokohama, "he would have to take the consequences."[1]

Bessie's sometime lover had been warned—and threatened, just as James wanted.

The next morning, when he spoke with Alan Rogers, James completely reversed himself. Now he wanted his best friend to tell Gibbens to inform Gower that James "could not take any further steps ... toward whipping Mr. Robinson." Those words baffled Rogers. Why had James changed his mind? he asked. James replied that he and Bessie had had a long talk the previous evening. She had been very persuasive: he must not harm Robinson. He promised her he would "do nothing more" to the man. And he meant to keep that promise.

So James wanted Rogers to tell Chandler Gibbens that he had withdrawn his threat to whip the offending Englishman. Rogers saw no need for that. It would be better to "take the chance that the fellow (Gower Robinson) might stay away." James concurred and agreed that they should "let the matter stand" and hope that would "keep the man away."[2]

There was hope of a sort for the next week that the warning tinged with a threat would do just that. It did not. On February 10, Gower returned to Yokohama. Suspecting that he had done so, James asked Rogers that morning if he knew whether the Englishman was back in town.

8. Death

Rogers didn't. Early that afternoon, James left the *Marion* to go ashore. He didn't try to find Bessie, for he knew she had gone on an outing in the country with the Lobanov family. Instead, he headed up Camp Hill to the Jujiya bookstore. That was on the way to Robinson's home on the bluff.

James took a cane along on his walk. He wasn't lame and didn't need its help. The cane was to be used if he encountered Robinson driving his trap. It would stun his wife's seducer, leaving him defenseless while James snatched his whip away. Then the wronged husband could give the man the whipping he deserved.

Clearly, James had changed his mind about punishing Robinson. The Englishman deserved it and the lieutenant was as obsessed as ever with giving it to him. But he could not—at least for a while. Just after lunch the next day, James came ashore intending to stay. A messenger from the *Marion* caught up with him, however, bringing urgent news. Alan Rogers was sick and James would have to take over his duties immediately. That kept him aboard ship until Saturday, February 13.

Reassurances are not necessarily good predictors of behavior. That certainly proved true in Yokohama on that Saturday. In the morning, just after quarters and muster aboard the *Marion*, James stopped for a talk with Captain Bartlett. He said he thought he could "get along ... if he only knew Robinson would stay away." That sounded quite reassuring to the captain, who had had his fill of the Robinson-Hetherington affair.[3]

Later that day, Paymaster Charles Ray stumbled upon Gower Robinson on the stairs of the back entrance to the United Club. He asked him if he was planning to attend the "hop" that evening—the regular informal dance hosted by the women residents of the Grand Hotel. Robinson replied reassuringly, "No, I won't go there anymore. It always means trouble." Ray smiled and said, "You know what is best."[4] But trouble, big trouble, loomed ahead.

The two reassurances that the rest of the day would prove peaceful, one from James, the other from Gower, proved to be nothing more than empty words. That evening, James Hetherington shot Gower Robinson.

We don't know how that Saturday started for Gower. Perhaps he checked in at his office to catch up on some work. Perhaps he stayed home and shared tiffin with a friend who had come along with him from Kobe. That friend, Martin Pors, was a German. He was a longtime employee of Paul Heinemann & Company, a firm that had metamorphosed from a tea and silk exporter into the sole agent for Japan's largest copper producer as well as a purveyor of all kinds of insurance. The two men had gotten to know one another years ago, probably when Pors had been temporarily assigned to Heinemann's Yokohama office.[5]

We do know that early that cold February evening, Robinson had his *bettō* bring his horse and trap around to the front of his house. He and Pors and the *bettō* climbed into their seats on the trap and headed down Camp Hill to the heart of Yokohama. About 6:00 p.m., they had just crossed the bridge over the creek and turned left toward the curve that would take them to the Bund and past the Grand Hotel. As they approached the main entrance of the hotel, they noticed the figure of a man standing between the two gas lamps that bracketed the hotel's main gate close to the curb. It was James Hetherington.[6]

He had left the *Marion* just after one that afternoon on one of the small boat shuttles headed for the boat landing close to the English Hatoba. He walked the short distance to the Bund and then turned left, as if he were headed for the Grand Hotel. But before he got there, he turned right onto narrow Odawara Street and then left again onto Water Street. Gower Robinson's office was located at #30 Water Street. James was clearly looking for someone just then but didn't find him. Continuing along Water Street until he reached the rear entrance of the Grand Hotel, he climbed the back stairs up to his room.

When he went in, no one was there. Bessie had gone out to visit a friend with baby Gladys and the *amah* in tow. He stayed in the room for some time, then went out to a shoemaker's shop in Aizawa, in the Japanese part of town, which was some distance away. When he returned, his daughter and her *amah* were there, but his wife was not. That didn't worry James because he suddenly remembered that Bessie had told him she was going to go to Captain Bartlett's for tea around that time.

He sat alone in the room for several hours, pondering what to do. Restrain himself or give Robinson what he deserved? If the Lord whispered "Vengeance is mine"[7] in his ear that afternoon, James heard Him not. By late afternoon, well after five, he knew what he must do. He got up, kissed Gladys, and left the room. Inside, his organs burned with rage. Outside he was cool, calm, and determined.

James walked down the stairs, past the hotel's main office, and through its front garden toward the gate that fronted the Bund. He stepped out onto the sidewalk, turned left, and then started to walk down the middle of the street toward the United Club. Suddenly he heard the sound of horses' hooves coming up from behind him. He turned to look back and see who might be in the trap. At first he couldn't make out any faces, for the lamps on the trap were bright and pointed toward him. When the trap got still closer, about 20 to 30 feet away, James could see three men in the trap. One of them was Gower.

At that moment, James swung into action. As the horse and trap neared him, he turned and pulled a navy-issue Smith & Wesson service revolver from his pocket. He had taken it that morning from the *Marion*'s small-arms locker. Then he shouted at Robinson, who was barely an arm's length away, "You damned scoundrel, you are back here in Yokohama, are you?"[8]

As the head of the horse pulling the trap came abreast of him, James reached out toward the trap. He thrust his right hand holding the revolver out, steadied it for a moment, and pointed the gun upward. Then he shouted "Stop!" Robinson and Pors looked over their shoulders toward him but made no effort to stop. James then fired the first of three shots into the air. At that point, Gower, who was driving, leaned forward to pick up his whip, and used it to spur the horse on. James again shouted "Stop!" and fired into the air a second time. But the trap moved ahead still faster, until it was about eight feet in front of him. Then James fired a third shot—toward the men in front of him.

At that moment, Martin Pors leaned forward and fell out of the trap sideways onto the ground. He rolled over several times. James still had three bullets in his revolver but he stopped firing. Pors got up and came toward him, saying, "Don't shoot any more. Those shots came very near hitting me." James said, "I am very sorry for you, sir," and then turned to look ahead at the trap. Robinson had finally stopped it some distance ahead of where he and Pors stood. Gower started to get down from the trap, and for a moment James thought he was going to either come toward him or run away. But Robinson fell to the ground. At that moment, James knew his bullet had struck his wife's sometime lover.

Precisely what James did next remains unclear. He later claimed that he was so confused at the moment that he did not know what to do. He gave contradictory accounts of what he did when he saw Robinson fall. He first said that he dropped his gun and gave himself up—"that was all." Then he said that he asked Martin Pors what he should do and the German replied that he didn't know. Later he said he handed his gun to a Japanese policeman who suddenly appeared. Giving him his personal card, he explained that he was an American, an officer aboard the *Marion*. The police officer wanted him to go with him, but James refused. Thinking he could return to his ship, he started running up a back street, so as to avoid the spot where his archenemy, Robinson, had fallen. Wanting to get a boat back to the *Marion*, he hailed a rickshaw and told the puller to take him to the English Hatoba.

Before they went very far, another policeman appeared. Realizing the law was after him, James told the policeman he was the person that was wanted and gave himself up. The officer wanted to take him to the police station, but James refused to go there for a second time. He insisted that he was an American officer and would not go anywhere other than the United States Consulate-General. That was where they took him—to #234, just a few buildings away from the public gardens nearby. James knew that he would be safely under American protection—and jurisdiction—there for whatever harm he had done to Robinson.⁹

Extremely agitated when he got to the consulate, he insisted that he, not the policeman, ring the doorbell. When the jailer and constable, Richard McCance, came to the door, James demanded that he summon the consul general immediately. He said he wanted to be placed in the constable's custody until that senior official arrived. McCance showed James into his own room, but that failed to calm him down. The lieutenant knew he was in trouble. But he still didn't know precisely what he had done to his nemesis, Gower Robinson.¹⁰

Neither did the man who found him lying in the street, opposite #12 on the Bund. That was Pietro Beretta, an Italian trader in silk and Asian fine arts, who was heading back from the United Club to his home and business at #10. With the help of Robinson's *bettō*, he picked up the wounded man, put him in a rickshaw, and ordered its puller to take him to the back entrance of the United Club, on Water Street.¹¹

That was where Dr. Stuart Eldridge, an American physician who had practiced medicine in Yokohama for 20 years, found Gower "in a very prostrated condition." The doctor called for help from those inside the club, and they carried the wounded man to the nearest room—#15, where his friend and fellow countryman Brooke Pearson was staying. They put Gower onto his bed, and Dr. Eldridge made his first examination of the victim. Finding Gower suffering from "excessive internal hemorrhage and shock caused by a bullet wound," the doctor quickly concluded that the man was dying.

Just then, Dr. Edwin Wheeler, an English physician who was Gower's regular doctor, burst into the room. He quickly examined him and reached a different conclusion. The patient was "in a state of collapse … but gradually rallying." The two doctors agreed to take turns over night watching Gower's condition.

News of the shooting got out from the moment it occurred. After all, it had happened at one of the busiest places in Yokohama, on the Bund between the United Club and the Grand Hotel. James had fired the fateful shots just when people who intended to go to the "hop" later in the evening were dining at the hotel. Perhaps Chandler Gibbens or Harry Henson, the club's secretary and treasurer, who had come into the room where Gower lay almost immediately after he was brought in, spread the word. Or Pietro Beretta could have managed in his broken English to have told Louis Eppinger, the hotel's general manager, what had happened. Given the gravity of the event, Eppinger likely suggested to the women sponsoring the "hop" that they cancel the dance.

8. Death

Just how Bessie got the news of the shooting remains unknown. But there can be little doubt that she was puzzled, emotionally torn, and alarmed by what James had done. How could he have shot Gower when he had pledged not to harm her sometime lover? Had she underestimated the depth of his passion and the strength of the anger he harbored and foolishly believed what he had promised? She likely felt sorry for Gower but angry at him, too. He had ignored her plea to stay away from Yokohama—and suffered the consequence. Did she feel fresh pangs of guilt, knowing that her actions in the past were in some measure responsible for what had just occurred? She certainly would have felt alarm and concern over what might happen if Gower died and James were hung or imprisoned, leaving her and Gladys alone.

Neither James nor Bessie likely slept easily that night. Gower apparently did so, for the next morning he seemed well enough to entertain a stream of visitors—friends; his partner Valdemar Blad; his attorney, John Frederic Lowder; and yet another physician, Dr. Thomas Hall Tripler, an American whose office was nearby. But as evening came on, Robinson's condition worsened. At 11:30 that Sunday night, with his personal physician Dr. Wheeler at his side, and his friend Brooke Pearson, his partner Valdemar Blad, and the wine merchant E.H. Andreis in the room, he died.[12]

It was Valentine's Day. How ironic! On that day, the day of love and lovers, the Robinson-Hetherington love triangle came to its end—in death.

James and Bessie did not learn of Gower's death until the next morning, Monday, February 15, 1892. That news likely produced mixed feelings in

John Frederick Lowder, Gower Robinson's solicitor and executor (FA86-095-01 from *Japan Gazette Yokohama Semi-Centennial...1909*. Yokohama Archives of History).

both of them. The man who had intruded in their lives and thrown their marriage into turmoil was dead. He would never bother either of them again. Relief. That was the good news. There was also bad news. There would be a reckoning for what James had done. Inquiries. An autopsy. A coroner's inquest. Eventually, a trial. That would open their private lives to public scrutiny and put James's life in jeopardy. That spelled more trouble, more anguish, and more anxiety—for James and Bessie.

Whether they liked it or not, that reckoning was sure to come.

9

Murder

That reckoning did not come in the way it would now.

If an American assaulted an Englishman resulting in his death in Japan today, all the investigative and legal procedures that followed would be carried out by Japanese authorities. Japanese physicians would perform the autopsy. Japanese investigators would amass the evidence in the case and charge the American with the crime. He would be tried, in accordance with Japanese law, in a Japanese court.

In 1892, none of that happened. Assailant and victim were shielded from Japanese legal authority by extraterritoriality. That privilege was guaranteed to them as foreign nationals under the terms of the 1858 treaties that opened the so-called treaty ports, Yokohama foremost among them, to residence by non–Japanese. James relied on that when he insisted to the Japanese police who apprehended him that he be delivered to the American consulate. And the procedures in the consular courts that had developed over the following years guaranteed Gower Robinson, even in death, that British officials would preside over the inquiries that took place immediately following his demise.

An autopsy, that is a postmortem examination of his body to determine precisely how he died, was the first of those procedures. It took place first thing on Monday morning, February 15, at Her Britannic Majesty's Royal Naval Hospital, at #15 on the bluff. A British physician, Dr. Edwin Wheeler, examined the body, and his American counterpart, Dr. Stuart Eldridge, took notes on his findings as they occurred. Three other doctors—Dr. Richard Fritz Theodor Kleffel, chief surgeon at the German Naval Hospital; a Japanese police surgeon; and Dr. Maurice Eden Paul, a Briton who had only recently arrived in Japan—stood by as observers.[1]

The cause of Robinson's death quickly became apparent to the doctors. A pistol bullet had entered his body through the left hip and passed through the ilium and various muscles into the iliac artery. It continued on through the abdomen and ripped into the small and large intestines. That,

Dr. Wheeler determined, had caused not one but two internal hemorrhages, which explained why death had come so slowly. The first one began the bleeding that produced a clot. The second one broke the clot, causing a massive loss of blood to Robinson's heart. Death followed quickly.[2]

Dr. Wheeler then extracted the bullet that had caused so much damage to Robinson's body. There could be no doubt that that bullet, fired from Lieutenant Hetherington's gun, had killed Gower Robinson. Dr. Rokkaku, the Japanese police surgeon, took custody of it for presentation at the coroner's inquest that followed.

Such an inquiry was standard procedure in Great Britain in the 1890s, where a minimum of 12 jurors determined whether an individual should be charged with causing a violent death. In the United States, especially in urban areas, the coroner's jury was already being replaced by the procedure familiar today—presentation of evidence by a district attorney to a grand jury that determined if indictment and trial of an accused should follow.[3] Neither American nor British procedure was followed strictly in this case. Instead, the British consul in Yokohama, acting as coroner, selected only three jurors. These men, as well as a crown prosecutor, questioned witnesses directly and were responsible for delivering a verdict.

The coroner's inquest into the death of Gower Robinson was a somber occasion held, appropriately, in the imposing British Consulate—the largest consular building in Yokohama. It sat astride one of the busiest intersections in the city—at #172 and #173, facing the English Hatoba, with the Bund at its front and the street leading past the recently built Kanagawa Prefectural Office to the Public Gardens at its side. The courtroom where the inquest would be held occupied a large space on the second floor of the building. It was as fully furnished as any in England—replete with a high bench where the judge sat, tables for barristers and solicitors, a witness stand and a docket for an accused, and benches to the side for jurors. This wood-paneled room also had ample seating for observers, who on Monday afternoon, February 15, 1892, filled it to capacity.[4]

Shortly after one, James P. Troup, the British consul in Yokohama acting as coroner, opened the proceedings. Silver haired at age 52, he had come to Japan as a student interpreter nearly 30 years earlier and risen through the diplomatic ranks to his current position. He was well prepared by experience—and his ample staff of six—to preside over what was to come. He first empaneled the jurors—George Henry Allcock, Thomas Holyoake Box, and A. Le Prevost. All three were engaged in the silk trade.[5] Then they were sent to view Robinson's body, which had been removed to the undertakers, Stibolt and Company, nearby.[6] When they returned, they found three observers acting on James Hetherington's behalf sitting at the solicitor's table: Captain Bartlett of the *Marion*; Lieutenant

9. Murder

Lazarus Reamey, Admiral Belknap's flag secretary;[7] and attorney Alexander Tison. Their presence attested to the U.S. Navy's very strong interest in the proceedings. A fourth man, John Frederick Lowder, Gower's attorney, observed on behalf of the dead man's family.

The crown prosecutor, Henry Charles Litchfield, acted as manager of the proceedings. He had lived in Japan for nearly 20 years and practiced law as a barrister in Yokohama. His first task was to instruct the jurors on their obligations.[8] They were to identify the body they had just seen as that of George Gower Robinson. They were to find the cause of his death and how it came about. Their third duty was to determine the means of Robinson's death and the "degree of culpability" pertaining to "the man who caused the wound"—Lieutenant James Henry Hetherington. Litchfield then called the first witness—Dr. Edwin Wheeler.

He first reported on how he found Robinson immediately after the shooting, and then summarized the results of the postmortem examination. In a dramatic gesture, he pulled from his pocket the bullet that had been taken from the body. His next words stunned those in the courtroom, for they described Gower on his deathbed. On the Sunday evening, not long before he died, Robinson, who was at that point "in a bad way ... suffering from great pain" but not expecting to die, gave the doctor his version of how the shooting had occurred. His words were important, but Gower's demeanor at the time was perhaps even more revealing. Dr. Wheeler said he had been reluctant to speak about how James Hetherington had assaulted him. He wasn't angry or thinking only about himself. He was modest. Robinson had protested, "It doesn't matter; it doesn't matter." Dr. Wheeler then retorted "it does matter."

The next witness, Dr. Eldridge, corroborated everything that Wheeler had just said. He added that the bullet they had extracted from Robinson's body came from a Smith & Wesson .35-to-.40-caliber weapon. That pointed to its U.S. Navy origins. Then he told the court what he had heard from Robinson about what had happened on the fateful Saturday evening. Although he had found him "moribund" at the United Club, the victim had managed to give him an account of what had happened immediately after he had been shot. He struggled to stop the horse. "With some difficulty" he got down from the trap. He saw Martin Pors grappling with his assailant and thought his friend might be wounded. He wanted to go to help him, but "from the moment of formulating the wish to go to his friend's assistance, he knew nothing more." Here was a second revealing vignette about the deceased. Even though he was wounded, he magnanimously thought first of helping his friend.

The next three witnesses then provided, for the jurors' benefit, their accounts of what they had seen and heard on the night of the shooting.

Testifying with the assistance of the Marquis Nembrini de Gonzaga, the Italian consul, acting as interpreter, Pietro Baretta told how he had found Robinson "senseless" on the ground and had him taken to the United Club. He added that he had not seen the man who fired the lethal shot but thought he had heard only two, not three, of them fired.

Kaneko Chūzō, Gower's *bettō*, said he had looked over his shoulder and seen the shot that struck his master as it was fired. But he couldn't see the assailant. The shot had come without warning, and no words had passed between the man who fired it and Robinson. When a Japanese policeman came to the scene, Kaneko told him, "This gentleman has shot my master, seize him."

The police constable who did so, Suzuki Mito (Kamita), next described how the sound of gunfire caused him to run to the scene of the shooting. He asked the *bettō* who had fired the shots but got no reply. Then he saw a stout man grappling with a thin man who had a revolver in his right hand. The thin man grasped his assailant's wrist. He then said in a mix of Japanese and English that the stout man was from an American man-of-war and had fired a shot from the weapon in his hand. The constable then grabbed the gun, and the stout man gave him his card identifying himself as an American naval officer. But then he started running, and Suzuki had to chase him down with the help of another policeman. The second officer held the man while Suzuki took the gun and the card to the police station and gave them to Inspector Okada Kantarō.

The inspector stood up and showed those present the gun. It was a six-chambered revolver with three cartridges remaining inside. Then he produced the card James had given Officer Suzuki. The evidentiary chain of evidence was plain for the jurors to see. The bullet taken from the body of Gower Robinson, the weapon that had fired it, and the name card were now in proper custody before their very eyes.

At that moment, Consul Troup abruptly adjourned the proceedings. He explained that a key participant in the shooting under examination was not available. The day after the attack, Martin Pors had left for his home in Kobe aboard the French steamer *Caledonien*. A telegram had been dispatched summoning him to return and give evidence. He had replied that he would not be able to do so until the following Thursday, February 18.

Troup rose and everyone present left for tiffin. The gentlemen "of the better sort" among them strolled over to the United Club for their meal. Their tables probably buzzed with talk about what had been revealed at the inquest that morning. But there were still questions about the shooting. Martin Pors had been there, and he claimed Gower was his best friend. He must have known that he would be a key figure in any investigation into what had happened. Why, then, had he left Yokohama so abruptly? What was he running away from?

During the break in the inquest proceedings, two things of importance happened. First, on Tuesday, February 16, Bessie penned an anguished letter to her parents. She took some responsibility for what had happened, admitting that she had been indiscreet. But Gower Robinson had fallen in love with her; and even though she told him never to speak to her again, he persisted in pursuing her. That left James with no choice but to become her "avenger." He had forgiven her, and she knew he would be acquitted. She still felt responsible, however, for causing the death of one man and jeopardizing the life of her husband. She longed for home and didn't think she would ever be able to enjoy "social pleasures" again. Bessie closed by apologizing for having caused her parents "great distress of mind"—precisely what she herself suffered from at that moment. When it later became public, the letter would serve Bessie well in the court of public opinion.[9]

Second, on February 17, officials at the American consulate reviewed the testimony given at the inquest and decided that they needed to charge James Hetherington with murder immediately. That would allow for his retention in American custody and guarantee that any trial would be held at the American, not the British, consulate.[10] In a word, they had to beat the British to the procedural punch.

The charge they swore out against James alleged that he "did ... feloniously, willfully, and of his malice aforethought, kill and murder the said George Gower Robinson against the peace and dignity of the people of the United States." Consul General Willard D. Tillotson then certified that he had "reasonable grounds for believing the contents of the foregoing complaint were true."[11] That act guaranteed that James would be tried in the American consular court.

When the inquest proceedings resumed at the British consulate just after 10:00 a.m. on Thursday, February 18, an additional observer was present. He was the German consul, Doctor of Jurisprudence Otto Schmidt-Leda, watching on behalf of Martin Pors, a German national, who was expected to be the star witness that day.[12]

The session began with questions from two of the jurors to the doctors. George Allcock wanted Dr. Wheeler to reaffirm his conclusions about Robinson's death. The doctor affirmed that the bullet Lieutenant Hetherington had fired was the sole cause of his demise. Allcock asked Dr. Eldridge if he concurred in that judgment, and the doctor readily did so. Then Thomas Box asked the American physician a different kind of question: Had Robinson mentioned any names to him while he was attending the wounded man?

Eldridge responded affirmatively. At some point after his first examination of the victim, Robinson had turned to him and said, "Doctor, if I get through this, I suppose he [Hetherington] will finish me next time, or some other time." Eldridge replied, "No, if you recover he will be out of the road of doing you any mischief." Robinson asked, "What do you mean?" "I said," the doctor replied, "he will be under arrest or out of the country." Gower had then protested, saying repeatedly, "Good God, that will never do, it will ruin the poor fellow."

Dr. Eldridge then revealed that the dying man had made an extraordinary request. Would he write a letter to Admiral Belknap for him? The doctor said yes he would. Then, "after speaking of the unfortunate occurrence of the evening before," Robinson told Eldridge to write: "If anything from me can render the position of Lieutenant Hetherington any easier or better I shall be very glad. I fully forgive him." Without commenting on how unusual Gower's request was—victims did not usually ask mercy for their assailants—Dr. Eldridge said he had answered Thomas Box's question.

What the doctor said about his conversation with Robinson on his deathbed was quite extraordinary. The victim had had mood swings. At one moment he was fearful of what James might do to him if he survived. At another he was magnanimous to a degree just short of amazing. In the letter he got Eldridge to write, Gower called on his attacker's naval superiors to go easy on James. He said he forgave him for what he had done. Dr. Eldridge's testimony portrayed Robinson not as a bitter victim but as a sensitive, caring individual.

Box's question itself raised questions, however. Why had he, in the midst of an inquiry into the medical and forensic cause of Robinson's death, raised a question of what he might have said to the doctor? Did he already know what Eldridge's answer would be? Might someone else, who had been present when the letter was allegedly written, have prompted him to ask the question in an attempt to portray the deceased in the best possible light? Could that person have been John Frederick Lowder, Robinson's attorney?

No one at that moment sought answers to the questions Dr. Eldridge's testimony had raised, and the rest of the morning's testimony was unexceptional. After tiffin, Martin Pors, who was both witness and participant in the shooting, stepped into the witness box. All eyes in the courtroom fixed on him as he introduced himself. He was a German subject residing in Kobe and "by occupation a merchant." Affirming that he was "well acquainted" with Gower Robinson, he added that the Englishman was "the best friend I had." He remembered how he and Gower had enjoyed watching the inter-port football (soccer) match at Kobe. Then he detailed what had happened on Saturday afternoon, February 13—before the shooting. He had met Robinson at the "English" (sic, United) Club and then was driven to his house. They stopped at the pharmacy on Main Street to pay a bill, and then drove around the back way, past the race course along the bay up to Robinson's house. After stopping there for about 30 minutes, they headed back down Camp Hill, crossed the creek bridge, and turned around the corner onto the Bund. "Nothing happened," Pors said, until just after they had passed the front gate of the Grand Hotel.

At that point, he continued, he saw a man running up toward the trap from behind. "The first thing" he noticed on him was a revolver. The man shouted, "Stop, you blackguard!" Then, without giving Robinson a chance "to do or say anything," he fired a shot. Pors heard the bullet whistling through the air and noticed that the man had hurt his hand on the side of the trap as he was firing. The shot prompted Gower Robinson to lean forward so as to gradually stop the trap. But then Pors added a vital detail: as far as he could see, the man firing the shot "never had the intention of stopping the trap before firing."

That raised a question. Had the shooter no intention of firing at Gower Robinson so as to harm him? Was the shot just a warning meant to scare him?

Pors didn't answer that question but continued narrating the sequence of events as he remembered them. After the first shot, he had tried to jump down from the trap. Just as he did so, a second shot was fired. At that moment, three things happened simultaneously. His friend called out, "Oh my God!" and sank over to his left side. Pors shouted, "Gower drive for your life. I will stop him." At that point—and he wasn't sure whether it was before or after a third shot was fired—Pors said he fell to the ground, somersaulted, and came up facing the shooter, who was only three or four feet away. Pors then stood up and hurled himself "with all the force I could muster" against the shooter. Throwing his arms around the man's neck, he had held on there and then tried to grab the assailant's right hand holding the revolver. He got it.

At that point, Pors said, he realized the shooter was stronger than he was. He couldn't stop him from doing whatever he intended to do. "I also had the feeling," Pors continued, "… that no imploring or begging could stop the man from doing further mischief." But when he tried begging the man to stop firing at his friend, "he at first would not hear of it. In fact he expressed his intention to continue firing." Pors struggled with the man for a little while, but then suddenly the shooter dropped his arm and let the revolver fall from his hand. Pors heard him say something like "I've done it." At that moment the firing stopped.

Pors first said he didn't know why, but then he proposed two possible explanations. He had managed to calm the man down by saying that he sympathized with him. He could say that because Robinson had told him "in effect that he pitied this person," that is, the shooter, Lieutenant Hetherington. "When I told the man this," Pors continued, "it seemed to disarm him." Or, Pors surmised, the shooter had stopped firing because he realized "that enough mischief had been done." Upon reflection, the German concluded that that was probably why the man stopped shooting.

In any event, Pors said, the assailant dropped the gun. He talked a bit more with him, and then the gunman asked him, "What shall I do now?" At that point, Pors said he had started to go toward Gower Robinson in hopes of helping him. But then a Japanese policeman who had heard the gunfire came up. The officer stopped Pors because he was confused as to who had fired the shots. Pors had had to convince him that the other man was the assailant.

The German then recalled the last words he had said to the shooter that night. "You may be a murderer at this moment. I hope not, and in this hope I will even try to help you away as long as you desist from firing further shots into my friend." Then he added that he had never seen the man before the shooting and never saw him again.

Pors portrayed himself as a hero of sorts on that night. He had tried to prevent more violence. He succeeded in calming the attacker. And he was certain that if he had not, the man would have continued shooting. His was surely the most gripping account of what had happened on the night of Saturday, February 13. But the jurors wanted to hear more.

Thomas Box asked if the shooter had appeared "in any way agitated." Pors responded that all he had seen of the man was his eyes—and the gun. He didn't even remember whether the man wore a beard or not. But "the whole appearance of the man" had given him the impression that the assailant "fully intended to continue his shooting." When he had had hold of the shooter's arm, he said, it had not trembled.

George Allcock then brought Pors back to the main point: Was he "perfectly sure" that the man he had just told the court about was the cause of Gower Robinson's wound? Pors shot back, "There can be no doubt about it." Was Pors sure of that? Allcock asked again. "Yes," the German affirmed.

Mr. LePrevost then asked Pors a troubling question. If he had never met or seen the shooter before, how could he have known that he was the person Robinson had previously been talking with him about?

Pors replied vaguely, "I had very good reasons for thinking so." That explanation was "scarcely an answer," the presiding officer, James Troup, interjected. Pors tried again, explaining he knew who the man was because that very afternoon he had heard from his friend Gower "that he was in

9. Murder

some trouble." That vague answer still didn't satisfy juror LePrevost. who pressed Pors for a clearer reply. What was it that had prompted Robinson to pity the alleged shooter? But the German demurred, saying, "That I am not prepared to divulge. I have given my word of honor. What little I know," he added, "would be of very little use to the court."

LePrevost didn't buy that. He retorted with a still more pointed question: Did Pors believe that the shooter "was provoked into attacking Mr. Robinson"? The German demurred once again. He was honor bound not to answer or even notice such a question. LePrevost pressed on, saying he wasn't asking Pors to detail Robinson's conversation with him about the shooter. That angered the German, and he said he wanted to cancel his first response to LePrevost's question. "I am not here to state what I believe ... only matters of fact—things that have occurred. Beyond that," he said tartly, "I am not required to answer any question."

Thomas Box then interjected that all they wanted to know was whether Pors had been "forewarned" about the man in his earlier conversation with Robinson and thus recognized him as the shooter. Pors then allowed that he had concluded the shooter was the man more because of what he had heard from "outsiders and others" than from his friend Gower, who really hadn't supplied him with much detail about why he "was in trouble," that is, why someone might be after him. He just knew, Pors said, the moment he grabbed the shooter "that this was the man Mr. Robinson meant."

Box pressed further: Did Pors know that from his earlier conversation with Gower that the person he grabbed and who had fired the shots was that man? That flustered the German still further. He asked that the record be corrected to state simply that the reason he declined to say what the deceased had told him about the assailant was because he had given his word of honor not to mention it. That was why he could not answer juror Box's question.

With that, Martin Pors stepped down from the witness box and asked if he could be allowed to confer with Mr. Lowder, the attorney observing on behalf of the Robinson family. James Troup snapped back: "The evidence was closed." There could be no communication between the witness and outside counsel. That prompted Thomas Box to ask if the witness could not speak privately to the jurors. Once again, consul and acting coroner Troup refused. "The witness's evidence is finished," he snapped. The coroner was not about to let the proceedings wander away from the facts of the killing into a discussion of the alleged assailant's motives.

Pors's testimony, however, left two important questions unanswered. Why was he so protective of whatever Gower may have told him? Had he spoken—in confidence—about his relations with Bessie? Even perhaps the details of what had happened during their midnight liaisons? That information would have explained Robinson's sudden visit to Kobe. More important still, it would have shed light on Lieutenant Hetherington's motive in shooting Gower Robinson.

Why, too, was Pors so eager to speak with John Frederick Lowder, the dead man's attorney? Had he conferred with him, or even been coached by him, on what to say—and what not to say—at the inquest?

Moving to bring it to a close, Coroner Troup summed up the evidence for the jurors. The fact that different witnesses gave different accounts of the number of shots fired didn't matter, he said. In the confusion of the moment, it was natural that they did not concur on that point. The evidence from the doctors left no doubt that a bullet fired on the previous Saturday night was the cause of Gower Robinson's death. Finally, what Martin Pors and the Japanese policemen had said about the card the shooter had given the latter identified Lieutenant James Henry Hetherington as the shooter.

The coroner then gave the jurors instructions on how they should reach a verdict. They had first to be sure that the body they had seen was Gower Robinson's. Then they had to determine the means of his death. Was it from the revolver that they had seen in court? Was the shot fired from the gun "unlawfully without warrant, or without excuse"? They must also make a crucial distinction. Was the fatal bullet fired "with malice aforethought, expressed or implied"? That question would be most important for them in determining "what crime was committed—if a crime was committed that evening by the person who fired the revolver." Was it murder?

Troup went on to explain the distinction between murder and manslaughter. The difference depended on the malice displayed—whether the shooter did or did not have "a deliberate intention of doing some corporeal harm to another." If the assailant had no such intention, then the crime was manslaughter. If he harbored that intent, even without the intent to kill and the victim died, the crime was murder. The jurors must also consider the question of provocation. "If the killing was done under provocation, while the ... [shooter] was under a paroxysm of passion," then there was no malice. But if the shooter had been provoked and had had time "to recover his mental equilibrium," then "the provocation was not sufficient to justify his action." "Provocation," he concluded, "was only allowable when it exists at the time" the shooter fired the deadly shot.

The coroner concluded his instruction with a stern admonition: the jurors must dismiss from their minds "all reports and rumors which they may have heard outside as to the circumstances which may have existed between the deceased and his assailant." Their verdict must be based solely on the evidence presented in court and what they had heard with their own ears. If they were satisfied that the name and address on the card they had been shown were in fact that of the shooter, then they must name him as the person who had caused the death. Troup then told the jurors, "I leave the case to you with the hope that a just, true, and equitable verdict will be returned."

The three jurors then left the room. While they were gone, everyone else waited, their minds weighed down with speculation about when they would return and what their verdict would be. Those in the courtroom did not have to wait long. Less than 15 minutes after retiring, Messrs. Allcock, Box, and LeProvost returned. Troup asked if they "were determined upon" a verdict, and they nodded in assent. The bailiff handed the note they had written up to Coroner Troup. At that moment, "a profound silence" descended upon the room.

Troup read, "We the undersigned jurors find from the evidence laid before us that George Gower Robinson, broker, of Yokohama, died on Sunday the 14th inst., near midnight, from a bullet wound inflicted by J.H. Hetherington, a lieutenant of the United States Navy, on Saturday the 13th inst., a little after 6 p.m., on the Bund, Yokohama, and we find the said J.H. Hetherington guilty of willful murder."

With that, the jurors and the coroner signed the necessary documents. Consul Troup then thanked and dismissed them. The inquest was over. As everyone left the courtroom, the last words of the verdict probably echoed in their minds: "Willful murder!"

But was it? Had Lieutenant James Henry Hetherington, as now both the American consul general and the British coroner's jury alleged, deliberately and with malice aforethought killed George Gower Robinson?

The trial that now loomed ahead would determine the final answer to that question.

10

Unquiet Rest

Five weeks passed between the inquest into the death of George Gower Robinson and the trial of Lt. James Henry Hetherington, U.S. Navy, for his murder. During that time, a lot happened. Gower was laid to rest in the Yokohama General Cemetery for Foreigners. He and Bessie and James became celebrities, the story of their love triangle spread around the English-speaking world. And an attorney, a stranger, came to Yokohama, determined to uncover its darkest secrets and save his client from the gallows.

There are no secrets in small, isolated communities. By the morning after Gower died, tongues were wagging all over Yokohama about his killing. There were no telephones as yet to spread the news. It was a Sunday, and church was where most people found out what had happened. The few people who knew beforehand spread the word to those who did not as soon as they stepped outside the church doors. The mix of scandal and violence that brought about Robinson's death was a story too hot for anyone to keep to himself. It was bound to create a firestorm of conflicting opinions about what had happened and certain to reveal deep divisions in the Yokohama foreign community.

Community leaders tried to dampen the flames of controversy. Gower's friends were eager to lay him to rest with a proper funeral and set a date for it—Tuesday, February 23. They hoped it would bring closure to his violent death and restore Yokohama to its normal, civilized and peaceful self. That, they believed, was the right way to maintain the flow of trade and tourists that brought prosperity to all.

Nevertheless, they could not stop people from talking about the events of Saturday, February 13. They failed because what had happened was unprecedented in their experience. To be sure, Robinson's was not the first murder, as officials at the British and American consulates had labeled it, to occur in Yokohama. Decades earlier, *rōnin* (samurai without masters) had killed foreigners to protest the opening of Yokohama and other

Japanese ports to foreign trade and residence. There was even another instance of violent death at the hands of an American naval officer back in 1859, when he had tried to subdue a rebellious sailor.[1] Brawls between young navy sailors of various nationalities and their merchant marine counterparts had also resulted in death in the past.

By 1892, however, nearly 40 years after Commodore Perry had "opened" Japan, Yokohama was no longer a "wild west" town on the Far Eastern frontier in which violent assault and murder were commonplace. James Hetherington's killing of Gower Robinson was so extraordinary because the port city had become a civilized and peaceful place. The alleged murder was even more tantalizing to Yokohama expatriates because the killer and victim were who they were. They were not drunken sailors but men who commanded respect in society—men of "the better sort," an English broker and an American naval lieutenant.

That fact, if for no other reason, was what made the Saturday the 13th attack and Valentine's Day death in Yokohama so compelling a story to the rest of the world. Locals talked about it. Reporters picked up what they heard from them. Newspaper editors embellished the story so as to gain more readers. And attorneys probed it for details that could be used in the trial that lay ahead to convict or exonerate the killer.

But before all that, Gower Robinson had to be laid to rest.

On Tuesday morning, February 23, 1892, Peter St. John Hellendale, the undertaker at Stibolt & Co.,[2] was dressed in his finest—black frock coat, freshly pressed pants, white shirt with black cravat, and a black derby. He went down from his quarters at #160 to check on preparations for the funeral and burial scheduled for later that morning. The coffin had been placed inside the glass-sided hearse. His *bettō* had hitched the horses to it and brushed their coats into the glossiest black one could expect on a winter's day. Mr. Hellendale had done everything that he could to make sure that everything for this funeral would be in proper order, for he knew it would be a special one. The time was at hand to celebrate the last rites for George Gower Robinson and give him a proper burial.

Shortly before 10:00 a.m., the undertaker climbed up onto the hearse. Picking up the reins, he clicked his tongue to signal the horses to start moving. They headed to Christ Church, Yokohama's principal Protestant house of worship. The big old wooden structure was one of the few public buildings to have survived the great Yokohama fire of 1866. When they stopped at its front lychgate, roofed as the canons of English church architecture dictated, the pallbearers and a crowd were waiting.[3] The former were Gower's closest friends—his partner Valdemar Blad, his neighbor Albert Read, and, of course, Chandler Gibbens and Brooke Pearson. They carried the coffin into the church, where men and women of Yokohama's "better sort" were already seated. Then reporters and the city's ordinary folk filed into the church.

The pallbearers came down its center aisle and placed the coffin on the catafalque at the foot of the altar steps. Chaplain Edward Champneys Irwine, garbed in black cassock, white surplice, and black stole, stood waiting for them. He bore the title "chaplain," not vicar or rector, because the church had originally been built to serve the needs of the British garrison that protected Yokohama's foreign residents from 1862 to 1874.[4] The reverend looked calm, for he had officiated at many Yokohama funerals, but he saw that this was no ordinary one. The church was packed, far beyond what was normal for such an occasion. Crammed, with people standing along the side aisles and at the rear, it looked as if it were Christmas or Easter Sunday. There was also a certain poignancy to the moment. None of the mourners present was related to the deceased. Gower's father was dead, and his mother had returned to England. His sister lived in Colorado with her mining engineer husband. His uncles who had come to Japan years earlier and distinguished themselves as *o-yatoi* (foreign experts employed by the government) had long since left. Gower Robinson had lived and died among friends and strangers, not family.[5]

His violent death had sent shock waves not just through Yokohama but also to treaty ports elsewhere in Japan and China and beyond across the seas to England and America. Thirty years earlier, as the church window dedicated to British merchant Charles J. Richardson attested, violent death in Yokohama was not unusual. Samurai protecting the anti-foreign *daimyō* of Satsuma had cut him down because he had trespassed on their lord's way.[6] But now? Violent death in Yokohama was almost unimaginable. And yet it had happened. The deceased was a murder victim. His death, preceded as it was by sexual scandal, had spread gossip and rumor and divided the city's English-speaking community against itself. That unhappy, potentially dangerous development had shattered peoples' images of who they were and what Yokohama was. They saw themselves as exemplars of Western, Christian civilization. Yokohama was Japan's preeminent treaty port, a model of peaceful and mutually profitable intercourse between East and West. Any threat to the expatriates' self-confidence and the image of the city they projected had to be quashed as quickly as possible.

That imperative explained why Chaplain Irwine saw unusual people as well as familiar faces in the congregation. Virtually all of Yokohama's "better sort" were present. The Yokohama consular corps and their spouses sat in the front pews. James Troup, Her Majesty's consul general; his younger American counterpart, Willard Tillotson; the Italian consul, Marquis Nembrini, who had served as interpreter at the inquest;

his German colleague, Herr Dr. Otto Schmidt-Leda, who had observed on that occasion; and, of course, Bessie Hetherington's friends, Prince Lobanov, the Russian consul, and his wife, the princess.

Yokohama's notables were arrayed behind them. John Frederick and Julia Lowder, of course. The doctors who had attended to Gower in his last hours, Edwin Wheeler and Stuart Eldridge, and Herr Doktor Richard Kleffel, who had participated in the postmortem. And, of course, the senior naval officers present, among them the new commander-in-chief, Asiatic Station, Rear Admiral David B. Harmony, for the United States, and Captain Charles J. Balfour, RN, for Great Britain.[7] Chaplain Irwine also recognized reporters for the local newspapers, one British-owned, the other owned and edited by an American, standing at the rear of the church. Their words would tell the community and the world beyond about what was about to begin.

The funeral service the chaplain was about to conduct would be not just a religious but also a civic event. It was meant to comfort those who came to mourn Gower Robinson, but it must also serve to repair the divisions in the foreign community that his murder had caused. The reverend would foster that healing through the familiar words and ritual prescribed by the *Book of Common Prayer* and hymns known to all. In this funeral service, he would use the ordinary to help quell the extraordinary emotions that the manner of the deceased's death had ignited in the congregation and the community.

What followed was a proper Victorian funeral service. It differed in tone and purpose from Christian funerals today. Nowadays a funeral is as much a celebration of life as an occasion for mourning the loss of the deceased. The words of remembrance and eulogy that come from mourners are often lengthier than those spoken by the officiating priest, minister, or rabbi. In 1892, a Christian funeral was a communal prayer to God asking Him to show mercy to the deceased and welcome that person into Paradise. Chaplain Irwine meant Gower's funeral to be precisely that sort of rite.

The chaplain first prayed for him. He read comforting passages from scripture that spoke of eternal life. Foremost among them were Jesus's words in the Gospel of John: "I am the resurrection, and the life; he that believeth in me, though he were dead, yet shall he live. And whosoever liveth and believeth in me shall never die."[8] Then the congregation heard the 23rd Psalm: "The Lord is my shepherd, I shall not want…" Chaplain Irwine asked all present to join him in reciting the Lord's Prayer, which they did in a loud chorus. He himself, at this point, likely said a few words—a very few words—about Gower Robinson. Better to say less than more about a man whose actions in life and manner of death were controversial. The congregation remained silent until Chaplain Irwine had raised his hand in blessing over Robinson's coffin. Then all joined in a final familiar hymn as the pallbearers carried it out of the church.

Undertaker P.J. Hellendale was waiting outside to help them replace the coffin in his hearse. Climbing aboard it, he shook the reins to signal the horses to start moving, and the funeral cortege began its march toward the Foreigners' General Cemetery on the bluff. Some but not all of those at the funeral followed along behind the hearse as it moved toward the burial ground. The road, then as now, was beautiful, affording views out over the city from between the trees that lined it. When the party reached the burial site in the English section of the cemetery, the pallbearers lowered the coffin into the grave.

Then for a second and final time, Chaplain Irwine spoke. He addressed the mourners—and the Divinity, using the words that the *Book of Common Prayer* prescribed:

> "Take on the soul of our dear brother here departed. We therefore commit his body to the ground; earth to earth, ashes to ashes, dust to dust; in sure and certain hope of the Resurrection to eternal life, through Our Lord Jesus who will change our vile body that it may be like unto his glorious body, according to the might working whereby he is able to subdue all things to himself."[9]

Silence followed. Then those present stepped forward, one by one, to complete the burial ritual. Each person picked up a handful of earth and tossed it down on the coffin. They paused, looked at the inscription upon it—George Gower Robinson, 1856–1892—and then turned away to leave as the gravediggers covered over the remains. Gower Robinson had been laid to rest.

As people walked away, they looked out at the cherry trees gracing the lower edge of the cemetery. They were bare as yet, for late February was still winter. Yet they bore within them the stuff of life that would produce their glorious blossoms in the weeks ahead. The view may have evoked feelings of hope in the mourners' breasts—hope for eternal rest for Gower, hope for justice for his killer, and hope for healing in the divided community that he left behind.

In the days immediately following his burial, Gower's friends and associates poured out their feelings in letters to Yokohama's newspapers. They said in them what could not be spoken at his last rites. Their eulogies were written to soften their grief at his loss and shroud him in good memories. In time they gathered enough money to commission a handsome grave marker for him. The stonemason at Stibolt's fashioned an elegant obelisk. On it he chiseled: "George Gower Robinson 1856–1892 Twelve Years a Yokohama Resident." That would lay him, his contemporaries

10. Unquiet Rest

George Gower Robinson Grave, Yokohama Foreign Residents Cemetery (courtesy Dr. Nagata Maruyama Motoko).

believed, in proper eternal rest. Erected later in the spring of 1892, the grave marker can be seen today in the English section of the Yokohama General Cemetery for Foreigners.

But neither tombstone nor eulogies nor funeral rites gave Gower eternal rest. The way he had lived, loved, and died guaranteed he would be remembered in Yokohama. What newspaper reporters were about to write about him; his killer, James; and his lover, Bessie, made all three of them celebrities whose names and deeds were known around the world.

11

Celebrity

Nearly two months passed between Gower Robinson's burial and the opening of James Henry Hetherington's trial for murder. During that time, Gower, James, and Bessie were catapulted from obscurity to celebrity. How did that happen? Did the celebrity-makers show the world who they really were? Why were people around the globe so shocked by what they learned about them? What difference did their celebrity status make for expectations about the murder trial that lay ahead?

To answer those questions, one needs to look closely at how news of what came to be called "the tragedy in Yokohama" traveled from the city to Japan and on to the world beyond. For there were differences of speed and physical means of transmission; of national perspective and journalistic culture; and of interpretation that shaped the way people viewed what had gone on, their expectations about the coming trial, and their sense of what the broader significance of the tragedy in Yokohama might be.

At one level, it might be said that the very nature of who they were and what they did made Gower, James, and Bessie celebrities. They were not just ordinary people but persons of "the better sort"—higher in social status and income than most, and better educated. They knew what the rules for a good life were, whether defined in today's secular terms as those necessary to preserve order in society or their time's religious terms. They knew the Ten Commandments and had broken them. Gower #9: he coveted another man's wife. Bessie, #6: she committed adultery. James, #5: he killed another man. By any measure, their actions were extraordinary, unacceptable, and shocking!

Yokohama residents learned what had happened directly, from one another. People outside the city—in Japan, beyond the seas, and around the globe—depended on newspapers and the men and women who wrote and published them to inform them about "the tragedy in Yokohama." These newsmakers were strongly motivated to publish whatever they could find out about it as quickly as possible. Sex, murder, and crime in print made money—lots of it—for newspaper owners. It made reputations and careers for reporters. And when news of it came from the exotic, mysterious Far East, from Japan, such news might even feed readers' desires to escape from their ordinary, everyday lives.

A story of celebrity misbehavior and murder committed far away was bound to shock and fascinate people around the world. It stimulated their curiosity. It stirred their hunger for more information about Gower, Bessie, and James. It fueled their speculation about who was responsible for what had happened. And it raised their doubts about whether the trial to come could determine truth and deliver justice.

The tragedy in Yokohama placed a heavy burden on the newsmakers. How they rose to the challenges they faced and what difference their reportage made varied from place to place. Yokohama's reporters and editors penned the very first stories about the killing on Valentine's Day weekend. Writing for the city's four English-language newspapers, three British and one American, they said little of the affair that preceded the killing and focused on its aftermath. Their readers got matter-of-fact accounts of the autopsy, inquest, James's arrest, and Gower's funeral. They left speculation about who was most responsible for what had happened and whether the killer should be found guilty of murder to Yokohama's rumor mill.

Japanese newsmen usually paid scant attention to what transpired in Yokohama's foreign community, but they could not ignore this story. Rather than presenting James, Gower, and Bessie as celebrities in the full sense of the word, they offered readers a brief, factual account of what had occurred. News of what they labeled "the Robinson incident" appeared on the front page of the *Tokyo Mainichi Shimbun* the day after Gower's death. Nothing more was said about the killer and his victim than one was an American naval officer and the other a British broker. Further articles in the Tokyo metropolitan press over the succeeding days and weeks about what was also called "the Hetherington affair" reported on events—inquest, funeral, and trial—rather than the persons involved in them. Those events commanded the attention of Japanese readers because they were exotic—an unusual killing of one foreigner by another in a hybrid city that most people knew little about. Thus James, Gower, and Bessie appeared more as oddities, albeit shocking ones, than celebrities in the Japanese press.[1]

They were certainly celebrities, however, in the treaty ports of China and beyond throughout the British Empire. Newspaper accounts there depicted them more as people to be pitied than transgressors of law and morality to be condemned. The first, most influential report of what had happened in Yokohama depicted Gower, Bessie, and James as if they were characters in a Shakespearian drama. A Yokohama-based reporter wrote it on February 18, just four days after Gower's death, and published it in Kobe's English-language newspaper. Telegraph and submarine cable then carried it to the *North China Herald and Supreme Court & Consular Gazette* in Shanghai. The article gave readers a vivid account of "the tragic incident of Saturday last ... that was currently the all-absorbing matter of interest in Kobe and Yokohama alike." Robinson, "in his usual health and natural buoyancy of spirit," had visited Kobe and then returned to Yokohama after receiving a message that he had left his home there out of fear. He was shot "under circumstances ... little better than cold-blooded murder." The killer, the report continued, was "a man of handsome physique and devotedly attached to his wife. Smothering his pride, [he had] ... warned Robinson [and gotten] ... his word of honour neither to approach nor communicate with Mrs. Hetherington again."

"Opinion is hotly divided," the report continued, about an affair that was "terribly sad and distressing [whether one considered either] the life so suddenly and tragically closed or the almost equally marred life of the outraged husband [who is] ... under arrest awaiting trial."

There was the story in its essence: two men in love with same woman. One of them killed by the other, who now faced the penalty that justice demanded. But the reporter added his own opinion about what had happened and appended a moral to the story. Robinson was not all bad, for he had penned a deathbed letter to his killer's superior officer, asking the navy not to go too hard on Lieutenant Hetherington. That act, the writer opined, was an "effort at reparation of a heart [that was] ... generous and able to recognize the right and true."[2] The real-life story ended just as one of Shakespeare's dramas would have: adulterous sex and violent death, followed by moral clarity with justice to come.

That article and a second based on an interview with Martin Pors, the only eyewitness to the killing, traveled via British-owned telegraph and submarine cables to Hong Kong and Singapore, Australia, India, and eventually all the way to England. These first reports made Gower, Bessie, and James instant celebrities for British newspaper readers. People wanted to know more about them and why they had acted as they did. One woman, a widow, Mrs. Adaliza Letitia Gower Robinson, had a particular reason for wanting to know more. What she read in the *Manchester Guardian*, the preeminent newspaper in the Midlands region where she lived, on Monday, March 7, was heartbreaking. Her son, Gower, was dead, killed by an American naval lieutenant. How and why had that happened?

She and everyone else had to wait for weeks for an answer to that question. They got only brief reports of the inquest and the killer's indictment. Why? Simply because it was so very expensive to telegraph more detailed information from Yokohama to London. And British travelers returning from Japan who might have passed along rumors and speculation about what had happened took so very long to reach "home." Thus James, Gower, and Bessie remained somewhat mysterious celebrities in Britain and its empire.[3]

In the United States, they became instant celebrities, in the fullest sense of the word, from Saturday, March 5, 1892, onward. That afternoon, the SS *City of Peking* was sighted gliding through the Golden Gate. Competing reporters from the *San Francisco Chronicle* and the *San Francisco Call* rushed to the Pacific Mail Steamship wharf, hoping to get newsworthy tidbits from passengers and their newspapers when the ship docked. Instead they got shocking news of a sex scandal, murder, and trial to come in Yokohama. Rushing back to their offices, the reporters wrote a blockbuster story that was splashed across the front pages of Sunday newspapers all over America. Its essence: "Shot fatal—A tragic death in Yokohama Lt. J H Hetherington of the American navy kills an Englishman."[4] That first word-of-mouth-based report tantalized newspaper readers all over the country. They clamored for more details about what had happened in Yokohama, and thanks to the transcontinental telegraph, regional wire services that shared information with member newspapers, and, most importantly, the canons of American journalism, they got a great deal of information quickly.[5]

Reporters in Dubuque and Wilmington rushed to tell readers how James's and Bessie's parents reacted to the news from Yokohama. Henry Hetherington got it at Dubuque Methodist Church. When the pastor prayed for those in affliction, he wondered whom he was referring to. But others in the congregation who had read their newspapers before church knew exactly whom the minister meant. When one of them told Henry that his son had been charged with murder, the old man burst into tears.

That same Sunday afternoon, a Wilmington reporter who had seen wire reports in the New York newspapers knocked on the Hewes family's door. When he told Bessie's mother the news from Yokohama, she couldn't believe it. Neither she nor her husband would answer questions. The Hewes home became "a sad and sorrowing place" and Mrs. Hewes "refused to be comforted." She became ill from "the sudden shock" of the news from Japan.[6]

Those local news stories touched the hearts of Americans, making them all the more eager for more news about "the tragedy in Yokohama." Who were the people caught up in it? Over the next 10 days, newsmen mixed fact, fancy, and flawed information to give their readers hastily drawn sketches of James, Gower, and Bessie.

James was perhaps the easiest for the reporters to portray. They found nothing about him to suggest he was capable of cold-blooded murder. He came from one of Iowa's best families. He was the son of a former Dubuque mayor and "a model young man." After winning an appointment to the Naval Academy, he had, in one reporter's telling, "graduated with high honors" (false) and gone on to become a fine naval officer (true). James was big—"a stalwart manly fellow, rugged in his manner and quick-tempered, but the soul of honor" (stereotypical supposition for no reporter had gone to the Naval Academy to find James's boyish graduation photograph). A Wilmington reporter tracked down one of the Hetheringtons' wedding guests who remembered James as a handsome, blond-bearded groom. (But he was neither blond nor bearded then.)

The reporters who queried his fellow officers, classmates, and former shipmates offered readers a stereotypical picture of James. He was an honorable and dutiful officer, appropriately nicknamed "the Judge." An officer who knew him from occasional duty at the Philadelphia Hydrographic Office remembered him as "a very quiet, gentlemanly young fellow." He was a proper sort of person who despised the "'silly antics" of those who indulged in "such frail amusements as dancing and eating [out] every other night." Given his social origins, his status as a naval officer, and what others said about his character, James did not look like a murderer in these early news stories.[7]

What was puzzling about him was not what kind of man he was but rather how he could he have done something completely at odds with everything known about him. American newspaper readers found the answer to that riddle in what reporters dug up about Gower Robinson.

First reports from Japan depicted him as "a rich banker and old settler in the Mikado's domain." Born in Yokohama (false) and educated in England (true), he had returned to Japan and become a cashier at the Yokohama branch of the powerful Hong Kong and Shanghai Bank. A quintessential young British gentleman, he "kept an English drag" (kind of buggy). He became a prominent member of the Union Club and "lived in great style and dressed in the height of fashion." Not surprisingly, Robinson was "very popular in society" with men and women alike. He also befriended American naval officers, and they greatly enjoyed his company. One of them remembered that when the USS *Richmond* had come to Yokohama years earlier, they had welcomed him to their wardroom during a voyage to Kobe. Another officer described Gower as "quite a swell"—a "masher"[8]—who hung around the Grand Hotel and presented himself as a leading figure in Yokohama's expatriate society.

Articles based on interviews with longtime Yokohama residents portrayed Gower as a perfect gentleman who had never been "mixed up in any scandal before." One old-timer recalled that when "some of the boys were twittering him about a certain married woman, he blushed like a girl" and demanded that such talk stop. Another man, who claimed to know Robinson well, insisted that reports of his maintaining a luxurious home where he had "received" Bessie Hetherington and "other married ladies" were "manifestly untrue." He could not have done so because fellow bachelors living there would have known about his "amours." Neither he nor the women, including Bessie, would have risked such exposure, the reporter's informant insisted.[9]

A third cluster of interviews painted a sinister portrait of Gower. Yes, he was a typical rich English playboy, a highly cultured man who spoke French, German, and Japanese (false). He was also a "gay sort of fellow who always had a love affair on." He looked like the villain in a Victorian melodrama, with dark hair and a mustache that he curled and waxed at its ends. Gower was vain. He brushed his hair up so that it looked like "it had been arranged by a Lady's hair dresser." But he was manly and "strong as an athlete." Considered "quite a horseman," he proved a strong competitor in Yokohama's many horseracing events. Gower boasted about "several" little "affairs" while giving the impression that he hadn't related even "half of his escapades" with women. Thus it was no surprise that the man depicted in these reports had entangled himself in a love affair with Mrs. Hetherington that prompted her husband to kill him.[10]

But what sort of person was she? Articles about her offered readers radically different portraits of Bessie. Her hometown newspaper first found it "improbable" that "the charmingly modest and handsome woman who was 'Bessie Hewes' here two years ago" could have, by scandalous behavior with Gower Robinson, given her husband just cause for killing the man. She could not possibly have been guilty of adultery.[11]

Some subsequent reports confirmed that judgment. Bessie was a young matron of high social status and great beauty. She was the oldest daughter of a family that "always moved in the best society." "Remarkably handsome, with a beautiful complexion, she was a willowy blonde of average height," readers were told. The cream of society in Wilmington and a popular summer visitor to Cape May, New Jersey, she would be "remembered in all the Eastern cities as a belle." She had blossomed into Lieutenant Hetherington's beautiful bride, and he had claimed her in one of the most lavish weddings ever seen in Delaware. One imaginative reporter wrote that a grand chorus of 35 had performed at the ceremony attended by a thousand guests—something clearly impossible given the modest size of the church. Another newsman more modestly and correctly described Bessie as a young woman with a naturally gay and outgoing nature that added to her physical charms.[12]

Readers got wildly differing reports of her behavior on the journey to Japan. A male fellow guest at her hotel in San Francisco said that her "most bewitching eyes, cherry lips, oval face, and wealth" of beautiful hair had made "susceptible males ... her willing slaves." If her husband had been there then, he added ominously, "a tragedy might have occurred ... and the victim would not have been George Gower Robinson." Another San Franciscan refuted that story, insisting that Bessie couldn't have behaved that way because she stayed only briefly in the city.

A former *China* officer described Bessie simply as an innocent but fun-loving young matron. Aboard ship, she had often dined with Illinois railroad millionaire Columbus R. Cummings and his niece. A well-known Democratic politician and the millionaire's secretary, "a handsome young man," frequently joined them. The two men vied for her attention in ways which she—and other diners—appeared to enjoy greatly. Her two faux suitors wagered one another as to who would become her favorite by the time they reached Yokohama. When the secretary "came out ahead" and the politician "fell back in chagrin," fellow passengers roared with laughter. Nothing serious had happened, and it all ended in good fun. Mrs. Hetherington had done no wrong.

Her behavior in Yokohama? Appalling! Dr. Edwin Norfleet, a former USS *Monocacy* surgeon returning home, reported that Bessie had been "a cause for gossip" from the moment she arrived in Yokohama. She was a "WEDDED FLIRT who ogled and giggled at handsome men." The doctor recycled a shocking rumor about Bessie. The night after the shooting, she had asked Frances Belknap if she should go to a formal dinner at the Russian consul's home. The admiral's wife snapped that she most certainly should not. Bessie spurned that advice, and when she appeared at the dinner, "clad in tulle and diamonds," jaws dropped. The other guests were so "aghast" at her behavior that they needed several minutes "to regain their composure."[13]

A final early report from Yokohama demonstrated how inaccurate and opinionated they could be. James was "a man of striking appearance because of [his] bright red hair." (His hair was sandy brown.) Gower was "a professional flirt" who exposed his "beautifully molded ... columnar neck" to attract women. And Bessie? The interviewee called her "the most worthless, brazen, senseless creature I have ever met," likely pregnant by her English lover. Capping his "authoritative" judgment on the tragedy in Yokohama, he predicted: "Time will probably show that Hetherington had abundant cause for perforating the gay Lothario who debauched his worthless wife."[14]

On Monday, March 14, when the SS *Oceanic*[15] arrived in San Francisco, the ship's most distinguished passenger, Rear Admiral George Eugene Belknap, recently commander in chief Asiatic Station, stepped ashore eager to talk to waiting newsmen. He was determined to set them straight about what had happened in Yokohama. He knew from personal experience, for he had participated in the events surrounding Robinson's death and Hetherington's arrest. His first words: "All talk of any strained relations between Americans and British in Yokohama growing out of the shooting is rubbish," the admiral snapped. He knew precisely why the tragedy in Yokohama had occurred. Gower Robinson was responsible for his own death. "He was told very plainly what would be the consequence if he persisted in … continuing his attentions to Mrs. Hetherington… [Lt.] Hetherington was a man who would endure no trifling. Robinson promised Hetherington by letter and his friends by word of mouth that he would desist, but he broke both promises. The shooting," Admiral Belknap proclaimed, "was simply the natural consequence of his failure to abide by his agreement as a man of honor."

The admiral then provided reporters with two previously unknown details about the tragedy in Yokohama. First, Robinson had written a deathbed letter to him. In it he forgave his killer and begged mercy for him from his naval superiors. He had forwarded it to the secretary of the navy in Washington. Second, although the dying man had said nothing in the letter about his or Mrs. Hetherington's guilt in their affair, one could infer who the most guilty party in the love affair that led to the killing was. None of Robinson's friends had come forward to speak in his defense at the inquest, and none had sworn a complaint against Lieutenant Hetherington.

Admiral Belknap then downplayed the significance of the murder charges against James. He himself had advised him to surrender at the American consulate general. Because a man couldn't be held there without a formal complaint, "we finally

Rear Admiral George E. Belknap, USN, commander-in-chief, Asiatic Station (NH56132, Naval History and Heritage Command).

persuaded the United States marshal at the consulate to make this complaint." As for the coroner's verdict of "willful murder," it "means nothing," the admiral insisted. Speaking with all the authority his rank could command, he confidently predicted: "Mr. Hetherington will never be convicted of murder." There would be a happy ending to this sad story.[16]

Although reporters proclaimed Admiral Belknap's statement "the clearest account of the affair" yet received, it was neither complete nor unbiased. He had not told them the full story of what had happened in Yokohama or his own role in it. What he said about events immediately following the shooting clearly departed from what British and Japanese witnesses had stated at the coroner's inquest. He barely mentioned his own role in getting an attorney to defend James. He put a positive spin on how the tragedy in Yokohama would end. The trial would be delayed until necessary legal documents, presumably ones that would strengthen the case for the defense, reached the city. The admiral predicted that James Hetherington would be acquitted. Killer though he was, the lieutenant had simply done what any man of honor, any normal husband, and any naval officer might be expected to have done under the circumstances.

After the admiral's stirring words were flashed across the country by telegraph, a long silence in the press about the extraordinary events in Yokohama followed. More news waited until the SS *Gaelic* docked in San Francisco on April 1, 1892. A few days later, a reporter caught up with former passenger R.M. Varnum at the luxurious Palace Hotel. The tea merchant had lived in Yokohama for nearly 20 years and claimed to know Gower, James, and Bessie well. Varnum told the newsman he wanted to discredit the "wild statements regarding ... [the] intimacy" between Robinson and Mrs. Hetherington that people in Yokohama had made and correct what had appeared in the press about them.

First, Gower. It was "manifestly untrue," Varnum said, that Robinson and other bachelor friends had maintained "luxurious apartments in a house they called The Niche." He could not have taken Mrs. Hetherington or other married women there because they would not have wanted "to advertise their amours" to his housemates. "Any meetings between them other than at social functions were held," he snapped "at the Grand Hotel." Then James. "He has always been regarded as a fine, manly fellow and made many friends during his short sojourn in Yokohama," Varnum said. When asked if he knew anything about Hetherington's current state of mind, he demurred, saying he hadn't seen the lieutenant since his arrest.

And Bessie? Did Varnum know "anything of Mrs. Hetherington's demeanor since Robinson's death?" the reporter asked. "She has kept quietly in her room," Varnum replied. She is "younger than you supposed [and] just as pretty as been represented and probably very indiscreet," the tea merchant added. "I have not made up my mind that she is guilty of all that has been laid at her door," he affirmed.[17]

So skepticism was in order. People would just have to wait until the trial, Varnum advised, to get the evidence needed to determine who was responsible for the tragedy in Yokohama.

But they didn't. Skepticism and doubt prevailed. People wanted to know—*now*—about the trial. When and where would it take place? How would it proceed? And if Lieutenant Hetherington were found guilty, would he hang for his crime?

Such questions would not have arisen if the killing had taken place in the United States. The defendant would be tried by 12 of his peers—a jury—in a courtroom in the local jurisdiction where the alleged crime had occurred. People knew that because they read about murder trials in their newspapers almost every day. The same would be true if the killing had occurred in England, where legal proceedings resembled American ones. Even in France, where the law derived from Roman rather than Anglo-Saxon tradition, justice would prevail. American newspaper readers knew it would because in the spring of 1892 they were savoring details about a "tragedy" at Cannes on the French Riviera that resembled the one in Yokohama. A wealthy Bostonian had returned from a business trip to Paris and found his wife, scantily clad, in their hotel bedroom with a handsome young French diplomat. The man was just putting his clothes back on, and the husband shot and killed him on the spot. No one questioned how and where he would be tried, for France was a "civilized" Christian country with a modern legal system that could be relied upon to render justice promptly.[18]

But Japan? Americans knew the country was modernizing. The Japanese had cast off the old "feudal" system of government and embraced "renovation" under the Meiji emperor. The country had a barely two-year-old constitution and had held elections for the Diet, its legislature. The Japanese were obviously striving to reach the level of institutional sophistication that prevailed in Europe and America. But … Japanese courts? Who knew anything about them or how they functioned? If an American were tried in a Japanese court, how could he, given the language barrier, even understand what was being said? Could Lieutenant Hetherington possibly get a fair trial under a Japanese judge?

Those questions revealed Americans' ignorance about Japan and its treaty ports. Peoples' anxiety about what might happen to James created a demand for accurate information about the forthcoming trial. What they got in their newspapers, however, was a potpourri of fact and fancy. Newsmen turned to "experts" who provided false or half-true information. A former Iowa state senator insisted that "Hetherington cannot be

11. Celebrity

tried at all." If an attempt to arraign him in Japan were made, "habeas corpus proceedings in the United States Supreme Court" would free him. Not so. Durham W. Stevens, a former American diplomat in Tokyo and current legal adviser to the Japanese legation in Washington, told reporters that the lieutenant would be tried in the American consular court in Yokohama. True. But if convicted, he could appeal to the American minister in Tokyo, who could "change the verdict." Not true.[19]

Eventually reporters found more accurate sources. Thomas F. Bayard of Wilmington, Delaware, a former United States senator and former secretary of state, stood foremost among them. He explained that Yokohama was a treaty port. According to treaties Japan signed with the United States and other countries back in 1858, foreigners enjoyed extraterritoriality there. That meant that an American citizen who committed a crime in Yokohama would be tried there by the American consul, acting as judge. He would select four men who would function like jurors. They would advise and he, as judge, would determine the guilt or innocence of the defendant. Bayard's words were reassuring. Lieutenant Hetherington was in no danger of being tried in a Japanese court. His trial would be as fair as any held in America.[20]

But would James hang if found guilty of murder? Enterprising reporters who dug deeper suggested that that was unlikely. While Americans in Japan had committed and been convicted of murder in the past, only one had ever hanged. Presidents had either commuted their prison sentences or pardoned them. If precedent prevailed, James Hetherington, even if convicted, would never die for having killed Gower Robinson. That was reassuring to the American public.[21]

But could the coming trial in Yokohama yield the truth about the tragedy that had happened there, determine individual responsibility for it, and deliver justice?

Only time would tell.

∞ 12 ∞

Opening Day

Early on the morning of Wednesday, March 23, 1892, Willard Tillotson stepped out onto the second-story veranda that ringed his family's living quarters at the American consulate in Yokohama. It was one of the first days of spring. If he glanced up, he would have seen a gray sky filled with clouds that held the promise of rain. It would not be the pelting rain of the Pacific storms he had known in Tacoma, but *harusame*, or spring rain. That gentle mist-like rain had inspired Japanese poets and artists for centuries, and its moisture would caress the cherry blossoms that made spring the loveliest season of the year in Yokohama. If Tillotson cast his glance toward the cherry trees in the Japanese-style garden that fronted the consulate, he might have seen but a bud or two, for it was too soon for the trees to be in full bloom. That was something he—and everyone in Yokohama—looked forward to seeing.

When Tillotson turned back into his rooms for breakfast, he was filled with anticipation about the trial about to begin. A year earlier, when he accepted the position of American consul general at Kanagawa (Yokohama), he could not have imagined that he was going to be the judge in a murder case. Now he was about to preside over the trial of Lieutenant James Henry Hetherington, U.S. Navy, for the killing of George Gower Robinson. It would be the most high-profile murder case ever tried in an American consular court.

Tillotson presented a striking appearance. He stood well over six feet tall, carried not an ounce of extra flesh on his bones, and wore a mustache whose wispy ends drooped down to his jaw. He didn't look like a judge, for he was only 31 and had not a touch of gray at his temples. Nothing in his previous experience prepared him for playing that role.

He had been born in Painesville, Ohio, the second son of a farming family. When he was nine, his family moved to Eureka, the county seat for Greenwood County, Kansas. Willard completed school there, and then worked on the family farm through his teens. Little is known of him

12. Opening Day

United States Consulate, Yokohama, Japan, trial site (140916-0019-PP, Kjeld Duits Collection, Tokyo).

thereafter until 1887, when he married Etta Kirkendall in Lyon, Kansas. The young couple subsequently moved to Tacoma, Washington, where Willard learned what he knew of the law while interning in the office of an attorney who specialized in real estate transactions. In 1890, the Tillotsons welcomed the first of their two daughters. Even as a new parent and fledgling attorney, Willard found time for politics. He won election to Washington's first state legislature as a Republican representative from Tacoma. When his term ended there, he netted the "spoils" of party loyalty. President Benjamin Harrison appointed him consul general at Yokohama at a salary of $4,000 a year.[1]

The Tillotsons arrived there only a few months before Bessie Hetherington did. Luckily for the new consul general, a very knowledgeable assistant was on hand to prepare him for his new job. That was George H. Scidmore, the vice consul. He had been born in Dubuque, Iowa, just two years before James Hetherington. His family moved to Madison, Wisconsin, and then on to Washington, D.C., where he graduated with a law degree from National University in 1876. He entered government service almost immediately thereafter, and after working in various European consulates, came to Japan in April 1881.

With brief exceptions for consular work elsewhere in Japan, China,

Judge/Consul General Willard D. Tillotson at the Great Buddha, Kamakura, Japan (Photograph 1950 166.1 Shasta Historical Society).

and Korea, Scidmore lived and worked in Yokohama until his death in 1922. As a bachelor and competitive yachtsman, he quickly became a popular and respected member of the Yokohama expatriate community. He hosted his sister Eliza for an extended visit in 1884, and she drew on his

12. Opening Day

knowledge of Japan to publish *Jinrikisha Days in Japan* (1891), the first American-authored guide to travel there. She went on to later fame as the first and most persistent advocate of bringing Japanese cherry trees to Washington, D.C., as symbols of trans–Pacific friendship. George labored on in bureaucratic obscurity.[2]

Scidmore supplemented his official income by teaching law at what is now Chūō University. His lectures there formed the basis for what became *Outline Lectures on the History, Organization, Jurisdiction, and Practice of the Ministerial and Consular Courts of the United States of American in Japan*, published in 1887.[3] That book became the *vade mecum* for the political appointees named to consular and diplomatic posts in Japan. In the spring of 1892, as the Hetherington trial loomed ahead, Willard Tillotson doubtless scoured it and picked George Scidmore's brain for good counsel on how to preside over a murder trial. By this trial's opening day, he was confident that he could do the job.

Just before 10:00 a.m. that day, a crowd of spectators surged into the courtroom. They had been waiting for some time outside at the front gate of the consulate. It was a modest wooden structure, not at all like its imposing British counterpart. Ringed by a second-story veranda and topped with blue-gray Japanese tile, its largest first-floor room was where the trial would be held. Those lucky enough to find a chair and sit down were excited, filled with anticipation for what was about to begin. Five weeks had passed since Gower Robinson was laid to rest. The days had been filled with speculation as to how the trial would proceed and whether the American consular court could render justice. Britons and Americans in Yokohama had differed sharply on that point, but by this time their antagonism had softened somewhat.

The spectators looked like a well-dressed audience waiting politely for a concert or play to begin. But their mood was more like that of those in the stands on race day at Yokohama's racetrack. Pure excitement.

People leaned forward in their chairs when the attorneys for the prosecution and the defense came in and sat down at their respective tables at the front of the room. They knew the man, or rather the men, who sought justice for Gower Robinson and punishment for James Hetherington. Henry Charles Litchfield, the prosecutor, had lived and practiced law among them for nearly 20 years. The man sitting next to him was the victim's lawyer, John Frederick Lowder. He had been a leading figure in the Anglo-American expatriate community from almost the first moment he set foot in Yokohama more than 30 years earlier. If the spectators had been at the track rather than in a courtroom, Litchfield would have been the jockey and Lowder the owner of the stallion favored to win the race.

The man who took his seat at the defense table was something of a mystery, a stranger to the crowd. He lived in Tokyo and had come to stay in Yokohama only a few weeks earlier to prepare for the trial. Some had seen him for the first time at the coroner's inquest, where he was a mere observer who spoke not a word. Now, everyone would hang on his words as the attorney for the defense. What Alexander Tison said in the flowery opening speech spectators expected him to deliver later that day might well determine whether James Hetherington lived or died.

Only a few in the audience had met and talked with Tison. He didn't look like much of a match for Litchfield, his older gray-haired adversary. Only 35, his hair and beard still dark, he had never tried a murder case. To the courtroom spectators, he might well have looked like David girding for battle with Goliath.

Appearances, however, can be deceiving. If reporters had interviewed Tison and given their readers an account of his background, they would have sensed that he would be a formidable opponent to Henry Litchfield. What he lacked in experience he made up in intellect. Tison boasted a stellar legal pedigree. Only a year younger than his client James, he had been born in Saint Louis, Missouri, and was raised in Olivet, Michigan. After graduating from the local Christian college with a degree in classics in 1878, he taught Latin at Olivet for five years. Then he went on to Harvard, where he earned his bachelor of laws degree in 1885. He studied for a year under a prominent New York City lawyer before passing the bar there and in Michigan. While at Harvard, he had caught the attention of President Charles Eliot, who had earlier befriended Japanese students who went on to become prominent officials in the Meiji government. When one of them advised him of its desire to have an American teach law at what would become Tokyo University, Eliot recommended Tison.

Still single and eager for adventure, he accepted the position and arrived in Japan in the spring of 1889. Over the next two years, Tison became a well-known figure there. In addition to his teaching, he practiced law and served as legal counsel, by courtesy, in the British as well as American consular courts. He also developed an academic interest in Japanese history and culture. That led to his joining diplomats and politicians, businessmen and missionaries in the prestigious Asiatic Society of Japan. By 1892, he served as its corresponding secretary. Little wonder, then, that Admiral Belknap and the *Marion* officers had wanted Tison to defend James Hetherington.[4]

Precisely at 10:00 that March morning, Willard Tillotson, now judge as well as consul general, entered the courtroom and took his seat at the front of the room. He ordered Marshal Richard McCance to bring in the defendant. When James came into the room from a side door, the spectators leaned forward from their seats hoping to catch a glimpse of the killer.

12. Opening Day

Those who knew him or had seen him earlier noticed something different about James. During the month of his sequestration at the American consulate, he had grown a full reddish-brown beard.[5]

The new facial ornament betrayed what psychologists today might argue was a clue to James's state of mind on the trial's opening day. What a man does with his facial hair is an expression of who he is and how he feels about himself. No one can know for sure, but maybe James had put on a new face because he felt he was no longer the person he had been before coming to Yokohama. Then he was a happily married new father and a well-liked junior officer with good professional prospects. Now he was a cuckold, a jealous husband, a man who had shattered his marriage and dimmed those prospects by killing his wife's lover. Now he was on trial for his life.

Was James afraid that morning? One suspects not—for three reasons. First, he sensed that Willard Tillotson was not a vindictive man determined to punish him. He had seen him several times during his sequestration at the consulate, and his confinement there had been more like house arrest than incarceration. As James explained in a letter to his father, he was well-fed, dining, as he put it, "at the consul's table." He had visitors. *Amah* Tome frequently brought baby Gladys to see him, and he played with her on the veranda or in the garden below.[6] Insofar as James could tell, Tillotson was a fair-minded man who had not already made up his mind about his guilt or innocence.

Second, James was confident he had the moral backing of his shipmates and the U.S. Navy itself. Captain Bartlett and his fellow *Marion* officers had contributed $350 to help cover his legal expenses. Now all in uniform, they were sitting right behind him, providing moral support. He may also have seen the latest newspapers brought from San Francisco, which printed Admiral Belknap's confident prediction: "Hetherington will never be convicted." The admiral would not have spoken that way had he not been certain that his superiors in Washington were doing everything they could to help Lieutenant Hetherington.

Third, James trusted Alexander Tison, who sat at his side. In a letter to his father-in-law, James described him as "young," never having lost a case, and "more than a match for the old fogy English lawyer who was conducting the prosecution." He and Bessie had gotten to know Tison during their pretrial preparations, and he gave advice that betrayed a shrewd understanding of human nature. James and Bessie must look innocent in the eyes of the court and the community—even if neither were free of responsibility for the tragedy that had occurred. They must stay together and never mention the word *divorce*. Whatever their personal feelings, they must present to the world the face of a couple completely reconciled to each other. Furthermore, Bessie had best not appear in court. Tison wanted to focus on the terrible wrongs Gower Robinson had done to her and James, not on her supposed misdeeds. With such an insightful defender, James had good reason to hope for acquittal or, if that proved impossible, punishment short of death.[7]

James knew his case was in good hands.

This first day of his trial did not proceed as expected, with the selection of assessors and opening speeches by the prosecuting and defending attorneys. Instead, it was given over to procedural matters and wrangling between the attorneys and Judge Tillotson. Alexander Tison pounced like a legal tiger even before the selection of assessors began. By objecting not once but five times to the trial going ahead at all. Why? His client should have been indicted by a grand jury. His client could not be held or tried without the presentation of an indictment. He should be tried before "a petit jury of twelve men in accordance with the common law as guaranteed him under the Constitution of the United States," not by mere assessors. His client had not been given prior notice of the names and addresses of possible assessors. The consular court had no jurisdiction, and there should be a change of venue to the court of the American minister in Tokyo. Judge Tillotson overruled these objections as quickly as if he were swatting flies.[8]

Those present unfamiliar with the niceties of procedural rules for American consular court trials must have wondered what was going on here. Those in the know, like vice consul general Scidmore and prosecutor Litchfield, knew that Tison's challenges to the court's jurisdiction would be overruled. Scidmore knew that Thomas B. Van Buren, a previous American consul general in Yokohama, had argued that anything other than a trial by jury conducted under the same norms as one in the United States was illegal. He also suspected that challenges to this court's jurisdiction would go nowhere. After all, when Congress a year earlier had rewritten the law governing consular court procedure, it had left unchanged trial by judge and assessors—without jury. The new law simply directed that appeals from a consular court's judgment go to the federal court of appeals sitting in California rather than to the state's supreme court.[9]

What, then, was Tison trying to do? Most likely, he sought to lay the grounds for an appeal if James was found guilty. He may also have reasoned that black-robed justices would find conviction for a capital crime without indictment or a verdict of guilty delivered by a jury to be unconstitutional. If they did not go that far, appellate judges might be inclined to temper whatever sentence Judge Tillotson imposed upon James Hetherington. Tison, the ambitious legal scholar, may also have hoped to give this case greater significance than its particulars might otherwise suggest.

12. Opening Day

Perhaps, as some forward-thinking American officials and certainly their Japanese opposites were hoping, the Hetherington case would demonstrate that trial of foreigners by their respective consular officials was an anachronism that needed to be put to an end.

Judge Tillotson then directed that they proceed with the swearing in and appointment of four assessors. The assessors were neither mere aides to him nor jurors who would determine the guilt or innocence of the defendant. They had to pass on a unanimously concurring opinion to the judge for his finding in the case to be final. If only one of them dissented, that set up an automatic appeal of his judgment to the court of the American minister (ambassador) in Tokyo. The assessors' function, viewed broadly, was to certify that the trial had been conducted in a fair and legally correct manner.[10]

The assessors were chosen in much the same manner as jurors are in American courts today. Their names were drawn by lot from a preexisting list like a register of voters. They were summoned to appear in court, where prosecuting and defending attorneys questioned them in *voir dire* fashion to determine their suitability for service as an assessor. If an attorney had reason to believe a prospective assessor was prejudiced or incapable of reaching an impartial judgment about the fairness of the court's proceedings, he could object. The judge would then rule on whether or not an individual could be retained as an assessor.

After a brief recess, prospective assessors were brought before the court. Tison objected to George Edwin Rice, a clerk working for a British machinery importing company, on the grounds that he might be needed as a witness for the defense.[11] Rice was excused. Litchfield then objected to A. Gilmore Smith, an American dentist who had been practicing in Yokohama since 1888, because he had a strong preformed opinion about the case.[12] When Smith testified that evidence would not dislodge that opinion, Tillotson dismissed him. Neither of the next two men presented—Samuel Sondheim, a British trader, and Eugene Samuel Booth, an American missionary educator who served as administrator of the Isaac Ferris Anglo-Japanese Girls School—harbored strong opinions about the case. They were quickly accepted as assessors. Two more men were sworn in as assessors—J.R. Simon, an American export-import merchant who had been born in France, and Nathaniel Ferdinand Smith, a British trader.[13]

At that moment, no one voiced further objection to the selection of assessors. But technically, not all of them were qualified to serve in that capacity. The rules governing procedure in an American consular court specified that in a capital case, the associates had to be American citizens "of good repute." Consul Tillotson may have been ignorant of that requirement. Attorney Tison was not. The Americans may have accepted two non–U.S. citizens as assessors in deference to local circumstance: the English-speaking foreign community in Yokohama was bitterly divided over this case. Everything possible must be done to avoid even the appearance of national partiality in it. Bending the rules so as to allow non–American assessors might also strengthen an appeal against a guilty verdict, if in fact Judge Tillotson handed one down.[14]

Reverend Eugene S. Booth, trial assessor (courtesy Dr. Stephen P. Johnson).

At that point, the crowd in the courtroom may have thought that they were going to hear a dramatic clash between prosecuting and defending attorneys in their opening statements. They did not. Judge Tillotson announced that the proceedings would have to adjourn because prospective witnesses had been subpoenaed to appear five days later, on March 28. That did not happen immediately because prosecutor Litchfield made a request: Could John Frederick Lowder, who had just been retained by Sir Hugh Fraser, the British minister in Tokyo, assist him as prosecuting attorney? When Tillotson asked Tison if he had any objection to that, the defense counselor most certainly did. Tison knew that Lowder had been Gower Robinson's attorney and that the dead man's friends and partner Valdemar Blad had solicited his help in this case. He also knew that Lowder would be a formidable opponent—a man best kept silent in court, if possible. He couched his objection to Lowder's participation in the trial in narrowly legal terms—with nationalistic overtones.

Tison asserted that Litchfield, a Briton, was by courtesy of the court allowed to serve as prosecutor just as he, an American, had been granted the same privilege of appearing before the British Court for Japan. Litchfield was quite qualified to prosecute and had no need for Lowder's assistance. Moreover, both British and American laws held that a private person could not serve as prosecutor. In this consular court, there could be

12. Opening Day

only two sides in a capital murder case: the People of the United States on one side, and the accused, James Henry Hetherington, on the other.

Willard Tillotson had studied the case law on this point and readily accepted Tison's argument. That probably triggered a faint smile on the defense counselor's face and a scowl on John Frederick Lowder's. He was angry—very angry. How humiliating it was to be denied a formal role in such an important trial! He was so angry that when he went home, he penned a letter that appeared in the *Japan Gazette* that evening. Lowder felt Tison had impugned his honor and professional reputation by suggesting that he had colluded improperly with Valdemar Blad, Robinson's executor. That absolutely was not so. He had simply told Blad and two of Gower's friends that if called to testify, they must tell the full truth about what had happened. He had not acted improperly but merely explained probable procedure in the coming trial to them. Burning with resentment about what Tison had implied about his professional integrity, Lowder closed the letter by insisting that he had done nothing improper![15]

Thus the first day of the trial ended with a pause, a note of bitterness, and perhaps distrust as well. Tillotson and Tison had been quick to exclude John Frederick Lowder from an official role in the proceedings. Quick, too, to agree on the relevant case law for doing so. Could they have colluded beforehand? And if they had, could Henry Litchfield possibly achieve justice in the American consular court for poor dead Gower Robinson? Might the trial that so many looked to for the truth about "the tragedy in Yokohama" turn out to be anything but fair, or worse still, a whitewash that let Gower Robinson's killer get off scot-free?

Obvious but unanswered questions as the trial's first day came to its end.

13

Guilty!

On Monday morning, March 28, 1892, the Yokohama American consulate courtroom was once again in crowded with expectant spectators. They rose when Willard Tillotson came into the room. Gaveling the trial to order at precisely 10:15 a.m., he asked the attorneys if they were ready to proceed, and they nodded in agreement. The judge then asked the defendant to stand. All eyes in the courtroom focused on him, as Tillotson intoned: "You are accused of the very serious crime of murder, and I will now read the complaint." Few paid attention to the legalese that followed—until he got to the last words of the document: "said J.H. Hetherington did, in the manner, time, and place, and by the means aforesaid, feloniously, willfully, and of his malice aforethought, kill and murder the said George Gower Robinson against the peace and dignity of the United States."

Looking directly at James, Judge Tillotson asked for his plea: "What do you say, guilty or not guilty?" Before he could speak, Alexander Tison interrupted, objecting three times on the same grounds that he had previously. The judge tossed the objections out immediately. Tison then directed James to plead. In a loud confident voice, Lieutenant Hetherington responded, "Not guilty!"[1]

Attention then shifted to prosecutor Litchfield. Courtroom spectators expected him to begin a florid speech outlining his case for the defendant's guilt. Instead, he made a request that turned into another long tussle with Tison. He explained that Martin Pors, eyewitness to the shooting, could not be present. He had returned to his business in Hyōgo (Kobe), and although he had been subpoenaed to return to Yokohama to testify, he had fallen ill with pneumonia. Confined to his room, he likely could not travel for some time.

Calling Pors "the most material witness on the part of the prosecution," Litchfield said he had agreed to be deposed and asked that the deposition be presented as evidence. He quickly cited the rule of procedure for

13. Guilty!

criminal cases in an American consular court that allowed that. He then asked that Pors be deposed and that court stand adjourned until copies of his statement were available.

Tison immediately objected to that procedure, challenging the history Litchfield had cited to support it. Back in the 1870s, the American minister in Tokyo, Charles DeLong, a layman "essentially unschooled" in the law, had written the rules of procedure the prosecutor had cited.[2] But the secretary of state ruled that DeLong had exceeded his powers in doing so. Congress then revised the law to reaffirm that evidence "had to be taken down in open court." If Pors were allowed to give evidence by deposition, Tison said, Lieutenant Hetherington would be denied the right, when "put upon trial for such a grave crime as this [murder], to be confronted by the witnesses against him."

That was a sound legal argument. But Tison's words hid the real reason for his objection: if Pors testified by deposition, he could not be cross-examined. The defense would lose the chance to plant seeds of doubt in the judge's and assessors' minds about Pors's recollection of events on the night of the shooting.

Judge Tillotson then asked Litchfield if he had any further information from the German. The prosecutor handed him two letters in which Pors explained why he could not be deposed anytime soon. He had had a relapse and couldn't even leave his room. His doctor had told him his prospects for going to Yokohama in two weeks' time were "very poor." His reluctance to testify about his friend Robinson's killing was not due so much to the physical duress of traveling "as the mental strain which we dread." Pors did not want to relive the terrible events of the night of February 13, 1892.

When Tillotson directed Litchfield to file the letters with the court, Tison objected, saying that they were not sworn testimony. The judge quickly overruled that and cut short any further wrangling over the matter. The letters, he said, made it "very doubtful" that Pors could be deposed or show up in court. "While I would very much like to have Mr. Pors here," he added, "it seems to me that we have witnesses enough without him." He then snapped, "We had better go on with the case."[3]

After a brief recess filled with murmurings among the spectators, Henry Litchfield rose and began his formal argument for the prosecution. He confessed to having "feelings of great pain" about the matter being tried. The "crowded states of the court" showed that the case had created "considerable interest, considerable excitement" in the Yokohama community. That being so, the assessors could not help being "imbued with certain ideas" that might "possibly warp" their judgment. Looking directly at them, he charged them to "dismiss as much as possible" any ideas and previous knowledge about the case that they "only too probably" had taken in. Their duty, he warned sternly, was to consider only the facts and evidence he would present.[4]

Litchfield then laid out what he intended to do. He would call to testify Japanese who had witnessed what Robinson and Hetherington were doing before their fatal encounter. They and others would attest to what had happened and how the victim had died. But then, his voice rising in an ever-more emotional tone, Litchfield made his quintessential point:

> There could be no doubt that James Hetherington had committed murder with malice aforethought. He had confronted Robinson on New Year's Day intending to do him harm—only to be restrained by bystanders. Five days had passed between the Englishman's return to Yokohama from Kobe and the night of the murder: plenty of time for the American to have cooled his emotions and restrained himself. "There was time to cool," (but) Hetherington "did not act with the hot impulse of an injury or insult upon him." "There was cooling time," he repeated and "there was deliberation. There was lying in wait. There was the use of the deadly, the fatal, weapon" by Hetherington "coolly and, I submit, deliberately. [That constituted] all the necessary elements to sustain the charge" of murder with malice aforethought that was before the court.[5]

Over the next day and a half, Litchfield called 11 witnesses. Five had testified at the coroner's inquest and would simply add detail to what they had said earlier. Six others, four of whom were Japanese, two servants and two police officers, would speak for the first time. From his list and the order in which he questioned these men, it is clear that he intended to argue this case the same way as he had at the inquest. If all went well, the American court would find Lieutenant Hetherington guilty of willful murder just as the British coroner's jury had done.

Litchfield began by calling Kaneko Chūzō,[6] Robinson's *bettō*, who had accompanied his master on the drive Gower had taken with Martin Pors on the afternoon of the shooting. The prosecuting attorney questioned him, as the person closest to the victim and sole Japanese witness to the shooting, about what had happened that evening. Kaneko spoke slowly, in translation provided by Miura Rikitarō, the consulate general's office clerk.[7] Detailing precisely where the trap was when the shots were fired, he gave a rough estimate of how much time had passed between the moment Hetherington cried "Stop!" and the time he grabbed hold of the side of Robinson's trap. Then he related how he had called for a policeman when his master fell, wounded, from it.

Judge Tillotson interrupted Kaneko with questions even before Tison could start cross-examining him. He doubted his ability to detail so precisely what happened at the time of the shooting. The Japanese could not state exactly how much time passed between Hetherington's shouting "Stop!" and the firing of his weapon. And he was facing toward the back of the trap, not looking forward as Robinson and Pors were, when the shots were fired. Tillotson interrupted with yet another challenge to the groomsman's credibility. After hearing once again his account of the trap's stopping just before the shots were fired, the judge picked up his copy of the inquest transcript. What Kaneko was saying now contradicted what he had said then. The judge obviously doubted the validity of what the first prosecution witness had said.[8]

When the proceedings resumed after a break for tiffin, Tison began cross-examining the *bettō*. He was determined to discredit the man's testimony by any means possible. The witness appeared to be confused and gave contradictory testimony. He went back and forth over whether Lieutenant Hetherington, before firing his weapon, had shouted "Stop!" or its Japanese equivalent, *Matte!* He insisted—twice—that the horses pulling the trap had stopped before his master was shot, and then claimed they had gone ahead some—"a little" or perhaps as much as 40 feet—before stopping. Tison pounced on these contradictions, and Judge Tillotson jumped in to point them out even more forcefully. Tison concluded by suggesting that the witness just wasn't answering his questions.

The second prosecution witness was Suzuki Mito, a Kanagawa prefectural policeman attached to the Yokohama Foreign Settlement police station. He had been the first to come upon the scene of the shooting, and Litchfield wanted him to verify that Hetherington, not someone else, had fired shots at Robinson. The policeman said they came from behind the moving trap, not, as some had speculated, to its side as if fired from someplace near Yokohama Bay. Suzuki said that when he came on the scene of the crime, he saw four men—Robinson and the *bettō* at the horse cart, and two more foreigners, one thin, the other stout, at its side. Leaning forward, Litchfield asked him if he saw the stout man now. Suzuki pointed to James, who was sitting in the middle chair at the front desk.

Judge Tillotson then directed: "Let him go down [from the witness stand] and put his hand on the shoulder of the man, if he recognizes him." At that moment, all eyes in the courtroom followed Officer Suzuki as he got up, walked toward James, and put his hand on his shoulder. He paused, then turned back toward the witness stand. The room was absolutely silent.

Prosecutor Litchfield waited a few seconds to let the import of the policeman's identification of the killer sink in. Then he segued into his next line of questioning: Had Officer Suzuki said anything to Lieutenant Hetherington then? "I asked him in Japanese [and by gesturing] to give me the revolver." James did so, gave Suzuki his card, and stood there just long enough for the officer to ask him to come to the police station. Then,

Suzuki said, he started to run. The policeman described how he had given chase, passed by the police station near the Customs House, and handed the revolver to another officer there.

Litchfield then motioned for the gun to be brought forward and examined by Officer Suzuki. Was it, apart from seals that had been placed on it by the time of the inquest, "in the same state now as when you received it?" he asked. The officer nodded, saying softly, "It seems to be just the same." Judge Tillotson must not have heard him, for he asked if the gun was "the same revolver" Suzuki had taken from the accused. It was, the Japanese replied.

The questioning, first from the prosecutor, and then from the judge, turned to the gun's condition when Suzuki got it. Was it loaded when Hetherington gave it to him? Suzuki replied that he hadn't examined it until he handed it over at the police station. He had found two or three bullets and realized that the weapon was "very dangerous." He just wanted to get rid of it. But were there any bullets or empty cartridges in it? Judge Tillotson asked. Suzuki reported that he had found two or three bullets—and no empty cartridges.

Tison then tried to render the policeman's testimony questionable, querying him rapidly. Had he accurately remembered the number of cartridges in the gun on the night of the shooting? Had James given him the gun voluntarily, or had he taken it by force? Was his memory of the number of shots fired correct or not? And didn't what he said today differ from what he had said at the inquest?

None of his probing came to anything.

Tison got nowhere with the remaining prosecution witnesses that day. Officer Masuda Akira[9] had helped Suzuki when James had resisted going to the police station and been taken to the American consulate instead. Tison tried to cast doubt on the accuracy of his testimony by asking him about the defendant's appearance on the night of the shooting. Did he wear a full beard, as he did now? No. Did he have on an overcoat? No. Was his hat that night one of the two the attorney picked up from the defense table and showed him? "Entirely different from either," the Japanese replied. Officer Masuda was not going to fall prey to Tison's theatrical tricks.

Neither was the last of Litchfield's police witnesses, Inspector Okada Kotarō. He gave the court a hazy account of the chain of custody of the gun on the night of the shooting. He had put it in his desk drawer for safe keeping, but he didn't recall when the Superintendent of Police had taken custody of the weapon.[10]

At that point Judge Tillotson adjourned the proceedings.[11] As everyone left the courtroom, the spectators doubtless voiced their opinions about what they had seen and heard. Prosecutor Litchfield looked good. Tough. He had given the American killer good reason to be worried. Tison didn't look quite so good. While he had pointed out contradictions in the groomsman's testimony and discrepancies between what the police officers had said earlier and their words now, he had failed to bring their testimony into question. The defense attorney was going to have to do better to discredit the prosecution's case against his client.

When court resumed the next day, Tuesday, March 29, Kondo Mokichi, Dr. Eldridge's *bettō*, was the first to testify. He had been waiting outside the P & O (Peninsular and Oriental) Steamship Company office at #15, to pick up Mrs. Eldridge when Robinson's trap came up from behind and passed him. Litchfield wanted him to tell the court what he had seen at the time of the shooting and to identify Lieutenant Hetherington as the killer. Kondo said the man who fired the first shot had been holding the splashboard of the trap when he did so. That attested to the fact that it had been fired from a low angle.

After that, however, Kondo's testimony descended into chaos. He contradicted himself when asked to answer yes or no to questions. First interpreter Miura and then Litchfield's Japanese assistant, Uchimura Rosetsu, intervened to try to explain that Japanese people responded to direct yes-or-no questions differently from the way Americans and Europeans did. Judge Tillotson did not buy that and reprimanded Uchimura for speaking at all. Confusion about the alleged presence of a jinrikisha man near the shooting site followed. Then Kondo seemed to have trouble identifying James. Even after he finally did so, much doubt about the validity of his testimony remained.

Alexander Tison attacked it with sarcasm. Addressing the judge, he said, "Your Honor, I should hate to have to shorten my canary bird's allowance of seed on this man's testimony—much less put a man in jeopardy of his life." That produced a ripple of laughter among the spectators.[12]

The early part of the afternoon that day was given over to testimony from Drs. Eldridge and Wheeler. They repeated what they had said at the inquest, telling the court how the fatal bullet had entered Gower Robinson's body, what immediate care he was given, and where it was found upon his death. What they said was unexceptional, but Tison in his cross-examination seized upon the doctors' words to call attention to what Gower had done. He got Dr. Eldridge to agree that the deceased had "paid more attention to ladies than some men." Tillotson didn't like that and snapped that the defense counsel's questions "were not germane to the doctor's testimony."

The rebuke did not deter Tison from continuing to try to plant seeds of doubt about Gower Robinson's character. Wasn't the man Dr. Eldridge had described precisely the sort of person who could have attracted—and seduced—Lieutenant Hetherington's wife? he queried. Then he asked a pointed question: Had Robinson made a will on his deathbed, and if so, who had witnessed it?

Wheeler replied that the deceased's attorney, John Frederick Lowder, had written it. He himself had given Gower a pen and advised him to sign it. The poor man could barely raise his hand to do so, he added. That detail was not as important to Tison as the preexisting will he wanted the court to hear about. If there was one, had it been destroyed when Robinson signed this deathbed one? he asked. There was a prior will, the doctor admitted, one that Mr. Lowder said Gower wanted to revoke. Lowder had given it to him to hold while the new one was being signed, he said. Tison followed up with a leading question: "This will which was revoked, wasn't it to be destroyed, revoked, canceled, burned?" Doctor Wheeler simply replied that he hadn't seen it.

That opaque answer served Tison's purpose nonetheless, for it raised questions about what had gone on at the time of Gower's death. Were those present—his friends, his attorney, and his business partner and executor—having him make a new will to cover up something suspicious about the old one? About something he had done in the past? Tison wanted the judge and assessors to have those questions in mind when he presented the defense's case.

Henry Litchfield put four more witnesses on the stand that day. Three of them gave unexceptional testimony. The fourth, however, gave him an opportunity to have a reluctant witness, Lieutenant Alan Rogers, James's best friend, confirm the premeditation behind the killer's actions leading up to the murder. Why had Hetherington sought out Robinson at the club on New Year's Day? he asked. "With the intention of horse-whipping him, Sir," Rogers responded, quickly adding that no such thing had occurred. What was the purpose of the warning message Rogers had taken to Robinson's friend Albert Read sometime early in February? the prosecutor inquired. To let Robinson know that if he returned to Yokohama "there was certain to be trouble again," Rogers replied. Litchfield then asked, "Did you specify the nature of the trouble or did you use those words?" "I think those are the words I used," Rogers said. Then he added in his soft Carolina drawl, "I knew at the time what it meant, though."

And what would that trouble be? Litchfield gestured to the bailiff to pick up the gun that was lying on a front table in the court and hand it to Rogers. "Is that a service weapon?" he asked. The lieutenant said he could tell if it was by examining the gun's stock. A hush fell over the room as he picked up the weapon and looked at it. "Yes," he replied firmly.

That clinched Litchfield's case for the prosecution. The gun that killed

13. Guilty!

Gower Robinson was a U.S. Navy weapon. Only the man already identified as the shooter on the night of February 13 could have obtained and used it. James Henry Hetherington, lieutenant, United States Navy, was indeed guilty of willfully murdering George Gower Robinson.

Attorney Tison used his cross-examination of two of the afternoon's witnesses to make valuable points for the defense. Richard McCance, the jailer and constable at the American consulate general, gave a vivid account of James's behavior and state of mind when he arrived there immediately after the shooting. The constable reported, "He was extremely excited, extremely excited, judging from the way that he ran in, pulled the bell, and insisted on seeing the consul general." He wouldn't sit down but paced "upwards and downwards from the window to the door throwing his arms about" while waiting for Consul Tillotson to arrive, he added.

"Before the Consul-General came, what did the accused say to you?" Tison interjected. McCance continued: While "walking up and down, excited, he said, 'Oh, if I had only followed my first thought—if I had got hold of that particular whip…. I tried to scare him [Robinson] but I lost all control of myself.'"[13] Those last words were gold for the defense, for they implied that James was not in his right mind when he shot Robinson. If that was so, Tison wanted everyone in court to ask themselves, how could he possibly be guilty of willful murder?

Tison then peppered Rogers with leading questions about what Albert Read had said when warned of trouble if Robinson returned to Yokohama from Kobe. Had Read said "anything about horse-whipping in connection with Mr. Robinson," his friend? he led on. Rogers paused as if trying to recall, then said, "Well, I think he did…" Then he corrected himself, saying that Read had only said "whipping." "What did he say about whipping?" Tison interjected. Rogers replied, "The way I understood it was that [Read said] something to the effect that Mr. Robinson had better come back and take his whipping, that it would do him good."[14] That was a very valuable remark for the defense. If Gower's close friend Read had said that he deserved a whipping for what he had done, then wasn't the Englishman the guilty party in the affair that led to the shooting and his death? Tison wanted everyone in court that afternoon to be asking themselves that question as he ended his cross-examination.

Henry Litchfield then announced that he had finished presenting the case for the prosecution. He had made a tight but limited argument. It had focused almost exclusively on providing incontrovertible evidence that James had in fact shot and killed Gower Robinson on the night of February 13, 1892. It relied on facts about his behavior to suggest the motivation behind his actions. His prior threatening behavior toward Gower and his taking a gun to stalk the man on the afternoon before the killing suggested deliberate, calculated intent at the time he shot Robinson. Litchfield had scrupulously avoided saying anything about the seduction and scandal that preceded that act. He wanted the judge and assessors to regard Gower Robinson as the victim, pure and simple, of James Hetherington's malicious intentions and actions.

But was he?

Alexander Tison did not want to address that question at that moment. Claiming that he needed time to prepare his speech, he asked for an immediate adjournment. One suspects, however, that his real reason for seeking a delay was quite different. He wanted to deliver his opening defense of James whole and uninterrupted so as to maximize its effect upon judge, assessors, and all who would hear it.

Judge Tillotson gave Tison what he wanted—with a twist. Because he and the assessors would be busy the next day, court would stand adjourned until Thursday morning, March 31.

∽ 14 ∾

Innocent!

That delay gave Alexander Tison the time he needed to refine his opening remarks, what would, in effect, be his basic argument for the defense. He had been preparing it from the moment he agreed to represent James. And he knew from the outset that winning acquittal for him would be difficult. There was no doubt that Hetherington had shot and killed Robinson. Now Tison, as counsel for the defense, had to convince the judge and assessors that that act was not "culpable murder." That Lieutenant James Henry Hetherington, lieutenant, U.S. Navy was innocent.

Tison knew that there were only two possible ways to do that. One was to argue that the killer was so crazed at the moment he fired the fatal shots that he could not have done so as a consequence of a rational decision for which he was legally and morally responsible. In a word, temporary insanity. The other was to argue that the circumstances surrounding the killing were such that the killer had no choice but to act as he did. The first line of argument would be narrowly legal. He would have to find a precedent to prove his client innocent. The second would require wider inquiry, not just into James's character and behavior but also into the broader circumstances in which he had acted. That demanded probing the darkest secrets of the Yokohama foreign community. He would also have to delve into the details of Gower's affair with Bessie and expose the Hetheringtons' private lives to public view. That would be embarrassing for them, but necessary. In short, he would have to get anyone who knew anything about what had gone on prior to the killing to tell all. That might be difficult, but putting all the facts before the court was the best—and only—way judge and assessors could be persuaded to find that James had been justified in killing Robinson.

Speculation as to how Tison would argue the case for the defense had rippled through Yokohama, spilled out into Japan, and floated back and forth across the Pacific to and from America and beyond for weeks before the trial began. The subject doubtless was the topic of mealtime and club conversations in Yokohama during the daylong recess, and it peaked on the evening of March 30. Betting money was on Tison taking a narrowly legal approach. Lawyers confidently informed reporters that precedent and case law would determine the defense's strategy. Tison, they suggested, needed to get a copy of the Sickles trial transcript. The precedent that case had set more than 30 years earlier could be the winning weapon in this one. The trial could not go forward until the defense attorney had become thoroughly familiar with it. That was the only way Tison could win a "not guilty" verdict for James Hetherington.[1]

Who was Sickles, and why was his case thought to be so vital for this one?

Back in 1859, Daniel Sickles, then a congressman and later a Civil War general, shot and killed Phillip Barton Key, whose father had written the words of "The Star-Spangled Banner." Key was the district attorney of Washington, D.C., Sickles's friend, and his wife's lover. Mrs. Sickles was quite open about the affair and had waved from her upstairs window to invite Key in for afternoon assignations. Sickles surrendered immediately after firing the fatal shot, went to jail, and recruited a stellar team of defense attorneys. Lincoln's future secretary of war, Edwin Stanton, led it. Sickles's lawyers readily acknowledged he was the killer but portrayed him as a defender of the sanctity of marriage and a husband who did what any man in similar circumstances would have done. The crux of their argument, however, was that Dan Sickles had been temporarily insane when he killed Phillip Key. He was so provoked by his victim's actions that he was incapable of acting rationally at the moment he pulled the trigger. The judge in the case instructed the jury that the claimed insanity "need not exist for a definite period, but only for the moment of the act" of murder. The jurors found Sickles innocent, and the case became a landmark legal event, setting the American precedent for verdicts of "not guilty by reason of temporary insanity."[2]

If in fact Tison got a copy of the Sickles trial transcript, he certainly would have read and used it in crafting a defense for James Hetherington. But he spent much more time during the weeks leading up to the trial ferreting out anything and everything he could find about the foreign community in Yokohama. He moved there, temporarily, from his usual quarters near Tokyo University and settled in at a hotel, probably the Grand Hotel. It was the social hub of the expatriate community, and that was likely where he interviewed people who might be able to provide information about the broader circumstances that led James to shoot and kill Gower Robinson. He spoke with Bessie at the Grand, getting her to reveal privately as much as she was willing to tell about her affair with the suave Englishman. He assured her she would not have to testify and

14. Innocent!

directed her not to attend the trial. Robinson's friends were much less forthcoming. Although they frequented the hotel, they proved reluctant to talk about the dead man. Tison also interviewed James at the consulate and his shipmates, either at the Grand or aboard the *Marion*. Back at the hotel, he observed the ebb and flow of people passing through its public spaces and their interactions with members of the hotel staff. Staying in Yokohama gave Tison the opportunity to learn how the city's elite behaved in public and pry into the private lives of "the better sort."

Tison's speech on the morning of March 31, 1892, drew more from what he had learned during his pretrial investigations than on the Sickles "temporary insanity" precedent. Unlike the short, clear, and dramatic opening statement that a defense counsel might make in a similar case today, it was florid, long, and emotional as custom demanded. Tison spewed forth a torrent of words, 10 times as many as Litchfield had used, to make his opening argument. He went on, and on, and on—for so long that the court had to break for tiffin before he finished speaking.[3]

Tison knew, however, that he had to gain the confidence, and even the sympathy, of judge and assessors if he were going to win this case. They needed to feel in their hearts as well as know in their heads that what he was saying, or getting others to testify, was the truth. So he began by calling attention to himself and his task. Tison depicted himself as an inexperienced David going up against a wizened legal Goliath—prosecutor Litchfield. "Never before," he proclaimed, had he been involved in a case "where life and death were in the balance." He had taken on this one out of a sense of duty and with a strong sense of purpose. "My eye," he continued, "can see but one person, my ear can hear but one voice. My business," Tison affirmed, pointing dramatically to his client, "is to defend this man: James Henry Hetherington, lieutenant, United States Navy."

He said he had to take a broad approach to doing so. That required scrutinizing the Yokohama community so as to understand the circumstances that led to Robinson's death. He promised to be discreet in doing so. Although his ear "had been turned ... into a common sewer through which ... most of the muddy impurities of social life in this Settlement for the last twenty-five years," were poured, he would reveal only what was pertinent to the case. "No catalogue of private sins" would be made public, he reassured everyone.

Getting to the truth of the circumstances that led to Robinson's killing had not been easy. Some who knew what had happened had proved reluctant to talk. Witnesses he would like to have called had gone away. Others had proved hard to find, and still others—"more than I can count on the fingers of my two hands"—had had to be compelled to testify by subpoena. Some of them had asked to be excused, acting as if they had "pad-locks on their lips for fear they will be asked to say something they know." Still others had impugned his motives in getting subpoenas issued, saying he had done so out of "narrow spite and petty malevolence." He had even been threatened with retribution if he insisted on calling a person who was the sole witness to the incident that led to the shooting on the night of February 13, 1892.

Someone, Tison spit out angrily, had suborned potential defense witnesses. Some of them had promised to tell the whole truth and then later denied "any knowledge whatever [about] … the matter before the court." Nonetheless, he intended to compel them to testify. Whether they would commit perjury, or had been suborned to do so, or say something different from what they had told others now sitting in the courtroom, Tison concluded, remained to be seen.

Then he appealed to the better nature of those who could shed light on what led to the tragedy of Gower Robinson's death. "The truth harms no one, least of all the dead," he argued, "for they alone stand in the presence of Truth itself." The living must tell the truth, lest on Judgment Day when they joined the dead and stood in fear of God they be reproached by being told that they had turned away when they had had the opportunity to "tell and know the truth." They carried an obligation to tell all, not just to the Yokohama community, but also to communities "across the sea": Hetherington's family, the naval service, and "the girlhood home of his unhappy wife [where] his child was born." Yokohama's citizens must not forget that in all of those places, "there are hearts that break because of what has been done here." They must come forward to make known the truth.

Tison then shifted his focus to the accused, James Hetherington. Who was he? The loving son of a respected Iowa family. An experienced and dutiful officer whose years in the navy had made him the kind of person he was. Not a rash man, as his patient courting of Bessie Hewes and kindly treatment of her after their child was born had demonstrated. He truly loved her—even to the point of giving up his naval career and seeking civilian employment as she had wished. When that had not worked out and he faced two years of sea duty, he brought his family to Yokohama to ease the pains of separation.

Tison next turned to the nature of the crime his client was charged with: "Willful and premeditated murder, a crime which, next to treason, is the highest crime known to our law." So heinous a crime had to be "grounded upon intent." A murderer had to have "a guilty mind or a dark and settled purpose of hate and death." The accusation of that crime—killing Gower Robinson—"requires the strictest proof. Nothing is to be, nothing can be … assumed, nothing taken for granted. Everything must rest upon the firmest and most unshaken demonstration of guilt," he insisted.

14. Innocent! 133

Why had Lieutenant Hetherington acted as he did on the night of February 13, 1892? Tison asked. The reason was simple: "the protection of his home." James was a husband and father, and as "God and nature made him ... protector" of his family. Seeing "that home ... threatened with ruin," Tison continued, he "put out his hand to save it." As a result, "the man who came to sow shame and dishonor in the place of joy and delight himself reaped the harvest he had meant for another." James intended to do "no more than was necessary for the protection of his home," Tison insisted.

That was not murder, Tison proclaimed. The defendant "had designs on no man's life.... He never thought that any man must die before he and his wife and baby could live their own lives in peace." "But," Tison asserted, his voice rising as he spoke, James "had provocation enough, God knows more, far more possibly than any of those who hear me could have borne." Robinson was doing him and his family wrong. "All he intended," Tison continued, "was that certain things must stop." Not "vengeance for his wrongs ... [but] only to guard the future." He never meant to kill Robinson. His mind "never went along with the wild and whirling work of February thirteenth." Shooting and killing there was "on that fateful night—but no reasoned, culpable intent to murder."

Tison then asked rhetorically, "Why had Gower Robinson" died a bloody "violent death"? The man brought it on himself by his inappropriate behavior. When Hetherington repeatedly wrote him letters demanding that he stop paying undue attention to his wife, Robinson wrote her a letter that "blisters the page, a most passionate avowal of love." When James discovered it and confronted his wife with it, that triggered his attempts to send her home, her threats to kill herself, and bitter arguments between the two. Eventually the husband "was melted, [and] for the sake of the baby only, he decided that the family should live together.... Apparently all was to be as it had been."

But that was not to be. Robinson did not abide by his word to stay away from Mrs. Hetherington. He demeaned her character, suggesting that she had lured him into scandalous inappropriate behavior. When her husband was at sea, he went to dances at the Grand Hotel and followed her up to her room, staying there a second time for nearly two hours. That prompted James, through his own and Robinson's friends, to warn him to leave Yokohama. He did so, but only for a time. Gower Robinson, Tison suggested, was not a man of honor, but a provocateur unable to stop pursuing Bessie Hetherington.

Tison then turned to his last, most crucial line of defense: James's state of mind during the days leading up to February 13. He started by saying that James "freely and fully forgave his wife" and promised her he would not harm Robinson. But then Tison took a swipe at those who blamed Bessie for what had happened to Gower. She had been comforting her husband "when some of these stories with which the town is rife would have her in a bacchanalian orgy with some of those gentlemen of fine feather whom ... the court will soon see in the witness box." That remark stunned everyone present. At that moment, no one doubted that Tison intended to go for the jugular in defending James.

Turning back to his state of mind on the eve of the killing, Tison insisted that something "so great and marked" had affected his behavior. He couldn't sleep. He flip-flopped. One day he swore he would horsewhip Robinson; the next he said, "I cannot do it; I cannot, and I will not do anything." Why? Because he had told his wife he would not do it. When he suspected that Robinson had returned to Yokohama, he insisted that he didn't want to see or find the man. But then he confessed to his best friend that "if Robinson did come back, he could not control himself." He would have to cane or horsewhip the man "even though he had ... promised he would not do so."

At that moment Tison paused for dramatic effect. Then, soaring into a lofty peroration, he promised: "What occurred at the time of the shooting I shall allow the defendant to tell in his own words." While it would be "like death itself [for him] to revive and tell that which has to be told in order to have the court properly understand and pass upon what he has done," Tison predicted, "he will do it."

If those words did not whet the appetite of those within hearing range to learn more about James Hetherington's killing of Gower Robinson, nothing could do so.

At that moment, Tison stopped speaking, turned back to the defense table, and sat down. Silence followed. Tison the orator had finished, Tison the interrogator was about to begin.[4] After a brief pause, he stood up and called his first witness: the Grand Hotel manager, Louis Eppinger. He was an American who had come to Yokohama barely nine months earlier to take the job.[5] Eppinger brought valuable physical evidence to back up what he said as a witness: the hotel's guest book and its accounting ledger that tallied the chits guests used in lieu of cash in the dining room.

Armed with that, Eppinger pinpointed when Gower began the affair with Bessie Hetherington. He was "properly" introduced to Bessie about a week after she had arrived, sometime between October 20 and 22, when all of the *China* party but Mrs. Hetherington and Columbus Cummings had gone to see the tombs of the shoguns at Nikko. Robinson had finagled that introduction through an intermediary who knew Cummings, so only the three of them were at the table when it occurred, Eppinger added helpfully.

He also reported that Robinson had changed his dining habits after the introduction. He "very seldom" dined at the hotel during the preceding nine months of 1891. But once he believed Mrs. Hetherington might be in the dining room, he appeared five times during October within two weeks. That was remarkable. Or, as Tison probably wanted everyone in the courtroom to surmise, suspicious. Eppinger then provided another hint that Gower was intruding himself whenever Bessie might be present. He had shown up at the *China* party's farewell dinner on October 30, even though he had not crossed the Pacific with them. Someone must have invited him. But who? Tison didn't ask Eppinger to answer that question, but left everyone wondering: Could it have been Bessie Hetherington?

He then called Herbert Maurice Bevis, manager of the Yokohama branch of the Hong Kong and Shanghai Bank, to testify. He had subpoenaed him hoping to get him to tell everything he knew about Gower's relationship with Bessie. Bevis spoke first, however, as a character witness for his fellow countryman. He had first met him in Hong Kong in 1877, when Gower had come from England to work at the bank's main office there.[6] He had found Robinson to be "a very nice young fellow indeed" and considered him an "intimate friend." Over time, especially after Gower left the bank to establish his own bill and brokerage firm, Bevis said, Robinson came to him for financial advice and friendly conversation—but never loans. The bank manager was clearly in a position to answer much more specific questions about what Gower had done.

What did he know about the events of Friday, October 23, 1891? Tison asked. That was the night Gower had whisked Bessie off to his home after returning from a concert in Tokyo. Picking up a copy of the program, which listed Robinson as a performer, he asked that it be put in evidence. Then he forced Bevis to reveal where and when he had seen Gower and Bessie together that night. Dining at the Tokyo Club before the concert and after when they took the same train back to Yokohama, the banker admitted. Tison interrupted him to note that the two had been seen sitting in the same compartment. Bevis quickly added that he hadn't seen them together after that—neither Mrs. Hetherington at Yokohama Station, nor Gower at his home, even though Robinson had previously invited him to come for a late-night whiskey and soda.

That was odd. It posed questions Tison wanted his listeners to ask themselves: If Gower wasn't home as planned, where was he? After spending so much of the evening in Bessie's company, could Robinson have been somewhere else with her—at her hotel or upstairs in his own house—in the middle of the night?

Tison probed further. What did Bevis know about Gower's feelings toward Bessie? Had Robinson ever spoken with him about her? "Yes," the bank manager responded, repeatedly—first about three weeks after the

Tokyo concert, very often thereafter, and then again just before he left for Kobe in January. Tison pounced at that to ask still more pointed questions. Did Bevis know that Robinson had made a will at the end of December? "I witnessed it," Bevis responded, adding that he hadn't seen its contents. However, Gower told him that night that he was leaving "any money he had to Mrs. Hetherington" and thinking of going to America on January 9. "Did he tell you why he was going?" Tison asked insistently. "I understood why," Bevis responded softly.

He didn't need to elaborate further, for it was obvious to everyone within hearing that Bessie was the reason. To make that crystal clear, the attorney fired off leading questions to Bevis. Had Gower told him that he expected to join Bessie there? Had he given her his sister's name and address in Denver, Colorado? "No, no," Bevis replied. Then, just to eliminate any supposition that Gower might have had a more innocuous reason for his proposed trip to America, Tison asked the bank manager if Robinson had said anything that night about his mother's address. "No," Bevis replied. And did he know where Mrs. Robinson currently lived? Tison followed up. "In England at present, yes," Bevis replied.

That answer left no doubt that Gower was not planning a trip to visit his mother. The person he wanted to see, to be with, to live with was none other than Bessie. He was, just as Tison had alleged in his opening remarks, intent on breaking up the Hetherington family.

The last witness of the day was Norman Ashleigh Walter, a 27-year-old Briton who had come to Yokohama three years earlier, worked for a merchant, and then taken a job as office clerk at the Grand Hotel for the last six months of 1891. Walter had saved money, made connections, and recently started his own bill and brokerage firm.[7] Testifying under subpoena, he was as uncooperative as he could be, answering questions reluctantly and with a selective memory. When Tison asked him if he had known Gower was sending notes to Bessie, he replied with a loud and firm "No!" But the other way around? He wasn't certain about that. Tison then handed him three chits from November 1891 written in his own hand. Were they not for delivering messages from Gower at his nearby office to Mrs. Hetherington at the hotel? he asked. "They are, yes," Walter replied softly, ashamed at being caught in a lie.

The former hotel clerk didn't want to tell anything more and stumbled into inconsistency when answering Tison's questions. He said he couldn't remember seeing Gower and Bessie together at dinner, but then became quite clear about seeing them dine with Lieutenant Hetherington. "You remember one and do not recollect another … time at dinner?" Tison asked incredulously. Determined not to play into the attorney's hands, Walter simply refused to answer. Trapped again, he fell silent. A long pause followed. Then Judge Tillotson admonished him for wasting the court's time. Couldn't he just answer clearly one way or the other? A second long pause followed. Then Walter finally admitted that he had seen Gower and Bessie "in company." "That is not the question," Judge Tillotson snapped and ordered the court reporter to repeat the question. Before Walter could say a word, Tison broke the tension with a witty interjection: the question "was put so long ago that I have forgotten all about it," he said. That got everyone in the courtroom laughing.

Humiliated and defiant to the end, Norman Walter then contradicted his earlier statements once again. At that point, Tison sensed that nothing more was to be gained from questioning him further. Prosecutor Litchfield's brief cross-examination of Walter proved as fruitless as his interrogation of the other two witnesses had been. Tison then asked for an early adjournment, and Judge Tillotson happily granted his request.

That evening as he returned to his hotel, Alexander Tison had good reason to be pleased by his day's work. He had delivered a moving speech outlining the argument he intended to present. The three witnesses had backed up the allegations he had made in it. The hotel manager presented proof that Gower had initiated the affair with Bessie. The bank manager had called attention to its crucial moment and to the intensity of feeling that fed Gower's designs. Clerk Walter's evasiveness demonstrated the desire in the community to cover up what had gone on.

All of that suggested to Tison that his plan for winning something other than a guilty verdict for Lieutenant Hetherington had gotten off to a good start. He could make the court and the community see things differently. Robinson the victim, not Hetherington the killer, was the real aggressor in what people were euphemistically calling "the tragedy in Yokohama."

15

Shipmates

By the time he strolled from his hotel to the American consulate on Friday morning, April 1, 1892, Alexander Tison had a clear idea of how he wanted the testimony of the day's witnesses to go. He would put the easier ones, all from the U.S. Navy and friendly toward James, on the stand first. Then, depending on the time remaining, he would question two or more of Gower's friends, men likely to be difficult. Cooperative or not, the witnesses would elaborate on the key point he wanted them to put before the court: Hetherington the killer, not Robinson the dead man, was the victim in this case. What better way to advance that argument than to call a woman to testify?

Shortly after 10 that morning, Mrs. Jeanie Bartlett was sworn in. As the captain's wife, she knew more about the *Marion*'s officers, their wives, and their behavior in society than anyone else.[1] Tison knew she would prove a very valuable defense witness. She could tell the court about the Hetheringtons' marriage, before and after Gower Robinson had intruded on it. She had seen James on the night of his greatest anguish. She saw Gower's egregious advances toward Bessie at a key moment in their relationship. He began by having her describe Bessie's reunion with James the day the *Marion* appeared off Yokohama. She said Mrs. Hetherington had gone to the pier with her baby and the *amah*, and then to the ship, like any good wife and mother, anxious to greet her husband. What had she seen of the Hetheringtons' "feelings of attachment" for one another? Tison asked. She gave him the perfect answer. Whenever she had seen them together, James had always shown "great affection and admiration" for Bessie, and she had spoken "with great affection" for him. "They seemed perfectly happy and contented. Their mutual love for each other seemed to be very strong," Mrs. Bartlett affirmed.

That was before James learned that Gower had seduced his wife. How was he afterward, on Sunday morning, December 27, 1891, when he had asked her to care temporarily for baby Gladys? the attorney asked. He was

15. Shipmates

a changed man, "very pale..., very much excited ... trembling very much and looking as if he was very much overcome. I could not tell whether it was [due to] anger, or grief, or disappointment," Mrs. Bartlett replied. But he said his wife "had been false to him" and had lied "to cover up her evil doings." Then he handed her a letter Robinson had written to his wife, saying "that man had ruined his life." But he also spoke of "the great love he had entertained for her," she added.

Mrs. Bartlett said she had tried to calm James by telling him that things were not as bad as they seemed. While Bessie had been "thoughtless and indiscreet," she was the "proper guardian" for baby Gladys. Did Lieutenant Hetherington say she wanted to keep her baby? Tison asked. "Yes," and that had helped soften his feelings toward his wife, she replied. She knew that was true because later that afternoon he had sent her a note saying that he had decided to let his wife stay—for the baby's sake, and he had promised that "to all outward appearances, their life would be the same as it had been before."

Those last words delivered precisely the message Tison wanted the court to get. James had acted in defense of his family, restraining himself, even at a moment of great emotional distress, at a time when, as Jeanie Bartlett reported, he denounced "the man who had entered his home and ... tried to steal his wife's affections." That showed that at this point, at least, the aggrieved husband had the capacity to reason and control himself.

That was in late December, but what about in mid–February, when he shot Robinson? those listening likely asked themselves. What had happened in the meantime to cause James Hetherington to act so differently?

In a word, Gower Robinson.

What kind of a man was he? Tison asked. "One of the most agreeable men I have met for a long time," Jeannie Bartlett replied. The attorney seized on her words to suggest that Robinson was something of a Svengali. "Were you ever in his company," he asked, when you saw "anything ... like an exhibition of the power to charm, if not to fascinate a woman over whom he sought to exercise it?" "I felt quite sure of it," Mrs. Bartlett replied.

Tison then turned to Gower's behavior at the Saturday evening, January 23, hop. Mrs. Bartlett reported that he "seemed to be always" where Mrs. Hetherington was. While she was dancing the Lancers, a popular quadrille, with others, he had passed a note to her chair. She left the dance, sat down, and wrote something back to him. The two exchanged glances and then abruptly left the ballroom before the dancing ended. "Did either of them return?" Tison asked in feigned ignorance. "No," Mrs. Bartlett replied. The attorney paused for a moment, leaving everyone within hearing to wonder if something inappropriate might have gone on between Gower and Bessie later that night.

Lest anyone in the courtroom surmise that whatever had happened next that evening was Bessie's fault, Tison quickly switched his line of questioning. Had Mrs. Bartlett seen her since the night of the shooting, and how did she feel toward her now? "Yes, I have seen her almost every day.... She has my deepest, warmest sympathy. I like her much better [now] than ever before," the captain's wife replied. The perfect remark to end her testimony.

If Bessie's behavior was as scandalous as wagging tongues had it, how could so highly respected a woman as the captain's wife still find her likeable?

That was something for the five men who would determine James Hetherington's guilt or innocence to ponder.

Prosecutor Litchfield declined to cross-examine Mrs. Bartlett, so Tison called her husband to testify. He would be a critical witness for the defense because he had seen and spoken at length with both victim and the killer. Tison wanted him to speak to the depravity and dishonesty of the one and the honor and anguish of the other. Captain Bartlett could detail his efforts to prevent a violent confrontation between the cuckolded husband and his wife's seducer. He could also show the court how Gower's pursuit of Bessie pushed James to the point of killing him.

Tison first asked Captain Bartlett how he came to know James, Bessie, and Gower. He recalled that he first encountered James a dozen years earlier in Washington, D.C., aboard

Captain John Russell Bartlett, USN, *Marion* commander and star witness (NH56109, Naval History and Heritage Command).

15. Shipmates

the steamer *Blake*. Then he really got to know him during the *Marion*'s Bering Sea patrol and voyage across the Pacific. He first met Bessie last November 2, the day his ship dropped anchor off Yokohama. When he came ashore, she was waiting at the English Hatoba and was "very anxious" for news of her husband. Could she "go off and see him?" she had asked, and he had offered her the use of his gig (small boat) to get to the *Marion* for a family reunion.

That was just the first impression of Bessie Tison wanted the judge and assessors to get: a loving wife eager to reunite with her husband.

When Tison asked Bartlett how he had met Gower Robinson and what his first impressions of the man were, he painted a mixed picture. Robinson had taken the initiative, coming to call aboard the *Marion*. Then he invited the Bartletts to his home for dinner, and they reciprocated by including him in a reception at their home, where, the captain remembered, he saw Robinson in "very earnest conversation" with Mrs. Hetherington. Then, at the Saint Andrew's Day ball on November 30,[2] the Englishman was spotted dancing with her, he snapped in indignation. When they next met just before Christmas at Robinson's home, "I talked ... [for] perhaps two hours" with him, and he "made himself very agreeable to me," the captain reported. The man behaved egregiously, but he was a charmer.

Tison then had Bartlett detail his efforts to prevent violence between Gower and James. They had begun on Sunday, December 27, after Hetherington had sent Mrs. Bartlett a note reporting that he had changed his mind about sending his unfaithful wife home. "I sensed that he was still very upset," the captain stated, "and I decided to go to the Grand Hotel to try to calm him down. I asked him to take a walk, and we strolled along the creek near the back entrance of the hotel for about a mile. Hetherington calmed down a bit and pulled a letter Robinson had written to his wife out of his pocket to show me. Not wanting to probe his marital secrets, I refused to read it," Bartlett reported.

Tison then interrupted with a leading question: What had Hetherington wanted to do to Mr. Robinson? "He was very excited. He said he must horse-whip him," Bartlett replied. "I told him I didn't want any scandal connected with any officer in the service and I would do what I could to prevent any ... horse-whipping." He told him "you are not calm enough ... not in your proper mind to know what you are talking about. I then asked him to let me talk with Robinson. If after that meeting some form of chastisement was still necessary, I would go with him to horse-whip the offending Englishman," Bartlett reported.

"Did he agree to that?" Tison inquired. "He did," Captain Bartlett said. "But before I went to see Robinson, Hetherington came to me saying he had another letter from the man to his wife and asked me to read it." "Did you?" Bartlett nodded as Tison showed it to him and asked him to summarize it. Bartlett remembered that Robinson had said he was going to leave town on January 9 and would stay away while the Hetheringtons were in Yokohama. At that, he continued, James had exclaimed, "If that man will leave town and stay away while I am here with my wife, I shall be satisfied.... But if he does not, why I don't know what I shall do. He must leave my wife alone." Then he cried, "If I only had some friend to tell Mr. Robinson, that is all I want." "That touched me," the captain said, "and I told Hetherington I would talk to Robinson on his behalf."

That exchange set up the first of Bartlett's two meetings with Robinson, which he reported on at great length. He said that when he went to Robinson's office on the afternoon of December 29, the conversation began pleasantly enough over a drink of port wine. Robinson revealed that he had written Bessie a letter meant for her husband's eyes in which he had agreed to leave Yokohama "for Mrs. Hetherington's sake and in order to prevent any scandal." He had looked into leaving on January 9 and made arrangements to rent his house, sell his trap, and cancel all his business appointments in the meantime. He had let it be known that he was leaving Yokohama due to "his mother's serious illness." Then, as if to give proof of his intent, the captain continued, Robinson said he had declined an invitation to the New Year's Eve ball—a leap year dance to which women invited men.

Unconvinced that Robinson was telling the truth, Bartlett said he had put the matter to him bluntly: he had promised to leave her alone, but the *Marion* "had scarcely left Yokohama harbor to conduct exercises at sea when he turned up at the Grand Hotel with Mrs. Hetherington." Robinson claimed she had invited him to come there at her invitation. He went on angrily, said Bartlett, saying she had "set her cap for me the day she got in here, ... followed me, tried to get me to meet her, and kept writing to me ever since."

If that were so, Captain Bartlett retorted, why hadn't he sent one of Bessie's letters to her husband so as to get him to put a stop to her unwanted behavior? Uncowed, Robinson had replied, "This woman, this is not the first time that she has done this thing." That only angered Bartlett all the more, the captain said, and he shouted back, "You are a damned coward.... You call yourself a man and try to lay the blame of this scandal on a woman." Then he reproached Robinson, saying, "I am trying to make peace, I don't want any scandal, but damn you, you are a damned scoundrel and a villain. If I was in Mr. Hetherington's place," Bartlett continued, "I would have come and put a bullet through you at sight when I saw the letter you wrote Mrs. Hetherington."

15. Shipmates

The word *bullet* rang in the ears of everyone present. Seizing the opportunity to highlight the emotional intensity of Bartlett's exchange with Robinson, Tison asked, "Do you usually swear, Captain?" "No, I do not," Bartlett snapped.

Continuing his account of the meeting, he said Robinson had suddenly turned contrite, saying, "Captain Bartlett, I deserve shooting for acting in this manner." Tison interrupted again, asking with feigned incredulity if Robinson had said he expected Lieutenant Hetherington to shoot him. Yes, the captain replied. Then he himself had shouted back: "Mr. Robinson, there is to be no shooting and no horse-whipping if you behave yourself. But if you don't ... I will come with Mr. Hetherington and see you horse-whipped."

How did Robinson take that? Tison asked. "He took it," Captain Bartlett snarled, but then seemed to back away from his promise to leave Yokohama. Robinson explained that his partner, Waldemar Blad, had cut his foot and would be laid up for about two months and be "unable to attend to business and it will all go to the devil." Nevertheless, he would be willing to give up his name, his business, and his friends in Yokohama—and go away. "Realizing that would be asking too much of the man," the captain reported that he told Robinson that he had come as a friend and did not intend that there should be any scandal about him, his friends, or "my navy officers." When he said he was willing to help, Robinson replied, "I will give you my word of honor what I will do."

"What was that?" Tison asked. Bartlett replied that Robinson had responded with a long string of promises: As long as Mrs. Hetherington was in Yokohama, "I will cease all attentions to her.... I will go nowhere to see her..., to no dinner party where she is.... I will not go to any of the hops at the Grand Hotel where ... she is often alone when her husband is away.... If I am asked, I shall find out if Mrs. Hetherington is to be there and if [so], ... I will decline. If I go to ... a reception and find [her] ... there, I shall make some excuses, or say I am sick, and go right away."

That was a solemn promise, was it? Tison asked. Yes, the captain affirmed. Robinson had then pledged he would give Lieutenant Hetherington "no further cause of complaint." With that, Captain Bartlett continued, the first meeting came to a pleasant end. Robinson thanked him "for the gentlemanly manner in which I had spoken to ... him" and shook his hand as they parted.

That prompted some in the courtroom to laugh in disbelief.

The next morning, Bartlett continued, he told Hetherington about his meeting with Robinson, and after "a good deal of argument and persuasion," the lieutenant promised to leave the man alone. The captain said he had sensed that Hetherington was unhappy with that pledge. On New

Year's Day 1892, Bartlett said, he thought his mediation might have succeeded. Lieutenant Rogers had come that evening and told him how he had gone to the club with Hetherington and persuaded him not to try to horsewhip Gower Robinson. But when he spoke with the lieutenant the next morning, he just said he wouldn't horsewhip Robinson—but only on condition that the Englishman "not give him any more offense."

That same morning, Bartlett recalled, he had found a note on his breakfast table from Gower Robinson asking him to call. He got a frosty reception when he did so. The Englishman wouldn't shake hands, saying he was "very angry," and insisted, "This thing has got to stop." He claimed he had "done his best to save Bessie's reputation in Yokohama," but her husband had "made a mess of it" (by trying) "to horse-whip me for something I never did." Protesting his innocence of any wrongdoing, Robinson spit out that Lieutenant Hetherington was responsible for the trouble at the club. He then insisted that he had lived up to his promise to stay away from the Hetheringtons and pledged again and again to "live up to his word as a gentleman" and keep away from them. Despite those promises, Captain Bartlett reported, his second meeting with Robinson had not ended cordially.

Tison asked Bartlett to specify when and how Robinson had broken his promises. The captain ticked them off: Robinson had gone to the January 9 hop at the Grand Hotel and engaged Mrs. Hetherington in "earnest talk." Two weeks later at the January 23 hop, he had written on her dance card, and then the two had left before the dance was over. "I was so upset about that," Bartlett said, "that I motioned to Robinson's friend, Chandler Gibbens, to meet me under the stair. I told him, 'This sort of nonsense has got to stop. Do you think naval officers are coming here to bring their wives and daughters … ashore to be at a hop to be insulted by any such black-guard as this [man]?'" Then he told Gibbens that he was going to see Lieutenant Hetherington early the next morning so that "this thing shall be stopped once and for all."

At that, Bartlett continued, Gibbens repeatedly said, "I can't believe that of Robinson." If he had given his word of honor to keep away from Mrs. Hetherington, "he would keep it." "When Mr. [Brooke Hyde] Pearson came up to us and was told that Robinson had broken his promises, he, too, at first said he didn't believe it, then grudgingly admitted 'Well, Gower Robinson is a black-guard.'" At that, the captain said, he had heard enough and left the hop.

So had Willard Tillotson. In a rare rebuke to Tison's line of questioning, he intervened, saying that all the detail about what had happened between Robinson and Mrs. Hetherington at the ball was immaterial. Mere "hearsay," he grumbled. Taking the judge's objection to heart, Tison asked Bartlett what had happened the next day. The captain reported that he had called on Bessie and told her he knew what had gone on the night before. He had advised her to tell her husband about it. She, he said quietly, "didn't deal frankly" with me in response.

There matters rested uneasily until around six that evening, Bartlett continued, until a "much excited" Chandler Gibbens came to his home and asked why he hadn't come to see Robinson. Puzzled, the captain retorted that he had no intention of doing so. "No," Gibbens replied, but when he and friends had gone to Robinson's house that morning, they had expected him to come and say everything between Robinson and the Hetheringtons had been resolved. When he hadn't shown up, everyone at Robinson's home had "a terrible day of it." At that point, Captain Bartlett explained, "I shook his hand. It was cold with perspiration and excitement."

Why was Gibbens so upset? Because Gower had behaved so irrationally, crying and threatening to take his life, Bartlett explained. Gibbens said that he and his friends had had to "exert ourselves to prevent him from actually killing himself." Fearing that Bartlett and Hetherington "would come with either fire-arms or horse-whips," they wanted to protect their friend. Then, the captain reported, Gibbens indirectly acknowledged that Robinson had done wrong by saying he and his friends would have let Hetherington horsewhip Robinson if he had come. The captain reassured Gibbens, promising there would be no shooting, no horsewhipping, "done by any officer of … [his] ship or in the service," unless it was absolutely necessary.

"My conversation with Mr. Gibbens ended," Bartlett said, "with conditional promises. If I would keep Hetherington ignorant of the fact that Robinson was still in Yokohama after having promised to leave, his friends would put him on the next ship bound for Kobe and Shanghai. They would keep him away as long as the Hetheringtons remained in Yokohama. I thought that reasonable and fair and replied, 'I will l connive with you … to prevent any scandal, provided you will promise to get Robinson out.'" Gibbens did so and their conversation came to an end.

Tison then asked Bartlett if he had talked with James about what had gone on at the January 23 hop. He had done so three days later, but their conversation didn't go as planned, the captain explained. When asked if he knew what had happened at the ball, Hetherington said he wanted to know the truth. So I told him "the whole of it," Bartlett admitted, but that wasn't the end of it. He said that the Grand Hotel mail clerk had told him his wife had put a letter addressed to Robinson in his box the preceding day. That had made him "very angry," he said, and he had asked what he should do.

"And you advised him to send his wife home?" Alexander Tison asked, fishing for a strong reply. He got it. Bartlett said he told Hetherington he must send his wife home on the next steamer. Despite his protest that that was a very short time, "I said in a strong voice, 'Send her [Bessie] away from this man'"—Gower Robinson. Hetherington replied that he hadn't the money to do so, and so Bartlett wrote out a check and gave it to him, the captain reported.

"But did he not send her away?" Tison asked knowingly. "He did not," Captain Bartlett replied. The next day he returned the check, saying, "I have decided differently." At that, Tison paused for a moment, then put another leading question to the captain. Did Hetherington say it was impossible for him to send Bessie away? "He did, and he wanted to tell me more," Bartlett replied. "But I didn't want to have anything more to do with the affair, and told him that Robinson was gone."

Tison ended his questioning of Captain Bartlett by asking him about James's character. He was "a peaceable, quiet man, seeking a quarrel with no one.... [He] was very fond of talking about his wife and child," Bartlett stated firmly. And Mrs. Hetherington? the attorney queried. She was so "attached to her husband" that she came almost daily to the *Marion* to see him. She had his sympathy, the captain added, for he felt she had been misunderstood by her husband and other people.

With that, one of the longest testimonies in the trial came to an end.

But there was more.

After Henry Litchfield's brief, ineffective cross-examination of Captain Bartlett, Tison called three more of James's shipmates to testify. The first would detail his anger and restraint at Robinson's provocation and prevarication. The other two would demonstrate the impact of Gower's pursuit of Bessie on James's state of mind.

Tison began his interrogation of Lieutenant Allen Rogers by having him establish his credibility as a longtime friend who understood Lieutenant Hetherington's temperament and behavior. Rogers obliged by telling the court that he had known James since they had roomed together at the U.S. Naval Academy in the 1870s. They became best friends, made their midshipman cruise together on the *Richmond* in 1879–80, and exchanged letters over the years until they reunited on the *Marion*.

Tison then jumped to the night of November 30, 1891, when Rogers had accompanied Bessie to the Saint Andrew's Ball. What had he known about Gower and Bessie's relationship at that point? Tison inquired. "A good deal of idle gossip," the lieutenant snapped. He had "rather guardedly" spoken to James about that shortly after the ball. His friend said that up to that point he had heard "nothing but good" about Robinson, but now his opinion had changed. He proclaimed that "he would see and have very little more to do with him." Restraint.

The attorney then asked Rogers to tell the court what had happened on New Year's Day 1892. He responded with a gripping tale. He and Ensign George Ralph Slocum had come upon James running down the hall of the Grand Hotel. He was carrying a rawhide riding whip and was so excited that Slocum thought his baby daughter must have died. But Rogers said he knew—or surmised—that Robinson was the source of James's agitation. He asked Rogers to go with him to the club, where he was going to horsewhip "that scoundrel [who] has just passed by and insulted my wife again."

Rogers said that he had tried but failed to persuade his friend to calm down and wait before doing anything so drastic. Then, Rogers said, "I grabbed him so strongly by the arm so as to stop him that Ensign Slocum thought we were fighting." While they walked toward the United Club, James told him why he was so upset. The Englishman was "paying very devoted ... and very conspicuous attention" to his wife. He had written the man twice telling him to leave her alone. Robinson had replied, promising to do so, but he "simply insisted on chasing her around and pursuing her."

Tison then peppered Rogers with more questions about Lieutenant Hetherington's state of mind on New Year's Day. Rogers said he had listened to James's litany of complaints about Robinson's broken promises to stay away from his wife. James had poured out his feelings, saying, "These things had been going on for a long time [and had] almost driven him crazy.... He couldn't stand it much longer.... He didn't know whether he was on his head or heels half the time." Rogers said James told him that it was Robinson's "insulting smile" to Bessie from outside her hotel room that afternoon that had left him determined to go to the club and attack the leering Englishman.

"How did you react to all of this?" Tison interrupted. Rogers said that he had tried again to persuade James not to do anything so drastic, but they went to the club anyway. James waited outside while he went inside and found Robinson in the billiard room. He told him that Lieutenant Hetherington was so excited that he "did not realize what he was doing," and begged for his help so as to prevent any trouble. At that point, Rogers continued, "Robinson professed ignorance ... of any trouble at all." He claimed he had lived up to his promises to Lieutenant Hetherington and warned angrily that if anything happened inside the club, he would have the American put out of it.

Rogers then said he had gone back to James and tried to persuade him to "see Robinson and fix it up." But Hetherington refused, insisting that the Englishman had been "lying from the beginning to the end." Rogers said he then went back into the club for a second time and got Robinson to promise that he would leave town shortly. When he gave that news to James, he replied that he was "bound to take the man's word for it and let the thing rest." After "a good deal of talking," Rogers said, Hetherington had calmed down.

But that didn't last for long. As they walked back to the Grand Hotel, James spewed out still more venom toward Robinson. "He told me," Rogers continued, "that the man had written his wife asking her to take the baby and go to Denver to wait for him to come and get a divorce." The Briton "not only wanted to rob me of my wife," James had cried out, "but he wanted the baby, too!" Hetherington had insisted that he "couldn't go around on shore as if nothing was happening" and repeated that Robinson's unwanted attention to his wife was "driving him almost crazy."

Those were precisely the words that Tison wanted the court to hear.

Then he switched his line of questioning to Bessie. Had Rogers said anything about her to James on that New Year's afternoon? Yes, Rogers replied, "I told him she had been very indiscreet." He replied that he knew that but insisted that "Mr. Robinson had such influence over her that she could not help but do as he said." Then he added ruefully that he didn't understand why that was so. As long as Robinson was away, he reported, his wife did her best—only to lose "control of herself" when he reappeared. Did Hetherington say anything about "fascination"? Tison interrupted. "Yes," Rogers replied firmly. He said that Robinson "fascinated or charmed her just like a snake."

Snake. The perfect word to conjure up a negative image of Gower Robinson in the minds of everyone in the courtroom. After all, hadn't Satan disguised himself as a serpent and gotten Eve to persuade Adam to eat the forbidden fruit?

Rogers continued, saying that when he went to the Hetheringtons' room later that afternoon, he found James lying on a lounge, face down, his head buried in a pillow. "He was played out" but not too weak to be unable to tell him that Robinson had made Bessie the beneficiary of his will, Rogers said. James and Bessie were "very much worried about it." Did he believe it was true? Tison asked. "No," Rogers responded, "I had no idea that it was true."

Tison pressed on. Had Mrs. Hetherington ever said anything about Robinson's threatening to kill himself? She had, Rogers replied, and she had said she was "very glad" things had stopped where they had. She knew Robinson carried a revolver, and if matters had gone further at the club that afternoon, "she did not know what might have happened." What did James say when a gun was mentioned? Tison asked. Rogers gave him the perfect answer: he wished he had been shot because he couldn't stand having the affair go on much longer. He would not have cared if he had been shot, Alan Rogers repeated.

"I tried to help him," Rogers said, "but James protested that because

15. Shipmates

I wasn't married I couldn't understand how he felt. If I were, he said, I might possibly realize the fix he [James] was in. I continued trying to console him for another half hour, but finally realized I couldn't," Rogers said. Then, he concluded sadly, "I left my friend in that terrible state of mind."

Could anyone who heard Rogers's story not feel sorry for James Hetherington? Perhaps even shed a tear for him?

After pausing for a moment to let that emotion strike everyone within hearing, Tison urged Rogers to describe James's behavior a month later. He said his friend had seemed obsessed with Robinson. On February 2, he had called him aside in the Grand Hotel's billiard room and said that he had heard the man was back in town. "I told him I thought he was mistaken about that," Rogers said. "James said he hoped that was so but, just to be sure, he wanted me to go to the United Club and tell the man's friends to please keep him away from Yokohama. I was to warn them of what might happen if he did not stay away. When I asked him what he meant by that, Hetherington replied, 'A horse-whipping.'"

Rogers said he did as asked, telling Robinson's friends to warn him that "there would be trouble" if he returned to Yokohama. The first friend balked, saying he wanted to wash his hands of the whole Robinson-Hetherington matter. The second man just said he would "catch him [Robinson] if possible." The first man then added that he doubted warnings would keep him away. Perhaps it would be best, he suggested, to let Robinson return and "take his licking."

"Later, when he came to see me in my cabin aboard the *Marion*," Rogers said, "James seemed to have calmed down. He said he had changed his mind about doing physical harm to Gower Robinson and had promised his wife 'to do nothing more.' He wanted me to go back to Robinson's friends and tell them 'all was off.' I told him I didn't think that was necessary. He should just take the chance that Robinson would stay away."

How did Lieutenant Hetherington feel about doing that? Tison interrupted. "Very ill at ease," Rogers replied. "Did you ever talk to him about the matter again?" the attorney probed. Rogers replied that James had come to him on Friday, February 12—the day before the killing—and asked if Robinson was back in town. "When I said I didn't know, he asked me again to find out if the Englishman had returned," Rogers continued. "I said I would do so 'incidentally' if possible." But that didn't satisfy Hetherington, Rogers added. "The next afternoon, Saturday, February 13, the day of the shooting, he came with the same question, and I told him again I didn't know Robinson's whereabouts." At that, Rogers reported, Hetherington left his cabin to board the next shore boat headed for Yokohama.

"When was the next time you saw him?" Tison asked, knowing what Rogers's answer would be. "On Sunday morning, after the shooting," the lieutenant replied tersely. That answer probably left those in the courtroom on the edge of their seats, expecting to hear more about the killer's demeanor then. Neither Tison nor Rogers said a word about that.

Instead, Tison ended his questioning of Alan Rogers just as he had with the Bartletts, asking for his impression of James Hetherington's character. The lieutenant described his friend as a "very even-tempered man [who had never been] in any trouble with anyone to amount to anything." What of Mrs. Hetherington? Tison followed up. Amid "all this trouble," he asked, had she visited James aboard the *Marion*? And had she come alone or with their baby? "Very often, yes…. Yes … [but] never with her baby," Lieutenant Rogers affirmed.

That vignette brimmed with innuendo about the Hetheringtons' marital relationship. They were just a normal couple, seizing moments of complete privacy in James's cabin. Happy together—until Gower Robinson intruded into their lives. Bliss before torment and violence, trouble and trial.

Tison's last two interrogations of the day paled in comparison with what had gone before. He had Dr. Frank Bates Stephenson, the *Marion*'s junior surgeon, who saw James daily, speak about a change in James's demeanor. He related two telling episodes about what he had seen. The first came early in February, just before James shot Gower. He and Marine Lieutenant (C. Marrast) Perkins were dining with him in the officers' wardroom. James looked "pale and worn and very much disturbed, [as if he were] laboring under some intense mental strain and commotion," the doctor reported. The marine agreed. James just didn't look right.

The second episode incident happened when James had gotten into a verbal row over something trivial with Dr. Frederick A. Hessler, the *Marion*'s passed assistant surgeon, the doctor reported. "Did that strike you as … unusual and peculiar?" Tison led on. "Yes," the doctor replied. Determined to show the court how very troubled James was at the time, Tison asked if he was often "quarrelsome and inclined to seek altercations or disputes." "No, sir. By no means," Stephenson replied.[3]

Enough. By that time it was nearly midafternoon, well past the hour for tiffin. Judge Tillotson mercifully adjourned the proceedings so that everyone could fill their stomachs.

16

Friends and Accomplices

When everyone returned from tiffin to court that Friday afternoon, the trial and Alexander Tison's strategy for the defense entered a new phase. Up to that point, he and prosecutor Litchfield had focused the court's attention on James Hetherington, the alleged killer. Now, and for the next two and a half days, the defense counsel put the victim, Gower Robinson, on trial. His aim was to lay bare before the assessors, the judge, and indeed the wider Yokohama expatriate community the character, the misdeeds, the lies and deceit of the deceased. He intended to show the court how Gower had transformed his friends into accomplices in his pursuit of Bessie. They, in turn, would in effect convict Robinson of the actions that prompted James Hetherington to kill him.

The witnesses resisted. Mindful of the ancient maxim "Speak no evil of the dead," they would reveal only as much about the dead man as they were forced to. What followed, then, was a tug-of-war between the next six witnesses and Tison. They preferred to keep what Gower had done in the dark. He was determined to bring the provocateur's every thought, word, and deed into the light of day. Once they saw the full truth about the man, he hoped, the court, the Yokohama community, and the world would understand why his client had killed Robinson.

Alfred Carter Read was the first witness to testify that afternoon. He was a British silk merchant who had come to Yokohama six years earlier and become Gower Robinson's friend and neighbor. Tison wanted him to tell the court what had happened at Robinson's home on Sunday, December 27, 1891. When he arrived, Read said, he was handed a letter that Mrs. Hetherington had written to Gower earlier that morning. In it she insisted that he "elope with her that evening" to Kobe, where they could catch a steamer and go on "to Europe or somewhere else."[1]

"Do you have the letter?" Tison asked, knowing that it had been destroyed. Read replied that he did not. Then he detailed his conversation with Gower about what to do. Bessie had said in the letter that James was going to send her away with only $50 and begged to know what she should do. Read, married and a new father, counseled his friend not to "accede" to her request. Doing so, he argued, would make any attempts at reconciliation with Lieutenant Hetherington impossible. It would be best, he advised, to just wait until they might have "more news" from Mrs. Hetherington.

That news came late that afternoon, around 5:30 p.m., Read recalled. Chandler Gibbens, who lived at Robinson's, was already there, and Waldemar Blad joined them. The three men advised Gower that the best thing to do, if her husband was going to send Bessie away, would be to let her go. "On no account" should he go with her. Better to stay in Yokohama for a while, then go to Europe and wait there "until he saw how things were to turn out." If there was "absolutely no chance of reconciliation" and divorce proceedings followed, then Robinson "could fulfill what moral obligations he thought were due." Whose idea was that? Tison interjected. Gibbens's, Read replied. They thought it was, he continued, simply "the best way out of a very bad business." That advice, however, became moot when Bessie's second letter saying that her husband had decided against sending her away arrived.

Tison then turned to the letters that had passed between Bessie and Gower. What did he know about them? Tison asked. A lot, Read replied. Robinson had shown him "20, 30, 40" and possibly more of them. I had been "blaming him very hard ... for his conduct," and Gower wanted me to read them "for his own justification." Did he try to demean Mrs. Hetherington by calling her "a foolish woman?" Tison asked. No, Read retorted. "He had simply given me letters and notes to read while he read bits of others and tossed them into the fireplace to burn."

That tidbit served Tison's purpose, for it showed the court that Gower had destroyed evidence of whatever had gone on between him and Bessie.

Tison then sought to put even more damning evidence about the Englishman before the court. "Did you never see, or Mr. Robinson never tell you he had made a will, in which he left all his property to Mrs. Hetherington?" he asked Read. That question in itself must have shocked those who heard it, for when would it have been proper for a bachelor to leave everything to a married woman?

"I saw the will," the silk merchant replied reluctantly, adding that Robinson had not shown it to him. "Well, when and where and under what circumstances did you see it?" Tison asked. "One night after Robinson's death when Waldemar Blad and I were burning the deceased's old papers," Read explained. "Was the will burned then?" Tison asked. "Yes, the first will," Read replied.

What about the second will? "Is it still in existence?" Tison shot back.

16. Friends and Accomplices

Read said it was, as far as he knew. He hadn't read it but had been told about it. The attorney seized the moment to make another shocking revelation: Did Read know that the second will directed its executor, Mr. Blad, to dispose of Robinson's property just as instructed in the first one—to Bessie Hetherington?

Read squirmed, saying he hadn't heard about that, but admitted, "Yes, I have heard outside rumors" when Tison pressed him for the truth. Tison then turned back to the letters Robinson had shown Read. Didn't they help him understand why the man had willed all of his property to Bessie Hetherington? Read had to acknowledge that they had.

Tison's interrogation of Albert Read did just what he wanted. It focused the court's attention on Gower Robinson's extraordinarily inappropriate behavior rather than James Hetherington's alleged crime.

Henry Litchfield was not going to let him get away with that. Cross-examining Read, he peppered him with questions about how conflicted Gower had been on Sunday, December 27. Who had suggested that morning that the letters between Gower and Bessie be burned? he asked. Robinson, Read replied, adding that his friend had said he didn't want to keep "anything which could damage a woman's reputation." And how had Robinson felt about leaving Japan when Bessie's first letter asking him to do so had arrived? "He said he ought to do what she wanted him to do," Read replied. Even though she had reproached him in the letter about his having been "attentive to other married women"? Litchfield asked in a tone of feigned surprise. That query was meant to suggest that Gower's feelings, and indeed his love, for Bessie were real. Read leaped at the chance to reaffirm that point. He reported that he and Chandler Gibbens had "had great trouble" in persuading Gower not to elope with Bessie.

Propriety had barely trumped passion.

By the time Albert Read stopped speaking, it was midafternoon. Tison was tired and meandered from one topic to another as he queried his next predictably uncooperative witness. Brook Hyde Pearson, who testified under subpoena, was a bachelor British tea trader who had worked in Yokohama and Kobe over the last six years. He lived at the United Club, where, Tison got him to admit, he saw Gower Robinson "very nearly every day." "I was one of his best friends out here, I think," Pearson added cheerfully.

That prompted Tison to ask him about the concert he had attended on November 10, 1891, when Gower had sung the ballad *Call Me Back* while eyeing Bessie. He wanted Pearson to tell the court about Robinson's inappropriate behavior. He balked. When shown the program for the concert and a newspaper review of it, he developed a sudden lapse of memory. Tired though he was, Tison realized there was no point in pursuing that line of inquiry further.

Instead, he jumped to a new line of questioning meant to reveal Pearson's—and others'—complicity in Robinson's misdeeds. He began by asking the tea trader about what had happened on December 28—the day after Gower had sent Bessie two letters. One, meant for James's eyes, told a lie: he promised to stop seeing her. The other, for her eyes only, told the truth: he wanted her to go to his sister's home in Colorado and await his arrival there. Hadn't Robinson asked him to deliver a note to Mrs. Hetherington? Tison asked.

Pearson said he had agreed to do so and gone to her hotel room at nine that morning. When he asked for her, the *amah* told him that she was bathing her baby. Pearson said he left, promising to return later, and when he did Bessie came to the door. He started to give her Gower's note, but she gestured for him to stop. Why? Because others in the hall might have seen and wondered what was going on, Pearson explained.

What was in the note? Tison interrupted to ask. Pearson first said he didn't know, but when pressed revealed that he had been told it directed Bessie not to write to Gower anymore and not to expect any more missives from him. Pearson continued, saying that he had tried again that evening to get the message, now with $20 in it, to Bessie. He went to dinner at the Grand Hotel, thinking he might find her alone but she was dining with her husband.

"You wouldn't have liked to give her the money in his presence?" Tison asked, hoping to get Pearson to acknowledge the impropriety of his actions. "Not very likely," Pearson replied. That triggered muffled laughter in the courtroom. Pearson then revealed that he had slipped the letter and money to Bessie later, telling her half of it was for silk for herself, the other half for the *amah*, "to keep her quiet" about what she might have seen. Although that implied that Pearson knew he had done something wrong, he wouldn't admit that he had done so. Indeed, he claimed that he had become Robinson's messenger out of gentlemanly concern to keep "a lady" from doing so.

Tison stung back. He told the court that Robinson had simply used Pearson as a dupe. He had warned Bessie in the note that Pearson was "a good friend and a good fellow, but he talks too much, and he has no common sense—he is not to be trusted." At that moment, Pearson may well have blushed in embarrassment at those words. But the point Tison wanted the judge and assessors to get was that Gower Robinson just used people—even his friends.

That exchange said more about Tison's skill than Pearson's mental capacity. He had gotten Bessie's active cooperation in preparing for the trial. Who else could have shown him the note—or told him its contents?

Brooke Pearson remained stubbornly uncooperative. When asked

16. Friends and Accomplices

if he knew that the lady he had saved from carrying written messages between Gower and Bessie had conveyed verbal ones and knew what had been going on between the two, Pearson couldn't recall precisely. Tison pressed harder: Hadn't the lady already told him a lot about Bessie and Gower just yesterday, when she knew he was going to have to testify today? "Yes," Pearson replied sheepishly. When Tison followed up by asking him if they had talked about the Hetheringtons, Robinson, or the trial, the Englishman couldn't quite remember.

Pearson's memory lapses angered Judge Tillotson, who interjected with a sarcastic question: "Do you remember any conversation you ever had with anybody?" he asked. "I talk to a great many people every day," the judge said, "and hear a great many things about this trial."

That cutting remark prompted Tison to change his line of questioning to Robinson's second will. Pearson had witnessed it and spoken with Captain Bartlett about it at the inquest. Did it contain "a secret charge or direction" to its executor to give Mrs. Hetherington the remainder of Robinson's property after his debts had been paid? Pearson denied knowing anything about that or having told Bartlett about it. Well, then, Tison pressed on, what had he told the captain about the will? "Simply that I signed it … but didn't know what it was about, leaving everything to [the executor] Mr. Blad to follow some instructions." "How did you know that?" Tison asked innocently. Because the will had been read to him before he signed it, Pearson replied. That admission exposed him as a liar, for he had told Captain Bartlett he didn't know the will's contents when in fact he did.

That falsehood rendered irrelevant anything more Brooke Pearson might say, so Willard Tillotson adjourned the court for the day.

As he walked back to his hotel late that afternoon, Tison had good reason to be pleased with the day's proceedings. His American witnesses had shown the court how Gower Robinson's actions provoked first anger, then restraint, and finally terrible anguish in James Hetherington. His two British witnesses had provided evidence of Robinson's ungentlemanly behavior, prevarication, and entanglement of others in his misdeeds. They set the stage for what others would testify over the next day and a half.

Refreshed by a good night's sleep, Alexander Tison came to court the next morning, Saturday, April 2, determined to squeeze even more incriminating information about Robinson from the friends he had transformed into accomplices.

Chandler Gibbens was the first of them. The American worked for the legendary shipping and mercantile firm Jardine, Matheson, and Company. A recent arrival in Yokohama, he had become close friends with Gower and even lived in his house during the last six weeks of 1891. Gibbens would testify under subpoena, so Tison knew he would have to work hard to pry information out of him. He wanted Gibbens to tell the court three things: what he knew about Robinson's affair with Bessie Hetherington before December 27; what had happened on that terrible Sunday at his home; and what had occurred during and after the January 23 hop at the Grand Hotel.

Gibbens testified that on the morning of December 27, 1891, he had been sitting at the breakfast table reading the newspaper when Gower came downstairs in a state of considerable agitation. He showed him the letter he had just received from Bessie saying that "all was discovered" about their relations and that her husband was going to send her away. Before Gibbens could say anything more, Tison backed him up: What did he know about relations between Robinson and Mrs. Hetherington before that date? A good bit, Gibbens replied. He had read him excerpts from his correspondence with her and shown him one that was "painfully unpleasant." So much so that he started pacing up and down and told Robinson that its contents were "more than I can stand." Then he added in a low voice, "I didn't know things were that bad."

Tison was much more interested in Gower's demeanor that morning than in Gibbens's reaction to Bessie's letter. He got the American to confirm that Gower was alternatively quite calm, calculating, and anxious about what to do next.

"Did he ask for advice, and did you think he ought to go away?" Tison asked. "Yes and yes," Chandler Gibbens replied. "Where to?" Tison followed up. "South, towards Hong Kong," Gibbens said. "Did he agree to that?" Tison asked. The American wasn't sure whether Gower had done so immediately or later that day. Had they discussed going to Europe? Yes, Gibbens replied, but Robinson hadn't wanted to go. "He didn't want to leave Yokohama," he added for emphasis. But, Tison objected, hadn't he subsequently decided to go to America, on the very next steamer after Bessie left for San Francisco? Gibbens replied that he had told Robinson that would not be a good thing to do. When Albert Read arrived later, did he concur in that advice? Tison asked. Grudgingly, Gibbens admitted that Read had, had reproached Gower for his behavior, and had agreed that he should leave Yokohama.

Tison then turned to the last event of that terrible Sunday, asking if Robinson had made out a will that evening. Gibbens replied that he had and volunteered that he himself had copied it and taken it to the bank the next morning. When Tison asked Gibbens if he had been consulted about, or agreed with, its provision leaving everything to Mrs. Hetherington, the American confessed that he agreed with what Robinson had done. And did Gower write to Bessie about the will? Tison inquired. "Yes, sir, I think he told me he had"—that night or the next day.

16. Friends and Accomplices

That tidbit provided the court with another clue about Gower Robinson's character. He had seduced her, but she was not just some casual conquest. His passion for her still burned brightly at year's end, and he was prepared to run away with her. But calculating as he was, he wanted her to know that if something were to happen to him, everything he owned would be hers.

Tison then turned the court's attention back to Robinson's deceptiveness—and, by indirection, his friends' complicity in it. Had Gibbens agreed, after they received Bessie's second letter saying she was not going to be sent back to America, to writing a letter meant to deceive her husband? It would say, in effect, that their affair was over and that he was leaving Yokohama. Gibbens admitted that he had done so. At that point, Tison dramatically picked up the letter and showed it to him. He denied ever having seen it. Incredulous, Tison asked, "The 27th of December, he [Robinson] didn't show you this letter?" "I couldn't say," Gibbens responded evasively.

Tison then turned everyone's attention to the January 23 hop at the Grand Hotel. Did Robinson attend—despite having promised not to do so "if Mrs. Hetherington was likely to be there"? Had Gibbens not told him he didn't think it right for him to be there? he asked. Yes, and yes, the American replied. When Gower wrote something—merely "goodnight"— on Bessie's dance program and then denied he had done so was he not being "altogether frank and open with you"? Tison pressed on. "Yes, but," Gibbens protested.

Before he could say another word, Judge Tillotson interjected incredulously, "He told you two different stories in regard to the card?" "Yes," Gibbens had to admit. Tison didn't need to ask anything more about that incident. Gower's American friend had given the court another clear example of the dead man's deceptiveness.

When Tison pressed him for what more he knew about events later that evening, Gibbens said he hadn't seen Robinson depart but knew he and Mrs. Hetherington had left the ball early. That answer gave Tison the opportunity to ask questions with information that could only have come from Bessie. Did Gibbens not know that his friend had spent an hour and a half in Mrs. Hetherington's room later that evening? he asked. No, Gibbens replied. Did Robinson ever tell him what had happened later that night? Tison followed up. Yes, the American responded. "A day or two later, he wrote me a note about it," he volunteered. Tison pressed on. Did it reveal that Robinson had gone upstairs that evening? Yes, Gibbens admitted. "Did he then or later tell you that he had written '11:30 Room 68'—Bessie's room—on her dance program?" No, Gibbens replied. But whatever Gower wrote on that note was so alarming, so offensive, so potentially damning about his conduct on the night of January 23–24, 1892, that he burned it, the American said.

That revelation likely left everyone in the courtroom, especially James, wondering if the very worst had happened. Had Gower Robinson slept with his wife that night?

That unanswered question ignited a fire in prosecutor Litchfield's belly. He began a tough cross-examination of Gibbens by posing a loaded question: "From what you had seen at the house at 172 Bluff, and from what you had seen of the intercourse between Mr. Robinson and Mrs. Hetherington at other places, had you any reason to believe, or did you know as a fact—know as a fact"—he repeated for emphasis—"that there had been any criminal intimacy [between them]?"

Criminal intimacy? What did those two words mean? Litchfield was old enough to remember when matters of family law—abuse, sexual intercourse in an adulterous relationship, and divorce—fell within the jurisdiction of British ecclesiastical courts rather than civil ones. But that was no longer true in April 1892. Tison knew that adultery was not a crime—in either the United States or England. Those who heard those two words from Litchfield's lips, however, knew exactly what they meant. Sexual intercourse in an adulterous relationship, even if voluntary by both parties, may not have been a crime, but it was a grievous wrong and a terrible evil. Wrong because it was a violation of the marriage contract. Evil because it constituted a threat to the family—the basic unit of society.

That was not what the words meant in the context of this trial, however. Litchfield used them like a rapier to pop Tison's balloon of hot air filled with allegations of Gower Robinson's wrongdoing and responsibility for his own death. Tison instantly recognized them as a threat to his basic strategy for the defense. They were meant to make the court doubt Robinson's primary responsibility for the events that led James Hetherington to kill him. Litchfield's words dripped with innuendo about Bessie's share of blame for everything that had occurred.

Trying to keep anything but favorable mention of her out of the court's ears, Tison protested that the question was irrelevant. Judge Tillotson asked Litchfield to repeat his question, then ruled it out of order. The prosecutor was not to be silenced so easily, however. He asked Gibbens if the parts of the letters Robinson had read to him gave him any reason to believe that there had been any "criminal intimacy." Tison instantly objected once more.

Willard Tillotson immediately told Chandler Gibbens "don't answer that." Litchfield defiantly tried again with the same question, and the judge again directed the witness to remain silent. Litchfield rephrased the question. Tillotson for a third time directed Gibbens not to answer. Then, in an

16. Friends and Accomplices

obvious show of chagrin, he said it wasn't necessary to take up any more of the court's time on that point. He added sternly, "The questions are ruled out of order." That silenced Henry Litchfield for the moment.

Tison, wanting that stinging rebuke to his adversary to linger in the minds of everyone present, realized that it was nearly noon on Saturday and immediately asked for adjournment until Monday. Judge Tillotson would have none of that. The court, he directed, would hold a short session after tiffin.

Tison questioned two witnesses that afternoon. Their testimony lacked the drama of the morning, but their words were not without significance. The first was Waldemar Blad, Robinson's sometime partner and executor, who spoke with his Danish accent. He had been reluctant to testify but did so because his consul had assured him all he had to do was to speak fully and truly. He revealed that he had seen Gower on the very first day he arrived in Yokohama back in 1888, gotten to know him well in 1889, and become his business partner in April of 1890.

Tison wanted him to tell the court what he had seen and heard at his partner's home on Sunday, December 27. Blad added little of substance to what Read, Pearson, and Gibbens had already told the court. But he captured for the courtroom audience the emotional intensity of that day. Knowing something extraordinary was up, he had found Robinson in a highly agitated state—nervous and weeping, Blad said. Had he ever seen his partner that way before? Tison interrupted. Yes, the Dane replied, Robinson had been like that, on and off, ever since he had met Mrs. Hetherington. More agitated and upset, Tison got him to admit, than he had ever been "with reference to any woman before." He had to explain, Blad continued, "everything" about his relationship with Mrs. Hetherington, and "I told [him] I considered it a bad business."

Those few words confirmed that all four of Gower's friends who came to his home that day had warned him to break off his relationship with Bessie. Everyone in the courtroom that afternoon, however, knew that he had not and that had led to his demise. In just a few words, Blad delivered exactly the message that Tison wanted everyone within hearing to get.

He then turned to Robinson's wills. Tison wanted to squeeze one last vital piece of information about them from Blad. Was the first one "made sometime in December or early in January still in existence"? he asked. Yes, Robinson's executor replied. And was that so because its provisions (leaving the remainder of Gower's estate to Bessie when all of his other financial obligations had been fulfilled) "are to apply insofar as the new will does not revoke them"? he pressed on. Reluctantly given, Blad's answer was clearer than anything the court had heard earlier. "In some cases, yes," he replied.

That less-than-definitive answer provided one more bit of evidence of Gower's passion for Bessie and his inappropriate behavior toward her. Satisfied, Tison sat down. Prosecutor Litchfield chose not to cross-examine Blad, so Tison called the last witness of the day, Ensign Creighton Churchill, to testify. He wanted him to attest to Gower Robinson's ability to corrupt and use people. Churchill was determined not to speak ill of the dead man. What followed turned into a tug-of-war between interrogator, witness, and, surprisingly, Judge Tillotson.

Tison began innocently by asking Churchill how long he had been in Yokohama and how he came to know Robinson. The ensign's answers suggested that he was something of an orphan in the navy and a waif in Yokohama's expatriate society. He had served on three ships—the *Charleston*, the *Alliance*, and finally the *Marion*—during the six months since he came to the city. But he hadn't gone to sea on any of them long enough to bond with his fellow officers, including James Hetherington. Churchill explained that his friendship with Robinson had developed slowly, and he hadn't been invited to Robinson's home until just before Christmas.

What happened there, Tison forced him to reveal, was at best unusual, at worst shocking. Gower had told him a lot about his relations with the Hetheringtons and shown him letters from Bessie. And what were those letters like? Tison asked. Terrible, Churchill replied. She wrote shocking things about her husband. "And did Robinson tell you about his promise to cease paying inappropriate attention to Mrs. Hetherington?" the attorney inquired. He did, Churchill confessed.

Why might Robinson have done so? And was it appropriate for him to pass along scurrilous information about Churchill's senior officer's marriage to him? Wasn't Robinson just using Churchill to serve his own ends—that is, wangling an invitation to Admiral Belknap's farewell ball so that Robinson could consort with Mrs. Hetherington? And didn't he succeed, for Churchill was the only officer voting against the proposal to exclude him from the list of invitees? Was that the right thing to do, knowing that Mrs. Hetherington "would certainly be there"? Had Churchill thought so then, and did he still think so now? The angry questions shot like bullets out of Tison's mouth.

Churchill's waffling reply drew a rare outburst from Willard Tillotson. "Have you no opinion about the subject? Do you hold an opinion at all?" he asked the young ensign, who said yes, and then, after a pause, no. That reply angered Tison. He pursued Churchill mercilessly with embarrassing questions. Was Churchill's friendship for Robinson not stronger than his sense of decency, stronger even than his loyalty to the U.S. Navy? It was then, Churchill confessed. Did he not know that when Robinson was asked why he was his friend, Robinson had replied that Churchill was

16. Friends and Accomplices

"the smallest thing," the only friend he had left in the U.S. Navy? Wounded by what his supposed friend had said about him, Churchill replied softly, "No, sir."

More evidence of Gower's callousness, if such were needed.

Tison couldn't resist asking one more damning question about Gower Robinson. He had said he wouldn't go to any social event where Mrs. Hetherington would be present. But on Saturday evening, February 13, the evening he was shot, he was on his way to a hop at the Grand Hotel where she was likely to be present. Did Churchill know who had invited him to it? Once again, the ensign responded evasively, saying he didn't know who had done so—but he had an idea as to who it was.

Tison didn't press him to reveal who that might have been. Churchill had done quite enough for the defense. His evasiveness suggested that he was trying to cover up for Robinson. His words showed the court just how bad the man had been. He had lied, broken promises, and used his friends to help him pursue Bessie Hetherington down to his dying day. That was the truth defense counsel Tison wanted to stick in the minds of his hearers. He had no more questions; neither did prosecutor Litchfield.

So Judge Tillotson adjourned court until ten o'clock on the following Monday morning.

Alexander Tison strode into the courtroom that day, April 4, 1892, determined to get everything he possibly could out of the sixth and last of Gower's accomplices, Henry Blanchard. Bessie had told him that Gower used him as a courier to carry notes to and from her. Judge Tillotson and the assessors may have dreaded the prospect of still more of his seemingly endless questions about Gower and Bessie's correspondence, but Tison felt he needed Blanchard to put more firsthand evidence of Robinson's depravity before the court. And he suspected that this last of Gower's friends would be a more cooperative witness than the five others who had preceded him.

Blanchard was an American who had come to Yokohama nearly a year earlier and taken a clerking job at the C.P. Low trading firm. He readily revealed why his testimony would be valuable for the defense. Robinson had befriended him late in December, confided in him during the weeks that followed, and then had him stay in his house while he was away in Kobe late in January and early in February. Blanchard also knew the Hetheringtons well and had even, with James's consent, danced frequently with Bessie. He could tell a great deal about what Gower, Bessie, and James had done during the days and weeks leading up to the shooting.

How had Robinson gotten him to become his courier? Tison began. Blanchard explained that Gower first told him that he needed someone more discreet than the person (Brooke Pearson) who had been doing the job. Then he proffered reassurances that it could be done without his being discovered. How? The Grand Hotel night watchman had been in his pay for some time and would not say a word about what he might see or hear. Blanchard could do the job in secret.

How many letters had he carried between Robinson and Mrs. Hetherington? And had there been more from him to her than the other way around? Tison asked. Blanchard replied that he had carried 10 times as many notes from Gower to Bessie than from her to him. He added that when she refused his notes, Robinson grew angry and insisted that he try again and tell her how important his message was until she relented and accepted what he had to deliver.

Tison then got Blanchard to tell the court something far more significant: how yet another, previously unrevealed midnight meeting between the two sometime lovers had come about. It had happened on January 9. That afternoon he had gone to a tea aboard the USS *Alliance*. Mrs. Hetherington was there, and he struck up a conversation with her. The *Marion* was anchored nearby, and they joked that James might be watching. So Blanchard told Bessie to drop her handkerchief. She did so, and when he in gentlemanly fashion bent over to pick it up, he put a note from Gower inside it.

The note, Blanchard said, contained a plea for her to meet him at her hotel room after the hop at the Grand Hotel later that evening. He, Bessie, and Gower—but not James, who had duty aboard the *Marion*—went to the dance. Tison interrupted to say, "Mr. Robinson asked you to go upstairs with him, didn't he, about midnight?" "Yes, sir," Blanchard replied. "Gower and Bessie spoke to one another briefly. Then she left the room one way and he motioned to me to follow him out another way." "He wanted to see her privately?" Tison asked. "Yes, sir," Blanchard responded. Then he added, "I suppose he wanted me to walk with him in case anybody saw him going up, they might have thought it rather strange."

Robinson had gotten Blanchard to provide cover for yet another suspicious midnight encounter with Bessie Hetherington.

In the midst of a welter of Tison's questions about what he knew about the messages he was carrying, the courier dropped another explosive bit of information: on the eve of the shooting, Blanchard said, Robinson "handed me a ten-dollar bill and said to give it to the night watchman at the hotel." Why so much? Tison asked. Blanchard replied, "He said he was a man who could give information that nobody else could ... [and] in case Lieutenant Hetherington went to him and offered him a few dollars more, it would be an inducement to keep his mouth shut."

That revelation surely raised questions in the minds of all who heard it. Was Gower, after all of his promises not to do so, after his sojourn in

16. Friends and Accomplices

Kobe, after his return to Yokohama, still determined to meet Bessie once more?

A possible answer to that question popped up when prosecutor Litchfield cross-examined Blanchard. "Were you," he asked, "in the habit of watching for the arrival of officers from the *Marion* and reporting the fact to Mr. Robinson?" Blanchard reluctantly admitted, "I always rode on horseback to tiffin, and after tiffin I always stopped to see the officers coming out of the shore boat." But he protested, he wasn't a spy or a snitch and didn't do so to gain "any information to better Mr. Robinson's position."

Litchfield shot right back: "Have you ever reported to Mr. Robinson, or been asked to report to him, what officers were coming ashore?" Blanchard gave a tantalizing reply: "I was asked on the 12th of February [the day before the shooting] to report whether Lieutenant Hetherington was going to be on duty or off duty" on the next evening. He added that Robinson "gave no reason for wanting the information."

Why did Gower want it? Was he afraid of encountering James? Did he hope to meet Bessie, in her husband's absence, at the Saturday hop set for that night? Or was he just intent on resuming his social life as it had been before he met the Hetheringtons?

Those questions remained unanswered as Tison queried Blanchard for the last time. "Had Robinson ever refused to take any letters from Mrs. Hetherington that you brought?" he asked. "There was only one I took him. He did not refuse it," Blanchard the courier replied.

By this time, Judge Tillotson was appalled by what he had heard. "Mr. Blanchard, did it occur to you that it was not proper to carry letters from one man to another man's wife, especially as boys and coolies are so cheap in Yokohama?" he said to him. "It did not occur to me at the time," the young American replied. "It does now?" Tillotson asked. "Yes," Henry Blanchard replied sheepishly. "I am glad to hear you say that. That's all," the judge said. And then he adjourned the proceedings for tiffin.

But there would be more, and still more damning, testimony about Gower Robinson to come that afternoon.

17

Servants' Tales

Alexander Tison returned from tiffin that afternoon more determined than ever to put the truth about what had gone on between Gower and Bessie before the court. He knew precisely where to look for it: from service people, hotel staff and servants. They had seen Gower and Bessie up close daily and in their comings and goings from midnight assignations. Though professionally committed to silence about what they had seen and heard, they could, through proper questioning under oath, be made to tell all. They would become, in effect, the carpenters who pounded the last nails into the coffin of Gower Robinson's reputation.[1]

Tison had already hinted at this strategy. His very first witness for the defense had been the manager of the Grand Hotel, who revealed how and when Gower began his pursuit of Bessie. Toward the end of the preceding day's court session, he had also put the manager of the Tokyo Imperial Hotel on the stand. He wanted him to suggest that Robinson had planned to share his bed with Bessie in the capital's finest hotel for a night. With a dramatic gesture, he picked up a letter and a telegram, both dated October 31, 1891, and showed them to Charles S. Arthur. "Both preferred the same request, did they not," namely a room for November 3, the night of the Emperor's Ball? he asked. "Yes, sir," the manager replied softly. Then Tison put words into the man's mouth. "You, for reasons and purposes of your own refused it … did not comply with it?" he queried. "Yes, sir," the manager responded—this time in a loud and firm voice. He then reported that Robinson and the Hetheringtons had stayed in separate rooms in his hotel on the night of the Emperor's Ball.

What had gone on here? Robinson had requested a double room and invited Bessie to share it after the ball. She, fearing that the *Marion* might arrive any day with James on board, declined her English lover's request. Out of discretion or on just a hunch, she scotched Gower's scheme for a second assignation. Robinson then had to cancel his request for a double room and ask for a single.

17. Servants' Tales

Tison knew that because Bessie had told him so during one of their pretrial interviews. He chose that earlier afternoon to leave the implication of the manager's testimony unclear—no more than a cloud of suppositions hanging over the heads of his listeners. Today was going to be different. Nothing would be left unclear. Nothing left unsaid out of discretion. Tison intended to make his witnesses tell all.

He would get that—and more.

Servants of foreigners ranked high in the Japanese working class. They had to be intelligent and understand English, and in return they were well paid.[2] The first of them Tison called to testify was Kaneko Chūzō, Gower Robinson's *bettō*. The stableman had previously testified for the prosecution about what he had seen on February 13, 1892, the night of the shooting. Today Tison wanted him to give evidence for the defense about another Friday—October 23, 1891. Those in the courtroom may have leaned forward in their chairs at that moment, expecting Tison to give them a clue of what was to come. He could have reminded them that October 23 was little more than 24 hours after Gower had been introduced to Bessie. But he said nothing about the possible significance of the date. He wanted Kaneko, an eyewitness, to tell the court the shocking tale of what had occurred on that fateful evening.

Tison began by asking questions designed to set the scene. Did Kaneko recall that he had gone to Yokohama Station to pick up his master that night? Was he returning from a concert in Tokyo on the last train, arriving around midnight? Did he get up onto his trap and take the reins? "Yes," the groomsman replied over and over. "He then drove along the Bund toward his house, #172 Bluff, did he not?" Tison led on. "Yes," the *bettō* affirmed. "Did he drive past the Grand Hotel without stopping?" the attorney asked. Yes, without stopping anywhere, Kaneko added. "And you were sitting behind him all the time?" "Yes" was the answer that came back again.

Robinson drove up Camp Hill, and then all the way home at a full gallop, Tison continued. Kaneko didn't want to acknowledge that. But the attorney trapped him into admitting that when they got to the house and he took the horse to the stable, the animal was so hot and sweaty that he had to rub it down immediately. "All of this time there was someone with Mr. Robinson, was there not?" Tison asked after a pause. "Yes," said the groomsman quietly.

At that moment, the defense counsel picked up a photograph mounted on a four-inch-by-six-inch card—a cabinet picture, in the parlance of that time.[3] Showing it to Kaneko, he asked, "Is this a picture of the person who was with him?" "Yes" was the reply that came back again. He hadn't known the person in the photo at the time but saw her later at a tea party, Kaneko added.

Prosecutor Litchfield then broke in to cross-examine the *bettō*. He tried to cast doubt on what the servant could have seen by asking him if the lights had been on when he stopped at the front door of the Robinson house. Kaneko said he hadn't been able to tell if the lights were on or not. That admission had little or no effect upon the court. Its potential significance was overshadowed by what Tison did next. Picking up the photograph that Kaneko had identified, he showed it to the judge and assessors.

It was, the court stenographer recorded, "a cabinet picture of Mrs. J.H. Hetherington."

Tison then suddenly recalled Henry Blanchard. He had previously told the court that Gower had spoken with him about his clandestine interactions with Bessie. Had Robinson ever told him about what had happened on that October evening? Tison asked. "Yes," Blanchard replied without hesitation. Regardless of the damage his testimony might do to Robinson's reputation, he spoke freely:

"Was Mrs. Hetherington with him?" Tison asked knowingly. "Yes," Blanchard allowed. "What did he [Robinson] say to her when they got into his trap?" Tison inquired. "He asked her if he might have the pleasure of driving her up to the hotel," Blanchard replied. "What happened when they got to her hotel?" the defense counsel led on. Blanchard said Robinson had told him that she had tried to jump down from the trap. "What did Gower Robinson say he did then?" Tison asked knowingly. "He said he prevented her and whipped up his horse," Blanchard replied. If that were not enough to indicate that Bessie thought that she was just being taken to her hotel, Tison clinched his argument with one last question to this American witness: "Did he say she was unwilling to go with him?" he asked. "Yes," Henry Blanchard admitted.

All of what he had said might in an American court today be challenged by a prosecuting attorney as hearsay and ruled inadmissible by the judge. The jurors would be told not to consider it. None of that happened in the American consular court in Yokohama on that April day in 1892. Prosecutor Litchfield made no objection.

Silence followed. Blanchard's testimony must have stunned everyone in the courtroom. It produced just what Tison wanted all to infer: Bessie, innocent and unsuspecting, had fallen that October night into the clutches of a determined and passionate lecher—Gower Robinson.

Tison next called a second servant to testify, Nakatani Masanosuke. He had been Robinson's houseboy for the last three years and he remained a loyal servant, all seeing but silent, even after his master's death. He didn't want to be in court now. When Tison asked him if he spoke English, he didn't answer. The attorney pried a "no" out of him through the interpreter standing by. Tison instantly alleged that Nakatani was lying because he had spoken with him earlier in English. Willard Tillotson then jumped in, asking Nakatani if he knew the attorney. "Yes," the houseboy replied in English. The judge didn't like that. "I thought you said you did not speak English," he followed up. That should have settled the matter, but when Tison asked him to affirm that he had served Robinson for three years, Nakatani wouldn't answer. Finally he snarled back "*He*" [pronounced "Heh"], an insulting, low-class way of saying "yes" in Japanese. Judge Tillotson didn't like that either. He asked again if the witness had been "Mr. Robinson's boy," adding, "You were, weren't you?" in a tough tone of voice. Chastened, the servant replied, "*Sayo de gozaimasu*"—the polite way a Japanese inferior would reply to a superior. Still angry and still not understanding the servant's reply, Tillotson snapped, "Why don't you say so, you understand what I am saying." Then he ordered the interpreter to translate for the rest of the houseboy's testimony.

It did not go smoothly.

Nakatani tangled with Tison when asked how many times he had carried letters from his master to Room 68 at the Grand Hotel—Bessie's room. At first, he said only three times. Then he didn't remember. When Tison asked him to swear that he never took more than that, he suddenly developed amnesia about how many times he had served as Gower's courier to Bessie. That angered Judge Tillotson, who directed the interpreter to warn Nakatani about the "penalties of perjury ... a very serious offense." Tison then trapped the Japanese in his evasions. A week ago, he told the court, Nakatani had answered these same questions very specifically. Why was he now saying he had never heard them and having so much difficulty in giving a straight answer to them? Nakatani understood what he was being asked, and he replied in the most contemptuous way a Japanese could: silence.

Judge Tillotson put an end to that. "I think we had better turn this witness over to the police," he quipped. The courtroom burst into laughter. Quick on the draw, Tison said he wanted to ask Nakatani "one or two questions before he goes." More laughter followed.

Nakatani didn't think anything was funny. When Tison gently asked him to just say yes or no if he knew Mrs. Hetherington's *amah*, he exploded in a torrent of Japanese words spoken "volubly and at length." Judge Tillotson tried to press him to tell the truth by asking if Inspector Okada of the Japanese police was present. Nakatani wasn't cowed by the threat. Tison said he was "indifferent to the witness's answers." But he couldn't resist asking Nakatani to tell the court what he had been up to—at his master's behest—with the *amah*. Didn't he ask her for her address in Japan Town? Didn't he tell her he needed it so his master could send her money for Christmas? Didn't she say she didn't want any money? "No." "I don't know." "I didn't hear that sort of thing." Nakatani fired defiant denials right back to Tison. Judge Tillotson got the same treatment. When he asked the servant if he had ever spoken with the *amah*, he got a "No, sir," tinged with contempt, back.

The American attorney had pounded on the Japanese nail. It didn't bend. The truth didn't come out. But Tison kept on trying to get the answers he wanted. He tugged, he pulled, and he pulled some more as he peppered Nakatani with questions about what he had witnessed on Saturday morning, October 24, 1891. The servant had previously told him what he had seen, and Tison was determined to force him to do the same in court. He spat out questions based on information only Bessie could have given him:

- Had the master not asked him to go upstairs and look for a scarf, a cloth used as colors at the horse races, and bring it down?
- Had he not shown it to Robinson and a lady who was there?
- Could that cloth not be used to cover one's face?
- Was he not sent to get a jinrikisha for the lady to leave the house in?
- And had Mr. Robinson in the lady's presence between five and six that morning not told him "he would be killed if he ever told what had happened"?

Nakatani shot back "No" to every one of those questions. But was he to be believed? Was he still protecting his master? Those were questions any defense counsel would have wanted judge and jurors to be asking themselves. But at this moment, one suspects, everyone in that courtroom would have been focused on what Nakatani, even in denial, had suggested about what had happened on the night of October 23–24, 1891: Bessie Hetherington had spent that night at Gower Robinson's home. And the couple had had sex.

That inference overshadowed doubts about the houseboy's veracity. It led, logically, to still more questions about what Gower and Bessie had done that night. Did he force himself upon her? Did she simply not resist his advances? Or was their intercourse consensual? Something, perhaps, that they both enjoyed?

Tison knew that only Bessie could answer those questions. She was not in the courtroom at his request. He was determined to reveal as little as possible about what she had done on that night or at any other time just before her husband shot Gower Robinson. He did not want to damage her reputation. He did not want to diminish, in the minds of the judge and assessors, Robinson's primary responsibility for what had occurred. At that moment, it was enough for his purposes that Robinson had told Henry Blanchard that Bessie had not wanted to go with him beyond her hotel that night. Tison wanted to move on and question a third eyewitness to the events of October 23–24, 1891.

Before he could do so, Judge Tillotson interrupted. He directed the interpreter to tell Nakatani, "I am inclined to believe that he has not been telling the truth." He felt it was his duty to turn the man over to the Japanese police. That gave Tison the opportunity to imply that the witness might have been "tampered with." While that was "a matter of the gravest concern, I would be loath to make charges," he continued, adding that would be "only too pleased" if Nakatani could "remove the least shadow of suspicion from anybody." Tison knew perfectly well that the houseboy was not going to tell who, if anyone, had gotten him to perjure himself.

Henry Litchfield was not about to let that insinuation stand. Cross-examining Nakatani, he asked if he had previously talked with him, or his clerk, about the testimony he would give. The servant replied that this was the first time he had seen the prosecutor. Did he know Mr. Blad or Mr. Read? Nakatani said he knew the one but wasn't sure about the other. Willard Tillotson then spoke up, telling Litchfield his line of questioning was a waste of time. The prosecutor protested, saying he only wanted to know if Nakatani had discussed what he should say in court with anyone. Tison jumped at the chance to reinforce his suggestion that witness tampering might have occurred. "I do not think we could believe him as to that," he snapped. Litchfield then asked Nakatani if he had discussed the matter before the court with any foreigners. Unable to give a straight answer, the servant replied, "I do not know." That was too much for Judge Tillotson. He ordered the witness to be taken from court and placed in Japanese police custody.

Henry Litchfield was not about to let matters rest there. "I do not know what Mr. Tison is going to make out," he snarled. Feigning any intention of implying anything, the defense attorney protested back, "I am not without knowledge going to make any suggestions or imputations, certainly not." But he had done so—secure in the belief that someone was trying to keep witnesses from telling the truth.

After that testy exchange, Tison's interrogation of Shiraishi Tome, the Hetheringtons' *amah*, must have seemed tame by comparison. She was cooperative and did not suffer from lapses of memory. Did she remember that Mrs. Hetherington had gone to Tokyo on October 23? the defense counsel asked. "Yes," the *amah* replied. He: "Did she say she would come back or not?" She: "She said she would come back at 12 o'clock." That was further evidence that Bessie, at least at the time she left to go to the concert, had no intention of going anywhere, upon her return, other than to her room at the Grand Hotel.

"Did she not come [then]?" Tison asked. "No," Tome replied. But "had she come in at six the next morning?" Tison queried in feigned ignorance. The *amah* gave him precisely what he wanted everyone to hear: "Yes," the woman said clearly.

Three eyewitnesses had now confirmed the essential truth about the night of October 23–24, 1891: Robinson had carried Mrs. Hetherington off to his home. They spent the night together. He swore his houseboy to silence about what occurred there. Then Bessie was returned incognito to her room, where her maid saw her.

Tison then got the *amah* to give damning testimony about houseboy Nakatani's delivery of Gower's letters to Bessie through her. She reported that he came sometimes two or three times daily, even at mealtimes. "Did he ever get letters from your mistress to take to Mr. Robinson that you saw?" Tison asked. "I never saw her send any," Tome replied. Had the houseboy found out where she lived and come there asking her to deliver letters from Robinson to Mrs. Hetherington, Tison asked. And had he come so often that "the neighbors thought he was your husband"? Tome replied that one of the hotel boys thought so.

The attorney then asked more questions meant to defame Gower Robinson still further. Had Nakatani not said his master was "a very bad man" and "catch" a new woman every two months? He continued in the pidgin English he knew she would understand: "He go Kobe maybe catch new woman?" The boy thought so, she replied. "And he was very glad there were no letters while his master was away?" "Yes," Tome replied, adding "no walk very much—all right." That provoked a rare burst of laughter in the courtroom.

Willard Tillotson was not amused. He cut Litchfield's cross-examination of the *amah* short and proposed to adjourn for tiffin. But Tison begged to have just one more witness testify before they took a break, and the judge reluctantly agreed. Tison speedily questioned the Grand Hotel houseboy who normally waited in the hallway outside the Hetheringtons' rooms. Shimada Tsunekichi confirmed what the *amah* had just said. When Robinson's houseboy came, he handed the hall boy letters and asked him to give them to the *amah*. That way, if anyone else passed by, they would think the letters were between two young Japanese, not Bessie Hetherington and someone else.

With that additional tidbit about Gower Robinson's devious ways, the court adjourned for tiffin.

Tison called only two witnesses to testify that afternoon. The first was Max Kaufmann, a German who had worked for the shipping and marine insurance firm Simon & Evers Co. He had lived in Yokohama for the past 11 years and known Gower Robinson well. He had also returned from Tokyo on the night of October 23 in the same late train as Bessie and

Gower. Tison wanted Kaufmann to tell the court what he had seen that night while riding home from Yokohama station in a jinrikisha.

"Were you overtaken by Mr. Robinson's trap?" he asked. "I was," Kaufmann replied. "Did you notice whether it contained Mr. Robinson and a lady?" he followed up. "I think I saw Mr. Robinson and a lady," Kaufmann dutifully replied. That was all Tison needed. Yet another eyewitness confirmed that Bessie had been taken to Gower's home that evening.

Tison then called the last witness of the day, the Grand Hotel's night watchman, Cesare Pachini. Anxious to avoid the confusion and evasion that had marked the Robinson houseboy's testimony given in translation, he had the Italian consul, Marquis Carlo Nembrini de Gonzaga, sworn in as interpreter along with the witness.[4] Seeing how very nervous Pachini was, Tison reassured him that all he had to do was answer questions. The interpreter replied on his behalf that he would "tell what he has seen." Those words must have pricked up everyone in the courtroom's ears: something important was about to be revealed.

Tison began by asking Pachini how long he had worked at the Grand Hotel. Four years, 10 months, and four nights, 6 p.m. to 6 a.m., as of last night, the watchman replied. What had he done for a living before taking the hotel job? Had he been a sailor? the attorney inquired. "Yes, I told you before, suppose you remember?" Pachini replied.

Tison continued, phrasing his questions so as to suggest he was repeating what the watchman had told him earlier. Did he know Gower Robinson so well that they sometimes spoke in Italian? Didn't the Englishman even boast that he was half-Italian? "Yes," Pachini replied. "And didn't you like him because he knew you, spoke kindly to you, and even gave you a little money for your children?" the attorney inquired. "Yes," the watchman replied once more.

Tison then asked his key question: Had Mr. Robinson given Pachini five dollars on January 23, 1892—the night he paid a long late-night visit to Bessie Hetherington's room? "No, he [Mr. Robinson] never gave me anything," Pachini protested. Tison found that unbelievable. Didn't he know that others had said Robinson had often given him money? he asked. "No, sir. He made a mistake," the Italian said. That prompted Tison to warn him that he was speaking under oath. But Pachini still insisted "the man never gave me a cent."

Tison's next question was meant to render whatever the night watchman might answer questionable: Did Pachini not know that Mr. Robinson had left him, after his death, $10 in the hands of a friend? "I do not know," the Italian replied, adding, "I should like to know who is the friend." That touched off a ripple of laughter across the courtroom.

Dead serious, Tison pressed on, asserting that Robinson had been seen talking with American naval officers in the parlor just outside the dining room where the January 23 dance was held. Probing for more corroboration as to exactly what had happened later that night and the next morning, he asked: Didn't Robinson give Pachini five dollars and promise 15 more if he would leave the hotel's rear entrance door open that night? "No," Pachini protested. Tison shot right back, revealing that Robinson had given the watchman as much as $20 between October and January. Pachini still insisted that Robinson had never given him a cent.

Tison then attacked the night watchman's credibility from another angle. Didn't he remember seeing Mrs. Hetherington come in the back door, the very one he had just denied leaving open at Robinson's request, about 6:00 a.m. on the morning of Saturday, October 24? he asked. The Italian replied that he had been "astonished to see a married woman there." He added that she was alone and went quickly upstairs. "You spoke to Mr. Robinson about that very soon thereafter, didn't you?" Tison followed up. "No, never," Pachini replied. A few moments later, Tison tried again, asking, "Didn't Robinson say he knew all about it when you told him about seeing the lady come in the back entrance at six in the morning? And didn't he also say he knew where she had been?" "No," Pachini replied, adding that Robinson had not said anything to him when he revealed that information.

That was another clear contradiction. How could he have told Robinson anything of the sort if, as he had said, he had never spoken to him about what he had seen that January morning? Tison knew at that moment that he had the Italian trapped in a lie—one that the judge and assessors had heard.

"Do you say now you have told truly all that you have said with reference to those questions which I have asked you?" he asked. "Yes, yes, everything is true," Pachini replied. "Everything he has said is true?" Tison asked the interpreter. "Yes," replied Marquis Nembrini, adding that Pachini says he has "some other things … [to say]." Before he could finish the sentence, Tison cut in with another question meant to cast doubt on the witness's character and credibility. "Oh well, you are quite sure Mrs. Hetherington is a bad woman. Didn't you tell me so?" Once again the Italian fell into Tison's trap—with another denial: "Everybody says so—not me. Every paper everyone says that—not me."

That remark was sheer gold for the defense counsel. Here was confirmation of what he himself had said in his opening remarks eight days ago: Yokohama was rife with rumors and prejudice against his client's wife. But he said nothing about it and pressed his case against Cesare Pachini. "I should like to have proper representation made to the Italian Consul as to

17. Servants' Tales

a witness of this sort, Your Honor!" he exclaimed. The judge thought that could wait until later. He wanted the interpreter, Marquis Nembrini, to affirm that the night watchman had been directed to "tell everything you know" in court and that Pachini had said he would.

Unable to believe the witness had done so, Tison angrily blurted out: "The man has not been so frank in the court as he has been in private conversation. He is full of vile things. Lies, lies, and more lies." At that moment, Tison may have believed that Pachini had said enough to suggest that the Italian had intended to blackmail Gower Robinson.

However tempting that line of inquiry may have been, Tison wisely chose not to pursue it at that moment. He kept his eye on the prize: convincing judge and assessors that what Gower Robinson had done was so evil, so monstrous, and so hurtful that James Hetherington had good reason to attack and kill him.

So Tison asked Judge Tillotson for an adjournment. He and the accused had suffered "supreme strain," he pleaded. Lieutenant Hetherington had had to endure hearing how Robinson had seduced his wife, and he himself had suffered through a parade of lying witnesses. He intended to call next the defendant to tell "the story of his sorrow," which would be best told and heard uninterrupted. But because the next day would be a mail day, when everyone would be busy reading incoming mail and dashing off letters to go out on a departing ship, Tison argued, it would be best to adjourn until the day after tomorrow.

Prosecutor Litchfield made no objection to that, but Tillotson was inclined to reject it. He and the associates all had other business to attend to and were "very anxious to have this matter finished as soon as possible," he said. But then, thinking better about going on, he declared the court adjourned until Thursday, April 7.

One suspects Alexander Tison walked out of the courtroom that afternoon feeling quite satisfied. What had been affirmed and denied over the past two days was enough to clinch the argument he had been trying to make about Gower Robinson's guilt. During the break in the proceedings that lay ahead, Judge Tillotson and the assessors could ponder that. And he would have more time to coach the next witness, the alleged murderer, Lieutenant James Henry Hetherington, on what to say.

18

Suspicion

Thursday, April 7, 1892, dawned a beautiful spring day in Yokohama. The last of the cherry blossoms fluttered down onto ground dampened overnight by *harusame*, the misty rain that fell only at this time of year. Those who crowded through the front gate of the American consulate brushed up against trimmed pines whose needles glistened with lingering drops of rain. When, shortly before 10:00 a.m., the bailiff opened the consulate front doors, those waiting outside pushed their way in and quickly filled the available seating. They wanted to see and hear what promised to be the climactic testimony of the trial: Lieutenant James Henry Hetherington speaking in his own defense. A clutch of reporters made sure they got to a place where they could witness everything about to take place.

When Willard Tillotson took his seat at the front of the courtroom, he launched into a tirade against the witnesses who had lied or perjured themselves during the last day's session. He issued a stern warning to those present and the entire Yokohama foreign community. "When a man is on trial for his life charged with … murder," he said, "and any witness [who] knows anything that might help him and yet refuses to tell what he knows—to tell the truth and the whole truth—and the defendant is convicted of murder, such witnesses would be accessory to his murder. That is to say," he clarified, "in case the defendant should be convicted and executed."

Tillotson's meaning was crystal clear. Could anyone bear the weight of guilt for that sort of miscarriage of justice if he or she knowingly lied or held back truths that might save a defendant from wrongful death?

After such strong words from the judge, everyone present expected Tison to call James to testify. Instead he summoned a surprise witness to the front of the room: Charles John Balfour, captain of HMS *Mercury*. He gave the court yet another account of the shooting that led to Gower Robinson's death. The captain said he had been walking from the British naval hospital on the bluff overlooking Yokohama toward the English Hatoba

18. Suspicion

on his way back to his ship just about six on the evening of February 13. As he turned a corner onto the front of the Grand Hotel, he heard someone shouting "Stop, stop" and saw a flash "high up in the air." He thought it might have come from a rifle or something smaller. And then he heard two reports of gunfire "in quick succession ... in a more horizontal direction."

Balfour's words might have seemed superfluous, but insignificant they were not. He was a respected British official speaking freely rather than under subpoena. That gave his words, which challenged prosecutor Litchfield's account of the killing, greater weight. If Hetherington had come to his encounter with Robinson determined to kill him, why had he fired up in the air rather than directly at his intended victim? If Balfour's eyewitness account was true, and there was no reason to suppose it was not, how could James be guilty of "willful murder"?

That question hung in the air as Litchfield tried in vain to devalue Captain Balfour's testimony. The Royal Navy officer simply reaffirmed what he had just said. The first shot fired from Hetherington's gun had indeed gone straight up in the air.

A pause, and then silence.

Then, nearly an hour into the proceedings, what everyone in court that morning wanted to hear began: James Hetherington testifying under oath in his own defense. He was called to the witness chair and sworn in. Tison had coached him thoroughly beforehand about what he must do now: speak loudly and confidently. Answer questions clearly. Express his feelings without hesitation, even though revealing his private thoughts and emotions would be difficult and possibly embarrassing. His words must strike judge and assessors with maximum force so as to elicit their sympathy and understanding.

Tison had a plan for getting the most out of James as a witness. First, question him about facts. Then tease out his emotional response to them. They would talk about his navy career and state of his marriage before he and his family had come to Yokohama. After that? He must tell the court how he had discovered and reacted to Robinson's pursuit and seduction of his wife. Finally, and most important, he would get James to lay bare before the court the state of his heart, his mind, and even his soul at the moment he shot Gower Robinson. Tison believed and hoped that all of this—information and emotions bound inextricably to one another—would convince judge and assessors, the Yokohama foreign community, and people around the world that James was not guilty of premeditated "willful murder."

It took a long time—a day and a half—for Tison to get James to tell his full story of how and why the killing had come about. He began by having him review for the court's benefit his early life in Dubuque, his becoming a naval officer and service at sea and on shore, and his courting and marrying Bessie. Those particulars need not be repeated here. What Tison wanted James to emphasize for the court was the probity of his character, his faithfulness to his profession, and the depth of his love for his wife. That came easily for James. He told how he had even, after 16 years of service and "with great deal of regret," resigned his commission. Why? Tison asked. "To be with my wife—and at her request," James replied. But when he hadn't found alternative employment and the navy asked him to reconsider, they decided he should stay in the service, even if his assignment to the *Marion* in the far Pacific meant separation. James said he thought the pain of that could be softened by bringing his family to Yokohama. His wife might even "enjoy living in Japan for a few years," he added.

How had the couple coped with months of separation before they reunited in Yokohama? Tison inquired. James said they had written each other letters daily. Had he been confident of Bessie's love and fidelity "without the shadow of a doubt" when they parted? the attorney asked. "Without the slightest doubt," James echoed in reply. "Even if you went away from her for any length of time?" Tison continued. "Any time," James affirmed. And during their separation, "Mrs. Hetherington and your child had been somewhat in your thoughts, had they not?" Tison led on. "Constantly!" James replied.

That portion of his testimony went perfectly. Anyone hearing it would have concluded that James was an honorable officer and a loving husband, that Bessie was a faithful and affectionate wife, and that theirs was a happy American naval family.

But then Gower Robinson.... Tison got James to recount the emotional havoc he brought upon their marriage. He first asked about their reunion on November 2, 1891. James explained how worried he had been when the *Marion* dropped anchor off Yokohama. Had Bessie and Gladys arrived there safely? He didn't know. A boat brought the local papers out to the ship, and one of his fellow officers showed him the list of guests at the Grand Hotel they contained. Finding Bessie's, but not Gladys's name, on the list, he became even more worried, fearing that something might have happened to his daughter. When he raced to their hotel room, he found it empty. He waited and waited. Finally his wife, their baby, and the *amah* came in with another lady.

Was his wife's "greeting what you expected"? Tison interjected. "No," James replied soberly. He had hoped for a warm welcome from Bessie but instead found her "changed ... not the same woman" that he had left back in Iowa. "Could you understand it?" Tison asked. "No," James replied in a soft, obviously unhappy voice.

"You stayed there at the hotel that night?" Tison asked in feigned

18. Suspicion

discretion. At that point, one could have heard a pin drop in the courtroom, as everyone present leaned forward in their seats expecting to hear a tidbit of marital intimacy. They were not disappointed. James reported that Bessie was "estranged and cold ... decidedly so." He couldn't understand her behavior but tried to pass it off as "something which..." Tison interrupted, saying "...would wear off in a few days?" "Yes," James affirmed. "You did not suspect anything was wrong, did you?" "No," the lieutenant replied sheepishly.

What a terrible reunion! What a disappointment! Could anyone in court that day not help feeling sorry for James at that moment?

At that point, a more aggressive, steely-minded prosecutor might have interrupted to call attention to the discrepancy between James's and the Bartletts' accounts of the reunion. Was Bessie waiting eagerly on the landing for her husband's arrival when the *Marion* reached Yokohama? Or had she been elsewhere, as James testified? Who was telling the truth? The captain and his wife, or the lieutenant? Henry Litchfield never raised that question. Perhaps he, too, was overcome by the emotion of the moment.

After a pause, Tison asked James to tell the court about his reaction to Bessie's behavior. He said he at first blamed himself for her frostiness. "You wished she had never come to Japan?" Tison queried. "Yes," James replied, implying that he had been wrong to bring her to Yokohama. Did he consider sending Bessie back home on the very next steamship bound for San Francisco? "Yes," James said. "And then you thought this would be giving up too soon, did you not?" Tison led on. "Yes" replied James. "And you remembered what your married life had been?" "I couldn't forget it," James affirmed. "And you dared to restore it?" the attorney continued. "I did," James responded bravely. That was precisely the affirmation of his character as a loving husband and father that Tison wanted the court to hear. "Your life has been unhappy since that day, hasn't it?" he prompted. "Yes," the lieutenant admitted.

Tison spent the rest of that morning questioning James about suspicion, the taproot feeling that led to everything that followed. How had his feeling that something wrong was going on between Robinson and his wife gotten started? What caused it to grow? And what had he done about it?

James obliged by ticking off Robinson's provocative behavior over the first month he and Bessie had been in Yokohama. November 4: he crowded into their train compartment on the return trip from the emperor's ball. November 10: he monopolized Bessie's attention at a charity concert for Christ Church in Yokohama. November 19: he invited them to his home for dinner but had a friend detain James while Gower talked at length to Bessie in another room. At dinner, he reached under the table as if to touch her, causing her to draw back in alarm. November 29: on a Sunday walk out to the racetrack and back along the seaside of the bluff, he twice rushed ahead of others to be alone with her. Back at his house, he followed her upstairs, where she had gone to recover her veil. Another ploy to be alone with her.

"I knew something was wrong," James said loudly. Tison pinpointed what it was. "Mrs. Hetherington had for a time refused you the privileges of a husband, had she not?" he asked. After a moment's pause to screw up his courage to answer such an embarrassing question about the most intimate details of his marriage, James softly replied, "Yes." Another silent pause followed, giving everyone present time to ponder the seriousness of what had just been said. In the Bible, Paul directed wives to be submissive to their husbands. In the 1890s, they were expected to yield to their husbands' sexual desires, regardless of what they themselves might feel. Why hadn't Bessie given James what he was entitled to? Had Gower Robinson completely alienated her affections for him?

Those questions hung unanswered over the court as James detailed his growing suspicion. Robinson had behaved badly the next evening at the Saint Andrew's Day ball. He had had the duty but arranged for Lieutenant Rogers to take his wife to the dance, James explained. His friend reported the next day that Robinson had been "very attentive" to her, sitting out dances in order to talk to her. "I wrote the man demanding that he stop such inappropriate behavior," James said, "and asked Bessie to tell him so in person." She did so at the skating party that evening and reported that he had shed tears. "That convinced me," James said, "that I had to take action. I wrote him a second letter, demanding that he speak with my wife only in a formal way so as to prevent unnecessary talk." An American naval officer and his wife dared not become the source of scandal. He had hoped that would be "the last of the affair."

It was not.

Tison pressed James to tell more. "This matter now began to take hold on your mind, did it not?" he asked. "Very seriously," James confirmed. And what made it so serious? his defender led on. "The next week we were to go to sea for target practice, to be gone … we didn't know how long," James replied.[1]

At that moment, everyone present was eager to hear more of James's tale of growing suspicion. But Judge Tillotson adjourned court for tiffin.

19

Rage and Remorse

The break for tiffin gave Alexander Tison an opportunity to step back from the morning's detailed testimony to the essence of what he wanted the court to hear that afternoon. He would have James tell more about his deepening suspicion. By revealing in shocking detail correspondence between Gower and Bessie, he would demonstrate how that suspicion drove James from reason to rage. Tison intended the afternoon to be a time of high drama in court.

He began by taking James back to the morning of December 7, 1891, the eve of the *Marion*'s departure for target practice at sea. The lieutenant said he had been so upset then that he thought of "refusing to live any longer" with Bessie. Instead, he hired police detectives to watch the Grand Hotel and report "whatever occurred between my wife and Mr. Robinson." When he started to pack up to go to the ship, she used "every means in her power" to keep him from going and so "I promised to try her again." After that, he continued, she burst into tears, their quarrel ended, and they went to Japan Town to buy things for their baby.[1]

That poignant vignette was meant to make listeners think that James and Bessie were trying hard to save their marriage. They were.

But James's suspicion refused to die. While he was away, he said, he felt "really very much afraid" the detectives would discover "something bad" was going on. "The first thing I did when my ship returned to Yokohama," he continued, "was to get their report." It revealed that while Robinson "seemed very desirous" of seeing his wife, she showed "no desire and no inclination" to see him. Later that day he heard things that made him think the detectives had done a poor job, and still later he learned that Robinson had "tampered" with their report. But at the time, James admitted it had a "very good effect" on his feelings for his wife. They had enjoyed good times together over the following weeks—going on a carriage drive, dancing at an informal leap year party and at a ball, sharing tiffin aboard the *Marion* on Christmas Day, and dining at Mr. and Mrs. Lowder's home that evening.

The morning after Christmas, James said, his suspicion turned to anger. When he went looking for a photograph Bessie had shown him earlier, "it had disappeared" from their room, he reported. He went to Farsari's photography studio and was told that a locket with pictures of baby Gladys and Bessie inside had been made there. At that moment, Tison pulled a locket from his pocket, showed it to James, and asked if it was the one in question. James nodded that it was. He had little doubt that Robinson had had a hand in its making. He also knew Bessie had to have given him the photographs for the locket. That had made me "very angry," he said, so angry that the feeling boiled over into the next morning, Sunday, December 27.

The court already knew from the Bartletts' testimony how terrible for the Hetheringtons that day turned out to be. Now it heard what had happened in even more shocking detail. James revealed that that morning, even before he was fully dressed, he had found a valise crammed with Robinson's notes and letters to his wife in their room. He took out and destroyed all but one of them. Just as he started to open it, Bessie came into the room. She watched, he continued, with an expression of horror on her face as he read the letter.

In court, Tison picked it up, showed it James, and asked, "Do you know this handwriting?" "I do [and] it is Mr. Robinson's," the lieutenant affirmed. "I will read the letter," Tison said. Silence descended on the courtroom as everyone present leaned forward to hear the dead man's words. They were his response to Bessie's plea that he stop seeing her. His words burned with passion, and Tison wanted them to singe everyone's ears as he read them aloud:

> My own, my pet, I don't know whether I should write to you or not, as upon my word I am scarcely responsible for my words or thoughts.[2] I got your letter when I got up this morning. I went to the Stones,[3] and I was thinking of you all the time and—I don't know—but I don't quite remember what happened for several minutes. I seemed all of a sudden to wake up and realized that I was walking about in my bedroom with tears running down my checks. [Tison paused to emphasize.] And laughing out loud. I believe I was mad for a few minutes. "Don't ask me to meet you again." I want to be a better wife and good night and good bye.' It seemed to be all mixed up in my brain. Good God, darling you don't mean you are going to throw me over after all that has passed. Do you realize that you have made me *love* you *worship* you, and are you now going to say I have had enough?—Good bye!—Well, of course you are right and have the right.
>
> As for me, I don't know what is the atter. I went downtown and saw you *smiling* at me as if *nothing* had happened. Have I been mistaken? Have you no heart? No, I cannot believe it. Those great big blue loving eyes looked so true into mine ad did not lie when they *looked* at what your lips said, "I love you" and yet you say "all is over."

19. Rage and Remorse

As for me—well, never mind. People remarked this morning, "What is the matter—are you ill? Your eyes seem to be jumping out of your head! You are as pale as a ghost," and so on, to which I replied that I had been sitting up late at the Stones and that it did not agree with me. My love my love see me *once* more anyhow, and I will swear to you as a man, and a gentleman, that I won't ask you to meet me again, as you don't want to. But let me kiss those lips and eyes once more, and the—well forget if I *possibly can*, "Those golden hours I passed with thee," as I sang to *you* in my song at the concert, I *love* you, my darling, and am crazy after you.

I don't insist, but if you want to do *one* kindness to me, meet me once more ere we part for good. I can't see [you] anymore, so goodbye, my own, my pet.

Yours as ever
G

Don't laugh at this letter, it comes from my heart and I cannot help it if it sounds ridiculous.

Friday *Evening* My Good *Tonight*

Tison paused to let the emotion of the letter sink in on everyone present. There, in his own words, was George Gower Robinson the seducer.

Breaking the silence, Tison asked James how Bessie had reacted when he showed her the letter and told her he was going to send her home without her baby. She was willing to go—on condition that he not show the letter to anyone, the lieutenant replied. And did he make "any threats ... as to what you would do to Mr. Robinson?" Tison queried. "I did," James confessed.

Then he plunged into a heart-wrenching account of the terrible argument that followed. Bessie said she wanted to stay in Yokohama and not be separated from her baby. He started to go and buy food for the child, fearing that if he didn't agree she would kill herself. When he returned, she was in tears. "She said she was going to throw herself into the creek, and she took off her jewelry and threw it aside—everything but her wedding ring. She started to go toward the door as if to go out, but I locked it and put the key in my pocket. She could not go," he reported. How long did the standoff continue? Tison asked. "A half hour or so?" "Oh, longer than that," James responded. Then he said he had relented and told his wife she could stay. How had he felt at that moment? And "did the child have anything to do with you relenting?" Tison asked. "Everything—almost," James replied. Did he think Bessie could be a good mother? "I knew it," James snapped. But for Robinson's influence, "did you think you would have no trouble?" the attorney led James on. "I knew I would not," he affirmed. "I thought she had tried to do right, [but] there was something I could not understand about the whole thing, that I couldn't believe. I did not want to believe that she had done wrong ... [but] that letter I found made me think so," James confessed.

Tison quickly pulled him back to the main point: Why had he let Bessie stay on? "For whose sake—your wife's or your baby's?" "For the child's sake," James answered. Always the dutiful and loving father. That was the impression he wanted everyone to draw from James's story.

Tison then turned to what led to James's clash with Robinson on New Year's Day. He began by reading Gower's letter of Sunday, December 27, 1891—the letter meant for James's as well as Bessie's eyes. In it, he said he would "*ostensibly*" leave Yokohama, "a small place and scandal rife," so that she would not suffer in any way. He apologized "if through my carelessness or worse I have done you any serious damage as regards your relations with your husband and socially here." Humbly begging her pardon, he said he was going to prove his contrition by leaving business, home, and friends behind. Closing with a flourish of chivalry, he wrote, "Allow me now to say good-bye, and say that I regret (more than I can write or express) for your sake and ours that we ever met." He promised he was doing everything he could "to shield your fair name, believe me dear Mrs. Hetherington." He signed the letter, "Yours sincerely, Gower Robinson."

Tison read those words in a skeptical tone. After a pause, he peppered James with questions: Had he known the letter had been written to deceive him? Did he know Robinson had proposed in a second letter that his wife run away to Denver and wait for him to join her there? Did he know that she had told Gower that James had found and read that second letter? Did he know that the very next day Robinson had gotten Brooke Pearson to deliver money to his wife? Sheepishly, the lieutenant admitted that he hadn't thought or suspected anything at the time. "And she did not tell you about that money in her trunk ... until long afterwards?" Tison followed up. "A long time afterwards," James groaned in reply. Was there any reason why his wife should have told Robinson that James had found the second letter? "No," James replied. So "it looked to you like treachery, then did it not?" Tison led on. "Yes, decidedly," James affirmed.

"What was your wife like while all this was going on?" Tison queried. "Very irritable," James answered. She had lost appetite and was losing flesh. "Did she show that she was unhappy?" "Yes," James said. "I tried to understand it. I did not know what it was. It occurred to me that it might be a strife in her feelings, or her feelings might be against me. I did not know." "Did you know that someone told your wife that it was not right to live with a man she did not love?" "Yes," James croaked. And how had he felt when he came ashore and saw his wife on New Year's Eve afternoon?

"Not well in my mind, no," James replied. When he tried to talk with her, she barely spoke. "That was the point when I turned on my heel, left

19. Rage and Remorse

the room, and walked downstairs. I hailed a rickshaw and went down to Japan Town and bought a rawhide whip about three to four feet long. I meant to use it to horsewhip Gower Robinson," he confessed.

He went on to explain how confused his feelings had been. He had left the *Marion* wanting to see baby Gladys but also felt a sense of danger. "I knew it was dangerous … to horse-whip any man. I didn't know whether he—Robinson—was armed or not. I didn't know what might happen." "Did you want to see your wife?" Tison interjected. "No!" James shot back. But when he returned to their room, "my anger toward her softened, and she focused on caring for our child," he added. "What did you do with the whip?" Tison asked. "I threw it on top of the wardrobe," James replied.

Tison then asked where he and his wife had gone that night. James said they had gone to a party at the American naval hospital. They tried to make it look as if nothing had happened between them and planned to leave early so as to reduce the risk of meeting Robinson there. James added bitterly that he hadn't known then, but did now, that his wife had written the man telling him to stay away until after they had left. That way others at the party would think he was complying with her husband's warning to stay away from events where she would be present.

Tison then had James describe his feelings on New Year's Day when friends customarily called on one another. He was terse. Upset when John Frederick Lowder spurned his invitation to visit. Happy when Julia Lowder came to see his wife. Very hurt when Alan Rogers and other *Marion* officers failed to call. What did he think the reason for that was? Tison asked. "The attentions this man Robinson had been paying her—my wife!" James snapped. He felt she had "lost caste, come to be seen as unfit to be the wife of a U.S. Navy officer." That saddened and angered him. "Right after that," he continued, "Bessie called me to the window and pointed at Robinson passing by." The Englishman had cast a lascivious leer at her. Tison interrupted to say that she had tried to persuade him that he was wrong about that, hadn't she? "Yes" and even now, he added bitterly, she insisted she hadn't done so. Obviously the anger he felt then smoldered on to the very moment he was speaking.

Tison pressed on. His aborted attack on Robinson… How did he feel about walking away from the club without doing anything to the man—right or wrong? "Worse, worse, worse," James repeated. "Worse for not having done anything to defend my wife's honor. Worse for fear I had besmirched my reputation. Worse at the thought others might see me as a coward. Worse for giving in to Alan Rogers's importuning and throwing the whip into the harbor."

"What was your state of mind when you went to your room?" Tison asked. "Down-hearted and disheartened.… [I had] a broken-down feeling,"

James replied. "I was consumed by rage, confusion, determination to act, and guilt over not doing so. Then I collapsed into broke-hearted calm," he confessed.

That admission was terrible, judge and assessors were meant to feel. A strong, proud naval officer had been plunged into an emotionally helpless state by Gower Robinson's relentless pursuit of his wife.

Still worse was to come.

It came in a 16-page letter Bessie had written to Gower some time after that terrible New Year's Day 1892. "He had saved it, and his executor found it and gave it to me," Tison explained. "Who had written it," he asked rhetorically. Without a word, he picked up a photograph and showed it to the court. It was a picture of Bessie Hetherington. The very same one he had used to get Robinson's *bettō* to identify the lady his master had carried off to his house on the night of October 23, 1891—the night Bessie had stayed there until dawn.

This was a clever way of letting her speak in her husband's defense—without giving prosecutor Litchfield a chance to cross-examine her.

Tison then proceeded to read the letter aloud.

It began with Bessie's anguished plea: "My God! Gower, why did you write me such a letter? Don't you think I have suffered enough already? I have never lost faith in you until now." She reproached him, saying she didn't believe it when someone told her he had tried to throw all the blame for the development of their relationship upon her. Now, worse still, even though he told her he had burned all her letters, "now you say you have them…. What do you mean by that?"

She explained why James had threatened to horsewhip him on New Year's Day and blamed herself for what had happened. The trouble began when she ordered photographs for him and refused to answer questions about them when James found them. So things "went from bad to worse." "Judge," the nickname he had her call him, "said he believed I was nothing more than your mistress," and he said he would not live with her. He apologized for that, but only yesterday he said "if he ever found out that I had deceived him he would shoot me without one moment's warning."

Their clash set the stage for James's crazed, erratic behavior on New Year's Day. Bessie explained that he had cried out, "Bessie, I shall have to leave the navy. I can't go back to that ship knowing that my brother officers think themselves too good to call on you, the dearest thing in all the world to me." "Poor Judge, he thought he was disgraced in the service," Bessie lamented. He felt even angrier when he went to their hotel room window and imagined "you looked at me…. Coming on top of all he had been suffering, it was too much…. I do believe he was insane for the rest of the day, for at that moment he turned to me and said, 'There is the man who has brought all this on me and, by God! I'll kill him.'"

That led to the aborted horsewhipping at the club, Bessie continued. She believed James "would have lost his mind" had she not reassured him that "every officer in the service was his friend." She sympathized and exclaimed, "Poor, dear Judge, what trouble I have brought on him!" Then she promised, "I shall do all I can to help him forget it. Of course, I promised him I would never receive or write another note to you."

She begged Gower, "You must understand, there is some good in me.... I'm not heartless, far from it. I have suffered, and I think you did [too] but neither one of us has gone through what my husband has, the innocent one."

Bessie's next works reeked with anger. "Can't you understand how I feel? Or is it true that you ran after me for what you could get? How dare you tell me that you supposed I had mounted the high stool of respectability!" Full of self-reproach and anger toward Gower, she added, "I never fell off that stool until I fell into your arms and shall never attempt to mount it again in my own mind."

Bessie then appealed to Gower on the basis of their respective self-interests. Things were getting out of hand. Rumors and misinformation about their relationship were spreading through the community. But all she had ever said about him recently was that she wished "Mr. Robinson will fall in love with the pretty widow." "I wished it from the bottom of my heart" because if he fell in love with someone else whom he could marry, "I would feel as though part of my sin were wiped out."

Her love for him, she said, was "like the dear dead, put away but not forgotten." She could never agree to run away to his sister's home in Colorado, await a reunion with him, divorce James, and then marry him. "If I had fifty divorces I would never be able to marry," she insisted. Why? Because "Judge told me that he would follow me to the other end of the world if he ever heard I had married you, and kill us both."

Bessie demanded that their relationship end because it was ruining relations between navy officers and their wives on the one hand and members of the larger Yokohama foreign community on the other. Just last night, she said, a man at the Grand Hotel had sent his card "with an insulting message on it" to a young woman visiting one of the navy wives. The hotel manager told Lieutenant Lazarus Lowrey Reamey, Admiral Belknap's flag lieutenant, and Captain Felix McCurley (of USS *Alliance*) what had happened. The two officers confronted the man and told him he would be shot if he ever came to the hotel again. Then they shoved him outside. James told her all about it the next morning and said all of his fellow officers were "very indignant about the way men looked at American Navy women." "He said that I had been treated with disrespect."

"We have brought this on ourselves; it can't be helped now," Bessie admonished Glower. "The only thing to do, for our own sake and for all the women in the hotel is to let it [their relationship] die once and for all." Then she warned her sometime lover, "The whole Navy out here is [up] in arms about the way their women have been treated, and it will end in some awful trouble unless we keep quiet."

With that, Bessie offered Gower a bargain of sorts. "I'll watch Judge and keep from saying and doing anything more," she promised. James assumed that Gower was going to leave Yokohama, and she didn't know what he might do when he found out that he had not. "But I will try to manage it," she vowed.

In return, Gower must "take back what you said, don't say you hate me, for I have done nothing to make you do so." James was "the only one who ought to hate me," she continued, but he was doing "all in his power to make life pleasant." So for the sake of "the love you used to have for me, and for my baby's sake," he must burn her letters and "never never write her another one."

"Gower, don't, don't, don't make me suffer any more than I have," Bessie pleaded in conclusion.

Tison stopped and allowed the silence to build. What he had just read was so gripping, so laced with love, and so full of James's rage and Bessie's remorse that he had no need to say another word.

Those in the courtroom that afternoon must have been stunned. Her letter was her confession of indiscretion, infidelity, and adultery—whatever one might call it—in her own words. Here was evidence of her determination to end the relationship with her English lover once and for all. Here was proof of the emotional instability behind James's actions toward her and Gower Robinson. Not least, here was her promise to do what her husband said he wanted her to do: act so as to protect the love and integrity of their family.

Willard Tillotson, like everyone else present, was caught up in the emotion of the moment. He paused, then gaveled the proceedings to an end for the day.

20

Confessions

Those who crowded into the American consulate courtroom just before 10:00 a.m. on Friday, April 8, 1892, might well have expected to hear more about Bessie's letter that had brought the preceding day's session to such a dramatic end. If they did, they were disappointed. Henry Litchfield said not a word about it, and Alexander Tison surprised the courtroom audience, too. Having led everyone to believe he would continue probing James's reactions to what Bessie and Gower had done, he focused instead on relations between James and Bessie. That would preface what everyone wanted to hear: the defendant's confession—his account of how he felt and what he did on the day he shot Gower Robinson.

Tison started by having James reveal that despite appearances to the contrary, he and Bessie had not gotten along well during the first three weeks of January 1892. Their married life was not the same after Robinson had intruded upon it. He had tried to make Bessie love him, he confessed, but not with as much affection as in the past. And he was increasingly afraid about what might happen when the *Marion* went to sea for a long time. James said he feared Robinson would take his wife and the baby, too. That seemed quite possible when he found out that Gower had made a will leaving his money to Bessie. He felt the man "was trying to use the influence of what wealth he possessed to draw my wife from me." Making matters worse, he had learned of the will when he himself was going into debt just to pay the family's Grand Hotel bills. He felt that he was "running a great risk, [that it] was not safe" for him to leave his wife and child in Yokohama while he was at sea. So "I decided," he declared, "that I should make another effort to get my wife to go home"—right away.

Before James could continue, Tison interrupted to point out that Bessie was, in fact, "full of fidelity" to him. In yet another dramatic gesture, he pulled a letter out of his pocket, explaining that Robinson's executor had given it to him. Bessie had written it to Gower barely 48 hours after he had come to her room in the middle of the night January 23–24. It was a stern warning—one made all the more ominous by Tison's tone of voice as he read it. Bessie wrote that she had made up her mind first "to go to no more dances without Judge," her husband, and second to spend her days with her trusted friends, Prince and Princess Lobanov. She advised Gower to "take my advice, stay away from Yokohama as long as it is possible." He needed to do so, she continued, to scotch the rumors floating around about their affair. "Be careful, for God's sake, Gower," Bessie warned in closing.

The letter was yet another proof, in Bessie's own words, of her determination to end the affair with her English lover.

Tison's next step was to show the court how James and Bessie had finally reconciled. He began by getting James to reveal just how frosty their relations had become. He admitted that he stopped kissing her and wrote formal notes to her. He had wanted to send her and the baby home—either to her family's home in Delaware or his father's house in Iowa—so as to "get her out of the influence of this man [Robinson and to a place] … where she would be among proper friends." He promised to continue supporting her and, Tison interjected, "the world would not know that anything had happened." But she was unwilling "to be separated from you," he led on. "Yes," James replied, affirming for the court's benefit her love for him.

They spent a "very miserable day," January 26, arguing, he continued. She was so insistent about not going that she had tried to stop him from reporting for midnight duty aboard the *Marion*. She cried, and cried, and cried, and would not let him leave until he promised she could stay in Yokohama. Fearing he would lose her and their baby if he didn't agree, James said he just gave in to her demand.

Tison then got him to describe his final reconciliation with Bessie. She took the initiative, he began. While they lay next to one another in bed, she started sobbing "as if her heart would break," pouring out her feelings to him in "a long [and] most painful" confession. Did it, Tison asked, "cover everything she had had to do with Mr. Robinson?" "Yes," James replied. She made that confession, he added, on condition that he not do or say anything "which would cause the matter to be … known generally." "Your wife had seen that she had lost your love … and how did that make you feel?" Tison probed. "It made me understand everything. I forgave her immediately [for] everything she had done," James confessed. Tison couldn't resist the temptation to add his own gloss on James's story: he had kissed her, "as a seal of your forgiveness." Then, as if he were reading from a romance novel, he said "she turned from you … fell asleep and slept like a child the rest of the night." "Yes," James replied, affirming the fairy-tale-like ending to this part of his testimony.

That touching account of the Hetheringtons' final reconciliation probably made some in the courtroom misty-eyed. Tison pressed on with questions meant to make them see clearly that all the fault for everything that had happened lay with Gower Robinson. Bessie's confession had "intensified" James's hostility toward him, had it not? he asked. James nodded in agreement but added that it also led to something akin to enlightenment about her seduction. Before her confession, he had "looked upon her as an outraged woman [and seen the] power [that Robinson] had over her." But now, after her confession and his forgiveness, "he understood it in a different way"? Tison led on. "Yes," James replied.

"You forgave your wife; did you forgive the man?" Tison asked. "No, I should say not," James replied. He was so angry that he couldn't sleep that night. And the next morning, although he had promised Bessie not to touch Robinson, he feared he lacked the strength to keep that promise. He had felt miserable while on duty aboard the *Marion* that night and worse still when he saw Bessie and Gladys the next morning. When he went on watch the evening after that, he couldn't put what had happened out of his mind. "I could not think of anything else," James admitted.

Then he confessed that he had deliberately committed a court-martial offense—falling asleep while on watch. So as, attorney Tison clarified, "to escape your thought." Yes, and worse still, James added, Ensign Churchill had seen him do so.

Dereliction of duty, for a United States Navy officer, was something so horrible, so opposed to everything James had been trained to do, so painful to his very soul, that there could be nothing worse. For him to admit that he had fallen asleep on watch was to reveal for the court's benefit the depth of anguish and confusion that he felt on the eve of Gower Robinson's return to Yokohama.

At this point, James had described so fully his emotional state by early February 1892 that only one more piece of evidence was needed to confirm his irrationality in the minds of all who heard him. Tison had James give his version of the hallucinations he had experienced about Robinson coming to get him aboard the *Marion*. His words repeated in essence what Dr. Hessler had already told the court. That was all that was needed to demonstrate that he was in extreme mental anguish. Betrayed by his wife, torn between love and distrust for her, anxious to be a good father to his child, disrespected—in his own mind—by his fellow officers, and made the subject of rumor in the wider Yokohama foreign community, and, most of all, frustrated in his efforts to find some way of driving the intruder out of his family's life—all of that suggested that James Hetherington had been a deeply troubled man when he shot Gower Robinson.

But was he capable of murder? Murder as a rational, willful act? A culpable act?

That was the question that Tison knew James had to answer to the court's satisfaction in his testimony about the events of February 13, 1892.

"When," he asked James, "did you first know Mr. Robinson had returned to Yokohama?" "On the 13th of February, about half past one o'clock," the lieutenant snapped back. But had he suspected the Englishman was back in town before that? When he asked Allen Rogers if he knew Robinson's whereabouts, the answer was "No." Then, James continued, he had gone ashore on Tuesday, February 10, to look for the man who had despoiled his wife. The man who would not stop pursuing her. He didn't find him at the Jujiya bookstore. "You looked about to see if you could find the man in person?" James confessed he had done so—carrying a cane he meant to use on Robinson in case he couldn't grab the man's whip and strike him with it. That sounded like malicious intent.

Before he could say anything more that might damage his defense, Tison pulled James back to events immediately preceding the shooting: what he had done on the afternoon of Friday, February 13. James said that had come ashore just after one and gone to their room at the Grand Hotel only to find her not there. Upset for a moment, he suddenly remembered she had told him she was going to be out with friends. He went outside and ... Tison interrupted him, asking, "Were you looking for anybody then?" "Yes," James replied, but he had not found "anybody." Then he went back to the hotel room, where he stayed until nearly 5:00 p.m., waiting for Bessie to return. She did not. Then, James said, he went out again, this time to the shoemaker's in Aizawa, before returning to the room a final time. Baby Gladys was there with the *amah* and he kissed her four or five times—a goodbye. Then he went downstairs and out the front door of the hotel, where he stopped for a moment on the sidewalk.

At that point, Tison interrupted. Had James been conscious then of his earlier nightmare about Robinson coming after him? "Yes, I remember that," the lieutenant affirmed. "Did your perturbation of mind [about this] grow less as you got further from it, or was it constantly with you?" Tison asked. "Oh," James admitted, "it was constantly with me." That exchange was meant to show the court that fear for his own safety had gripped James's mind just moments before the shooting.

What had he done next? Tison asked. James described how he had come upon Robinson, with a man [Martin Pors] alongside him, heading down the Bund in his trap. He wasn't sure it was the Englishman until the trap got about 20 to 30 feet away from him. At that point, he continued, "I stopped and turned and drew my revolver, and said to Robinson, 'You damned scoundrel, you are back here in Yokohama, are you?'" Tison interrupted to ask James why he had been carrying a gun. "For self-protection and also for the purpose of bringing him to a stop; of holding him up," he answered. Well, Tison pressed James, did Robinson stop or use his whip to drive his horse on? He did not, James explained, "so I started running alongside the trap. I held my right hand and elbow over the wheel and splashboard, holding my pistol up and…" Tison jumped in, asking if he had said anything at that moment. "I called out 'Stop!'" James replied. But Robinson and Pors did not halt. I waited "a perceptible time to see if they made any effort [to halt]." "They did not?" Tison asked. "I fired … into the air," James responded. "I said, 'Stop, God damn you, stop.'" The attorney shot back, "And you fired again?" "I fired again," James responded "… but not at him [Gower Robinson]." Tison queried, "In your mind, was this meant the same way as before?" "Yes," James replied.

Tison cut in to hammer home the key point: "You as a sailor, or a man of the sea, are familiar with firing across the bow to bring a vessel to…." "Yes," James shot back, "there was something of the sort" in his mind at that time. But the trap kept going faster and faster, and he was getting out of breath. Robinson whipped his horse to make it go faster, and "in a short time" after that, James admitted that he had fired a third shot. Just as he did so, he saw a man fall sideways out of the trap. That scared him. "I thought he must be shot … and I stopped there right in my tracks." "What did you intend to do then?" Tison asked. "I was scared. I didn't know what to do," James answered.

He said he then waited for Robinson's friend to get up and come toward him. He didn't know whether the man had been harmed or not, until Pors complained, "Those shots came very near hitting me." Realizing that the man was not wounded, he apologized, "I am very sorry for you, sir." James said he then focused on Robinson, prompting Tison to ask what Pors might have said about him at that moment. The German replied that his friend said, "He is very sorry for what he has done; he has just been telling me all about it." That prompted James to ask back, "If he is sorry, why does he come back to Yokohama?"

Tison then asked how he had kept his arm while he spoke with Pors. James obliged dramatically, saying it had been "Out this way, yes, [bent slightly at the elbow and] with the revolver, not quite straight, with the revolver up, not extended." Tison: What did he remember then about Robinson's being armed? James: "I did not have any doubt in my own mind but that he was armed. I did not see how a man could come back here after he was warned, without being armed himself—after what he had done."

James then said he had watched Robinson stand up, get down from the trap, and turn toward him. "What did you expect him to do?" Tison asked. James replied, "To come for me, or try to get away, one of the two." At that moment, he thought that was his chance "to get the whip [from the trap] and horse-whip him." That did not happen, because only a few seconds after Robinson got out of the trap, he fell where he stood. Then "a number of Japanese" ran up to the Englishman and stood around him.

"Was that the first idea you had he was hurt?" Tison asked. James: "The first I had he was hurt at all." Tison: "You had no intention of shooting him?" James: "No." "The most you meant was to bring him to a stand?" Tison led on. James: "To bring him to a stand and horse-whip him," James replied in a firm voice. "What did you do when you saw him fall?" Tison pressed on. "I dropped my pistol and gave myself up, that was all," James answered.

That was his confession about how he had shot Gower Robinson. But Tison went on, coaching him to make the key point in his own defense crystal clear: he was behaving rationally. He had fired two warning shots—in the air—and then a third from an awkward position at a figure in a vehicle speeding away from him. If he had intended to kill Robinson, and not just to snatch his horse whip so as to attack the man, would he not have fired again? There were, as Tison had reminded the court, still three more bullets in his pistol. If "willful murder" had been his intent at that moment, he could have fired again, again, and again so as to finish Robinson once and for all.

But he did not. He hadn't even moved closer to Robinson so as to shoot again. Instead, James said, "I dropped my pistol and gave myself up, that was all." He turned instead toward Martin Pors and asked what he should do. The German replied he didn't know but "was very sorry and sympathized with me," James continued. At that moment, Tison told the court, a policeman came up and James gave him his weapon. He told the officer who he was, gave him his card, and explained that he was an officer from the *Marion*. Then, James continued, Pors came up to him again and said, "'My dear sir, I am very sorry for you. I want to shake you by the hand." At that moment, James continued, "I shook hands with him and thanked him for his kindness." Cool, normal behavior. It was as if a man crazed and tormented had suddenly turned into a figure of icy reason.

After that remark, all that was left was for James to explain how he had come into the custody of the American consul. After refusing to go with the policeman, he walked for a bit, hailed a jinrikisha, and headed for the English pier, he said. But then another policeman had come up, wanting to take him to the police station. He had objected, stating, "I was an American officer and would not go anywhere but to the Consulate." Again, rational behavior under the circumstances.

At that point, a day and a half after James had begun testifying, Tison sensed that he had said all that he could in his own defense. "That is all the witness has to say … and that is the defendant's case," he intoned. Henry Litchfield indicated he had no wish to cross-examine. Surprised,

20. Confessions

Judge Tillotson asked if he had anything to say in rebuttal. "No," Litchfield replied, the judge could "take the case of the prosecution as closed."

Tison then asked for an immediate adjournment, but Tillotson denied it, saying that he didn't want any more delay in a trial that had already gone on for 10 days. He and the assessors had other business to attend to. Tison objected to continuing. He protested that at the moment his mind was "not in order; the whole matter is disjointed and disordered" and pleaded for more time to prepare his summary defense. Judge Tillotson then decreed a short recess so that he could consult with the assessors about how best to proceed. When they returned, he declared the court adjourned until the next morning.

The courtroom fell silent, and the reporters present scurried to their offices to begin writing their accounts of the day's proceedings. Did they or anyone who read their words later that evening believe that James had, in the words his attorney had coaxed out of him, shown that shooting Gower Robinson had been a reasonable act?

Alexander Tison had one more chance to convince them that they should.[1]

21

Summing Up

Saturday, April 9, 1892. The 11th day of the trial. The day that Lieutenant James Henry Hetherington's fate would be decided. Determined to make that happen, Judge Tillotson gaveled court into session early—at 9:15 a.m., to be precise.[1] Then he directed Alexander Tison to begin his summing up.

He obliged by pointing to James sitting at the defense table and proclaimed, "This man has been in hell [but] I have felt for days that [his] case … was won." Some have said, he continued, that because an American was on trial before an American tribunal, the result would be a foregone conclusion. However, he believed that "the day the truth was known the defendant would be safe in the hands of a jury of Hottentots." Then he called the judge and assessors' attention to the importance of the case they were about to decide. It "is one of the great murder trials of the world," he proclaimed, "a unique murder trial … [that] will be remembered long after we have been forgotten."

Tison then changed his tone completely, spewing forth the anger he had felt while listening to Robinson's friends testify. They had not told the full truth about all that they knew. He had made only "some breaches, some openings" in the wall of silence that surrounded Robinson in life and death. "A society has been formed," he intoned, "in which … concealment … was made to wear the … appearance of virtue." He had persisted, he said, with the help of others who knew the facts, even if Robinson's friends withheld that knowledge. Pointing to James, he said proudly, "I believed he could be saved in spite of them."

"I venture to suggest," Tison continued, "that a body of friends, a 'youthful parcel of noble bachelors,' banded together not to talk … [so] as now to prevent this community … from … understanding what had occurred. But Mr. Blanchard is an exception. While he had done wrong by serving as messenger between Gower and Bessie, he came to tell the truth about it." Tison then shot back at local people who had complained that the trial had been delayed so long because of the difficulty of obtaining evidence. "But there had been no difficulty in knowing the truth. I knew that in its ghastly horror ... the first time I saw the defendant."

Tison then attacked John Frederick Lowder, albeit not by name. The preeminent barrister in Yokohama had had in his possession letters from Mrs. Hetherington to Robinson "that I presumed did not exist." Worse still, "while I was getting this story in sobs from a broken-hearted woman, distracted by a fretful child," there was "a gathering of gentlemen who ... over a dinner in the midst of their wine were reading aloud these letters."

That may have been why the British minister (Sir Hugh Fraser), Tison alleged, "spared no effort to bring himself here."[2] The law was against that. "More than a hundred years have passed since any one representing the sovereign of England could assume to say who should take part in an American court of justice.... Does Queen Victoria ... send her chief representative here in Japan as counsel to intervene, to add the weight of his strength to tear down a sinking man who has smitten to death the ravisher of his wife?"

Tison then attacked those who had said "the head of the defendant ... should be pounded into a pulp for what he has done." Thanks to them, he asserted, "Injurious lies have been carried from this place to America [and] been sown all over that country. In the bloody sweat of this agony, Lieutenant Hetherington has been stung by pismires [ants smelling of urine]." The English press had been no less wrong in its coverage of this affair, he continued, for it put out "that this matter causes a division of feeling which may result in collision between English and Americans residents in Japan. Nothing could be farther from the truth," he snapped. "No one thought of mob violence or lynch law."

Tison then attacked those who had given false witness: Mr. Robinson's boy (Nakatani Masanosuke), who confessed to lying. "The Italian Pachini, the night watchman," who "continues to go about the streets" spewing "falsehoods ... about Mrs. Hetherington." Tison could not rid himself of his disgust for the man. Pachini would "as soon stab a lady's reputation as to do any other dirty piece of work." But rather than condemn one false witness, he would rather reproach "those fine gentlemen and ladies who profess to have a more elevated standard [but] who have been the hucksters round about" of false stories.

They had prejudged the Hetheringtons, Tison alleged. Bessie was not "all bad." That was clear from her 16-page letter to Robinson that he had read aloud to the court. Remember, he appealed to his listeners, that "amidst her sorrow and disgrace," she had praised her husband, James, as the real victim in this case. And he had done the right thing by taking her back after she confessed her infidelity to him. The defendant, Tison said with a flourish, had given him a quotation, paraphrased from the prophet Malachi and written in his own hand, that explained why he forgave his wife. "Tears," Tison intoned, "are shed on God's altar for one who forsakes the love of his youth."[3]

How, at that moment, must James have felt? Could tears have fallen from his eyes and from those of others in the courtroom?

Tison then shifted his tone from pathos to anger against yet another group of Robinson's friends who tried to pervert the course of justice. They repeatedly suggested to him, he revealed, that "if I would tell them all that I knew about this affair, enough to get the defendant acquitted," they would obtain the help of "certain other persons ... to see that a plea of guilty of manslaughter was accepted by this court." That was, in effect, a plea bargain, a proposal that could only have sprung from the mind of a lawyer. Tison suspected that had been John Frederic Lowder but again, out of discretion, did not mention his name. He simply said, "I did not see my way ... to barter and traffic with a man's life or his liberty in that way." Lest that sweeping charge be misunderstood, Tison quickly added that prosecutor Litchfield had not been part of that effort to convict Lieutenant Hetherington of manslaughter.

There would be no plea bargain in this case.

Tison then continued in dramatic fashion, alluding to the terrible earthquake that had shaken Japan just when Robinson began his affair with Mrs. Hetherington. A portent of trouble to come. He noted that Gower's cart in which he had abducted her to his house in the middle of the night, the same one that later carried him away from her hotel room after another tryst, still traveled the streets of Yokohama. He pulled from his pocket the two ten-dollar bills that had been given to the Hetheringtons' *amah* to buy her silence. Another proof of the deceased's deceptiveness. Concluding this portion of his argument, Tison proclaimed Gower Robinson was "a man of rare and engaging manners, of infinite charm, so radiant and full of life, and potent in its activities" that he deceived Bessie Hetherington and used his friends to hide his misdeeds. The man was shameless.

Bessie and James? They, by contrast, knew in the end what was right and what they must do. Remember, he argued, what had gone on between them on New Year's Day 1892. She had come to him with "the scarlet mark" (the letter *A* for adulterer in Puritan New England as Nathaniel Hawthorne had told the tale) upon her forehead. She sobbed and confessed that she had sinned. Yet he did not respond like Othello, the wrathful and jealous husband in Shakespeare's play who killed his wife in the mistaken belief that she had given herself to another man. Instead, James, the husband who had sworn "his wrath against her ... [had] take[n] that discarded wife to his heart."

21. Summing Up

Why had he done that? That was "the riddle of the sphinx"—unless one thought back to the testimony that James himself had given. Did it not demonstrate his nobility, his commitment to family, and, most important, his love? Love, true love for his wife and daughter, was the reason James forgave Bessie. Love for his family was also the motive behind his actions on the night of February 13, 1892.

At that point, Tison pleaded again for sympathy for James. "Who has woe like this man," he asked, "whose wife and baby had come halfway round the globe, who he thought were coming to a civilized community—who were pounced upon?" For the villain, the blackguard, the seducer Robinson, stealing away "one was not enough—both must be taken." James "saw that there was no help." What could he do?

Then Tison apologized for jumping to a very different subject. He knew many people had expected him to introduce in evidence Gower Robinson's deathbed letter to Admiral Belknap—the one that begged mercy for his assailant and proclaimed, "I fully and entirely forgive him."

"I have that letter in my pocket now," Tison said, putting his hand in his pocket for emphasis. Others may have thought that "the expressions of magnanimity which it was supposed to contain" would be used to produce "their proper influence on this court." That is, to make it show mercy toward Lieutenant Hetherington in whatever judgment it handed down.

Tison would have none of that. He proclaimed, "I would rather see him go, and the defendant would rather go, with level and unfaltering step to the gallows than owe his life to what some people have called the magnanimity of the man who is dead." He hoped Mr. Robinson's friends would understand the truth: despite his "gay and debonair manner, [despite] the smile on his lips, ... there was a worm at his heart." Robinson had drunk "the delirious and forbidden cup of the moment and put behind him a world of happy days."

That lofty language was meant to remind everyone of the ugly, the uncomfortable, and the essential truth. George Gower Robinson was the villain in all that had gone on leading to his death. He had seduced Mrs. Hetherington. He had tried to take her and her child from her husband. He left James Hetherington no choice but to act against him in order to defend his honor and his family.

Tison then hastened to close the case for the defense. Turning the court's attention back from facts and emotions to the law, he pointed out that there were legal precedents for bringing in a verdict of acquittal. The Sickles case, for one. In it, "the intent of the injured husband went hand in hand with the deed (murder) and yet a jury in the capital of our nation saw no blame in the accused." There was also another precedent—in England.

In the case of a father who killed the man who had molested his son, "an English jury on English soil refused to call that murder."

Then there was the common law, which "excuses and applauds self-defense." One could defend one's person or property and, if need be, take the life of another man in so doing. That was what had happened on the night of February 13, 1892, Tison asserted. He argued that "an offense against the family is worse than robbery or assault on the person." "Shall a man not be permitted to defend his wife and his baby?" he asked rhetorically. Tison conjured up a vision—not one of rage, jealousy, or revenge. It was, rather, an image of James's wedding, of the vows he had exchanged with Bessie barely three years earlier. James, Tison said, "remembered his vow to love, cherish, and protect her—aye, against herself if need be, against all other harm—to protect her at any cost." Those promises, Tison insisted, demanded in his mind that he attack Gower Robinson.

But was the lieutenant insane at that moment? Was temporary insanity the reason why the court should find him not guilty? Tison vigorously rejected that argument. "What we are trying to show is how sane Lieutenant Hetherington was," he reaffirmed. "I could have called experts for testimony; but if I did so they would not have been physicians. I should have sought for a man who had a happy home and a wife who loved him and had his love."

In other words, the defendant had only done what any other man in the same situation would have done. That was no crime. With those words, Alexander Tison brought his defense of Lieutenant James Henry Hetherington to a close.

He then addressed a final appeal to Judge Tillotson and the four assessors. He was glad to have brought the defendant before them. "I leave him in your hands with confidence, assured that you are about a right and true deliverance to make, restoring him to his liberty, to his country and ... to those whom he wears in his heart's core."

A moment of silence followed. Willard Tillotson then directed Henry Litchfield to sum up the case for the prosecution.

Litchfield was a patient man. He had sat through days of defense witnesses' testimony and rarely objected to what they said. He was a serious, sober man. Only once—when three times he had asked if there had been "criminal intimacy" between Gower and Bessie, only to have Judge Tillotson direct the witness not to answer that question—had he shown any sign of emotional intensity. He was a quiet, scholarly sort of lawyer—a man with an almost religious sense of the majesty of the law. He approached the task before him that April morning with a sense of grave responsibility. He intended to prove James Hetherington's guilt in precise legal terms, rationally, with all the intellectual force of English understatement. The facts, he believed, when presented in tandem with the terms of the law, would produce justice.

Beneath his sober demeanor, however, Litchfield was as emotional as any man. By the time he rose to speak, he was angry. Very angry at Alexander Tison, for what he had just said and for the way he had said it. He knew he had to give vent to that anger before he could proceed to make his case in a sober, coldly rational way.

So Litchfield lashed out against Tison.

Unlike him, he would be brief and matter-of-fact. Tison had done wrong three times. First he had painted a misleading portrait of the three principals in the love triangle that led to the murder. Then he had alleged that key witnesses had been suborned to give false testimony. The night watchman, the Italian Pachini, he insisted "had certainly plenty to tell." And Robinson's boy Nakatani "had been thinking for himself." Tison had been naive to rely on his testimony and that of other Japanese witnesses. "When the defense counsel had a little more experience of the Japanese," he said, "he will find that when a Japanese thinks for himself, he almost invariably thinks wrong." That remark betrayed his belief—one shared by many other expatriate residents of Japan—that the natives simply did not measure up intellectually to white Americans and Europeans.

Topping off his attack on Tison and the validity of the evidence he had presented, Litchfield said that Robinson's friends, whose testimony Tison had questioned, knew their own minds. They had neither lied nor concealed facts but simply spoken the truth.

Litchfield then reminded everyone that his obligation as prosecutor was to show "that a human being who was identified, was on a certain date done to death within the jurisdiction of this court, and that the person who inflicted the wound by which that human being was destroyed was within the jurisdiction of this court and was acting deliberately and unlawfully." "Those were my sole duties," Litchfield asserted. He had fulfilled them. "There can be no doubt," he said forcefully, that the points he offered in evidence "have clearly and satisfactorily been established."

In other words, his facts were absolutely correct while those the defense had presented were dubious.

Litchfield then challenged Tison's depiction of Gower Robinson as a kind of Svengali, a man who overnight changed from being "a paragon of good" to a person who succumbed to "vices and vicious propensities [and] used the power that was in him to undo the wife of the accused." That was not how the love affair that led eventually to murder had begun, Litchfield asserted. Responsibility for it did not rest solely on Gower Robinson's shoulders. It was not a one-sided affair.

Science, the prosecutor claimed, not singular passion, explained correctly what had happened. "One power is useless until it finds some affinity with which to come in contact," he said. "When the positive and negative currents of an electric instrument meet," he reminded the court, "they cause mischief." But apart, they "are harmless." That was a way of saying that Bessie was as responsible as Gower for what had developed between them.

Litchfield then turned back to the law, "the law which holds the life of man sacred, which says you shall not take life without excuse or justification, you shall not for your own purpose recklessly endanger life." He went on to remind everyone that murder in the common law was "the deliberate killing of another unlawfully, willfully and with malice." The law also allowed that when a man "upon gross provocation" inflicts such injury, "the circumstances of provocation shall be taken into consideration as palliative of the offence." That would be true if an attack followed "in hot haste and hot blood" upon the provocation that the attacker had suffered. But the law, Litchfield insisted forcefully, "will not allow a man [to] take vengeance by himself, after he has had time to brood over his wrongs, to consider and act upon them." That, he implied, was exactly what James Hetherington had done.

He then reviewed for the court's benefit how James had brooded once he discovered Gower's letter to Bessie professing his love for her. He had taken deliberate steps meant to harm Robinson: going to his office intending to horsewhip him, only to be restrained by his own friends. Then again, on February 10, just days before the attack, he had gone in search of Robinson "armed with a stick or a cane." And on the night of the attack, Hetherington had admitted that he sought out the man, intending "to horse-whip the deceased with his own horse-whip." There was proof, Litchfield insisted, of intent to harm.

The prosecutor then challenged James's statement of how the attack on the night of February 13 had played out. His claim that he intended to use Robinson's own horsewhip to attack him was not credible. "A cane or a birch or a cowhide would be a more convenient, a more apt and more probable instrument to use to inflict punishment upon a fellow man." The notion that he had fired shots in the air to get Robinson to stop his trap was equally implausible. Would a man who heard shots be likely to stop?

And then there was the weapon that the defendant used—a revolver, a weapon of offense, not defense. If Lieutenant Hetherington had gone out that night carrying it, would not its very weight and size have reminded him that he was armed? And would that not have given him "time to reflect [beforehand] on his actions and upon the consequences?"

That first rhetorical question was meant to elicit a firm "yes" in response to the second in the minds of the judge and assessors.

21. Summing Up

All of that, together with Hetherington's own account of how he had followed Robinson's trap, Litchfield insisted, belied the notion that he was armed for self-defense on the night of the shooting. Coming up behind the trap, he would have had the advantage if, as had been alleged without proof, Gower Robinson had drawn a weapon with which to shoot at him. Hetherington had not acted in self-defense on that night, Litchfield insisted. Nor was there "recklessness in his action." "He—the assailant—goes into the fray armed, reckless of human life, and that fatal deed is done," the prosecutor proclaimed.

"I have to ask you, sir, and you, gentlemen," he said, addressing Judge Tillotson and the four assessors directly, "whether this was not deliberate; whether this did not come within the definition of the common law." He then offered to refer, "for your Honor's guidance," to the law on the subject. Finding that suggestion demeaning, Tillotson shot back that he "had [i.e., he knew] the law."

Litchfield finished by reaffirming his most basic point: the defendant had acted with deliberate intent on the night he shot and killed the victim. The court must consider "whether in the face of the clear evidence I have submitted, substantiated by the evidence of the accused, there was deliberate shooting" when Hetherington encountered Robinson riding in his trap. Or, alternatively whether what happened at that moment was "such a reckless use of the weapon, such an utter disregard of human life, that taking this man's life was in the circumstances unjustifiable, willful, and premeditated." In either case, James Henry Hetherington would be guilty of murder.

The two summary statements—Litchfield's for the prosecution and Tison's for the defense—put the question the judge and the assessors would have to decide squarely before them: Was James Hetherington guilty or innocent?

Willard Tillotson, the man ultimately responsible for answering that question, was not ready at that moment to consider, let alone answer, it. He simply adjourned the court for two hours for lunch.

22

Verdicts

Judge Tillotson had adjourned the court until 2:30 p.m. that Saturday. By that time, the courtroom was packed with spectators eager to hear the final verdict in this case. Would Lieutenant Hetherington, who sat quietly next to his defender, Alexander Tison, at the front of the room, hang? Go free? Be sentenced to prison? Minutes ticked by in suspense. Murmurings in the crowd gave way to expectant silence.

Then, after someone noticed that Henry Litchfield was absent from the prosecutor's table, another wave of muffled conversation passed from the rear to the front of the courtroom. Where was he? Why wasn't he here? Didn't he know that the culminating moment of the trial was at hand? Nearly an hour passed as people quietly exchanged thoughts about Litchfield's absence.

Finally, around 3:20 p.m., the door at the front of the room opened. The four assessors, followed by Judge Tillotson, came through it and took their seats. Another few minutes of silence passed. Enough for people to ask themselves more questions. Why were the five men late in returning to the courtroom? Had they disagreed about a verdict? Or were they just discussing what it should be? Was the verdict going to be given any minute?

Willard Tillotson gave the spectators an answer to their questions. He said he was "very sorry that the honorable counsel for the prosecution is not present." He "certainly expected he would be." Then he offered an excuse—a plausible reason—for Henry Litchfield's absence. Perhaps the prosecutor had misunderstood when the proceedings were to resume. Did the judge not speak with a note of sarcasm in his voice?

Whatever the reason for the prosecutor's absence, Tillotson was not going to delay the proceedings any longer.

If this had been a trial in a 21st-century American or British court, he would have at that point instructed the jurors. They would then have left the room. And everyone would have had to wait still longer for them to return their verdict, which would be read to the court. But this was a

22. Verdicts

19th-century American consular court in Yokohama with its own, unique procedures. The assessors were not jurors—only advisers to the judge. He would read his verdict and then they would formally announce their concurrence with it.

Willard Tillotson began reading his verdict by thanking both attorneys for the evidence they had presented. "I don't know how we could have got along without them in ascertaining the truth," he said. And, he added, neither of them had left anything undone in presenting their respective arguments.

This case, he asserted, was "of such unusual nature" for three reasons. First, the audience it attracted. Not just "residents in the entire East," but also "a vast number of people throughout the whole world" were paying attention to it. Second, its principals. The victim was a man "so prominent and universally known" that his violent death came as "a great shock to this cosmopolitan community." The accused is both "a man of … rank, bearing an honorable record" and the cause of the victim's death. That "naturally created the presumption that the deceased had given him great provocation." Third, its impact. "A heavy burden … has pressed upon the minds of the people of this port for nearly two months." At this point, Tillotson continued, "there is a general feeling of relief that the trial is now at an end."

At this moment, James may well have felt anything but relief. His life, his future, his career, his marriage—all hung in the balance of what the court's judgment might be. Willard Tillotson did not provide quick relief from that tension.

Instead, before turning to the legal basis for his judgment, Tillotson assured everyone that he and "the associates who have so patiently and attentively listened to the testimony" [had] "tried to make the most searching inquires possible into the facts and law of the case." He then explained that three judgments were possible under the "rules of law governing our Consular Court." The first was murder. The second was manslaughter. And the third… "If we find that the accused shot and killed George Gower Robinson, and other facts existed which justify or excuse him, he may be found not guilty."

The judge then recited from the legal authorities defining "what constitutes murder, reduces the crime to manslaughter, or what justifies or excuses homicide." "Murder occurred when a person of sound memory and discretion unlawfully kills any human being … with malice … or aforethought either express or implied." But "malice," Tillotson continued, was so broad a term that it was sometimes necessary "on account of peculiar mitigating circumstances" to "reduce the crime to manslaughter even where malice exists." Manslaughter was simply the unlawful killing of another "without any malice express or implied."

Justifiable homicide could be that committed by a lawful executioner; an act committed "as a necessary incident to an arrest." It could also be an act taken to prevent "any atrocious crime." Or it could be an act committed by a defendant who "at the time of the fatal blow was deprived of the power of self-control by the provocation he had received." In that instance, the key question would be "whether any ordinary man would under the same provocation probably be deprived of the power of self-control."

Tillotson then pointed out that the purpose of law was "to prevent, not to punish crime." If a man had done "only what an average man would do if placed in the same circumstances," it would be "persecution" to punish him. That would injure rather than protect society. "The law," he intoned "does not punish to avenge the dead but to protect the living."

He then posed the essential question before the court: "Was the defendant in such a condition that he was deprived of the power of self-control in the evening for February 13, 1892?" The defending and prosecuting attorneys had already reviewed that question extensively so there was no need for him to go over it again. Thus all that remained was for him to give "the conclusions arrived at by the court."

Doing so required him to retrace the "long train of circumstances" leading up to "the culminating point in this sad affair," His very first words about what had happened hinted at what his judgment would be. "For more than two months ... the defendant had been trying to avert trouble." But the deceased "continued to pursue the wife ... almost fiendishly." Throwing the blame for what followed on the woman did not affect the defendant's position. He believed that his wife and his child "were *his* castle.... For reasons of his own, he was battling to hold his home together for the sake of his child." The provocation he suffered was not ordinary but continual, and the longer it went on "the fiercer the flames would rage" in his heart.

Tillotson then pointed out that during "all those long weary weeks that the conflict of emotions was contending in his mind and heart," the defendant never made any suggestion of shooting Gower Robinson. Instead, he "seemed to think that if he could get at him ... [to] cowhide [whip him] and by so doing humiliate the man, his wife would probably be safe from pursuit."

When was the turning point in James Hetherington's behavior? Tillotson asked. Early in December 1891, he had learned that his suspicion that Robinson was the cause of his wife's changed behavior was correct. Then on February 2, Bessie confessed, telling him of "that wild midnight ride to Robinson's house" on October 23, 1891. She told her husband "everything" of the Englishman's "threats and pursuits—whether all or more than actually took place," the court could not decide. The point was that by early February, "the deceased having broken his word of honor so solemnly given so many times" not to continue his pursuit of Mrs. Hetherington, "the defendant was undoubtedly ready to believe anything" about the man. From what the officers of the *Marion* testified, it was clear that the defendant "was evidently laboring under great mental disturbance. From the wrongs inflicted on him by Robinson as detailed in court," Tillotson concluded, "I can readily believe that he would not probably be able to control himself" if they met.

Tillotson then parsed James's actions on the night of the attack. The lieutenant, he concluded, "undoubtedly intended to inflict some chastisement, but when he found Robinson was getting away, he lost his self-control.... I believe he did not exactly know what he was trying to do, or wanted to do, or how to do it. His one object seems to have been to protect his home and save the mother of his child from ruin." Judge Tillotson then concluded, "I cannot conceive how any man, under the same circumstances, could have maintained his self-control on meeting the cause of his sorrow that day."

Up to that moment, everyone in the court had listened "with the most profound silence" to Tillotson's reading of the judgment. But that last sentence caused the audience to applaud vigorously and loudly. So much so that the marshal, Richard McCance, had to shout "Order! Order!" repeatedly. When the noise finally died down, Judge Tillotson read out his official opinion and his verdict:

"I think he [James Henry Hetherington] should not be convicted of murder or any other crime. There is no evidence in this case of premeditation, at least satisfactory to the court. But I do find the defendant had such provocation that under the pressure of grievances his mind had been strained to such an extent that he was not responsible for his actions at the moment the fatal shot was fired. Therefore, I find him 'Not Guilty.'"

Those words triggered another outburst of applause. This time Marshal McCance did not even try to silence it. The noise was joyous and judgmental all at once. An innocent man had been found free of crime. The court had come to the right conclusion. And, at long last, the trial that had gripped the emotions and attention of the Yokohama expatriate community was over.

When the clapping ceased, the four associates affirmed their concurrence in Judge Tillotson's verdict. That made it official and complete.

Alexander Tison had the honor of speaking the last words at the trial. Rising slowly from his chair, he turned toward Judge Tillotson and the associates. He thanked them on behalf "first of my client and then on behalf of his wife and child" and then himself. Then he addressed Henry Litchfield's absence. It was regrettable, but he was sure that the prosecutor would have wanted him to thank the court for "the courtesies which he, as well as myself, has received from the first to the last in this trial."

A third round of applause, rendered in praise of Tison's final words, rippled across the room. Then Judge Tillotson and the assessors rose and left the courtroom. At that point, if reporters' accounts are to be believed, James Hetherington and Alexander Tison turned toward one another and shook hands vigorously. They then retreated in opposite directions—the attorney toward the front door, the freed defendant toward the rear door of the consulate building. The trial of Lieutenant James Henry Hetherington, U.S. Navy for shooting George Gower Robinson, Esq., was over.

What happened immediately thereafter had been carefully devised to avoid any appearance of national prejudice within the Yokohama expatriate community. An open carriage, hired by a committee of "some 260 gentlemen, chiefly English and German," and without a single American in its number, waited outside the front gate of the consulate. A congratulatory banner had been prepared, and a group of men had volunteered to replace the horses and pull the carriage with the vindicated lieutenant in it through the streets to the Grand Hotel.

That did not happen. Instead, at James's request, the horse and carriage drove around to the rear entrance to the consulate. He came out the back door, climbed into the carriage, and took his seat. Then, amid repeated cheers for "'the defender of our homes,'" he was driven to the Grand Hotel, where Bessie and little Gladys awaited him.[1]

That end to the trial had, obviously, been carefully scripted. Those who planned it were certain James would be found not guilty. Alexander Tison was sure that would be the verdict as well. James himself must have been confident to have acceded in advance to such a carefully nuanced, triumphant but not taunting end to the trial.

No one underestimated the damage that the affair, whether termed "the Robinson murder" or "the Hetherington affair," had done to the harmony of the Yokohama expatriate community. Justice had to be seen to have been done. And the damage done to the social fabric of the community had to be repaired. Indeed, the reputation of the community, which in the words of a later historian was an "outpost of civilization,"[2] had to be restored. The world, no less than the local community, had to believe that justice had been done.

But was it? Did the American consular court in Yokohama deliver justice? Was it right that Gower Robinson lay dead in his grave and James Hetherington walked out of court a free man? Willard Tillotson had delivered his judgment, but his verdict was far from the last word on this case.

No sooner had he finished speaking than reporters rushed from the courtroom to their offices to begin writing their accounts of the trial's

22. Verdicts

end and telegraph them to the world. Captain Bartlett was not far behind them. He hurried to the *Marion* and drafted a brief message to the secretary of the navy: "Hetherington acquitted." He handed it to a junior officer who took it to the Yokohama telegraph office as quickly as he could.

The captain was scooped by James himself. Immediately after hugging and telling Bessie the verdict, he dashed downstairs to the hotel's mail and telegraph clerk's office. He drafted a nine-word message: "Yokohama April 9.-Acquitted. Bessie vindicated. Notify Dubuque. Hetherington." He addressed it to Emlen Hewes, in Wilmington, Delaware, knowing Bessie's father would send it on to his own. James handed it to the clerk, and what would be the first word of the verdict to reach America went out on the wire immediately.[3]

News of the verdict raced west around the world by telegraph, reaching Paris, London, New York, and Washington before April 9 ended in local time, just in time for Sunday morning editions of local newspapers. In America, headlines joyously proclaimed "Hetherington Free!" In Britain, only a few somber sentences announced the verdict in the killing of George Gower Robinson. Those first reports portended many differences of opinion over the verdict in the case of United States versus James Henry Hetherington, Lieutenant, United States Navy.[4]

Those differences proved sharpest in Yokohama. While the *Tokyo Asahi Shimbun* gave its Japanese readers only a brief matter-of-fact report on the verdict in the trial, the English-language newspapers reported strong differences of opinion within the expatriate community over it. "Broils," that is to say sharp verbal encounters that threatened to boil over into fisticuffs, were reported at the United Club. Britons and Gower's staunchest defenders disputed the court's findings. Americans and people inclined to view the trial outcome more in empathetic than in strictly legal terms found no fault with the verdict.

Those differences were reflected in newspaper accounts that appeared immediately after the trial ended. The British-owned *Japan Herald* called the proceedings "a farce" and the verdict an "astounding decision." The assessors "did not take into proper consideration" the evidence that had been presented at the coroner's inquest. Hetherington had been perfectly rational when he killed Robinson. That, owner John Henry Brooke and his editor daughter, Gertrude Smith, concluded, was perfectly obvious from the fact that he had armed himself, stalked his victim, and shot the man "in one of the most vital parts he could choose … [so as] to make certain of taking his life." Nonetheless, the *Herald* conceded, Tison the defense attorney had "behaved in an exceptional manner in … this sad affair." "We congratulate him," the paper concluded.

Captain Francis Brinkley, the Anglo-Irish owner-editor of the *Japan*

Mail, was not at all sure that praise was deserved. If Robinson had truly "outraged," that is seduced or raped Bessie Hetherington, why had he not been "arrested and held to answer in a court which might be relied on to ensure justice being done"? he asked. There was "no more serious charge short of murder itself." And if proven, "it would have relieved the husband of the responsibility of taking any other steps against the violator of the sacredness of his married life." That would have been "the most effectual shield" of his wife's honor he could have used. In short, the actual trial that produced a dubious verdict could have been avoided.[5]

The correspondent for the *North China Herald*, who had come up from Kobe to report on the trial, put forward a more nuanced view of the verdict and the local community's reactions to it. "The feeling is, I think, one of guarded disapproval" of the verdict, he wrote. People thought Lieutenant Hetherington "should have been given *some* punishment." But at the same time, they sympathized with him because the trial revealed that Robinson's conduct toward Mrs. Hetherington was "utterly unprincipled and abandoned." His treatment of her husband was "false and hollow." Indeed, for anyone who "knew the man's fair and captivating manner, his characteristically affable and agreeable bearing," it was "hard to believe him the paragon of blind self-indulgence and evil" that the trial proceedings "represent him to have been."

The trial, in this observer's view, did, nonetheless, strike a balance in revealing truth. "Private accounts" spoke of much more that could have been revealed to "blacken the case." But attorney Tison showed "highly credible guard" against bringing a lot more presumably "salacious and/or defamatory material into court."

This correspondent could not resist proffering his own verdict on the broader consequences of the trial. Its "unsavoury proceedings" revealed "anything but health and soundness in some quarters of the Yokohama foreign community." There were those who preferred to hide the truth, to put a "brazen face on things and seek to bluff and 'brave' it out." They were wrong. If it "cleared the air somewhat ... the terrible affair will not have wholly evil effects." If "this sad affair in all its details ... introduces a healthier moral tone in some of the elder men of Yokohama as well as the younger fellows," then Gower Robinson "will not have died a merited death in vain."[6]

What they read in the Yokohama papers likely mattered little, however, to James's fellow officers on the *Marion*. They knew justice had been done and wanted to reward Alexander Tison for his part in obtaining it. Much to his surprise, they approached Captain Bartlett just after quarters on the morning after the trial ended with a purse containing $200. They asked him to use the money to buy a gold watch for Tison in recognition

22. Verdicts

of his services. The captain ordered the gift to be made and inscribed at Farsari's jewelers. The officers looked on later with pride when Bartlett presented the watch to Tison and thanked him profusely for what he had done. In their view, he had made a brilliant defense of their shipmate and won what most certainly was a just verdict.[7]

Britons in China and Australia and those "at home" in England did not vent their feelings about the justice of the trial or appropriateness of its verdict as fervently and quickly as their countrymen in Yokohama. They had followed the trial daily, thanks to brief summaries of its proceedings sent by telegraph. The *Manchester Guardian* editor who published them knew that the scandal, murder, and trial in Yokohama had stirred intense feelings among his paper's readers. He planned to profit from them by printing and selling a 40-page pamphlet capped by news of the verdict. It appeared right away, but six weeks passed before a full account of the trial's ending and the official text of the verdict brought the pamphlet to an end.

If she read the barebones account of the trial's end in her newspaper or, worse still, the full version of "the tragedy in Yokohama" in the *Guardian*'s pamphlet, Adaliza Letitia Robinson, Gower's mother, may have felt her grief and sense of loss at his death deepen. She, and others who had known him, may well have concluded that the American court had rendered anything but a just verdict.[8]

In the United States, the predominant opinion about the outcome in the Hetherington case was just the opposite. Justice had been done. A sense of satisfaction rippled across the country as first James's and Bessie's parents and then newspaper readers across the country learned of the verdict. Henry Hetherington went to church on Sunday morning, April 10, with a smile on his face, knowing that his son had been acquitted. The cloud of anxiety he had felt ever since getting word of the killing had been lifted. When friends came up to him after the service to congratulate him on the good news, he said he was delighted that his son's long ordeal was over. Justice had indeed been done. Bessie's parents in Wilmington felt the same way when they got news of the trial's outcome. That their daughter's reputation had been cleansed and their son-in-law acquitted was news they received "with much favor."[9]

A similarly triumphant mood was reported at the Navy Department in Washington. Officers there who knew James welcomed the verdict. Some claimed they had been confident from the moment they heard that he been charged with murder that he would be acquitted. Admiral Belknap, who had predicted that outcome, must have been particularly pleased.

That sense of satisfaction—the feeling that justice had in fact been done in Yokohama—ran through the first American newspaper reports on the verdict. They described "a perennial wellspring of joy" over Lieutenant Hetherington's acquittal. That sentiment, however, predated the arrival, weeks later, of details about the trial proceedings aboard the *Empress of Japan* and the SS *Belgic* in Vancouver, British Columbia, and San Francisco, respectively. Summaries of testimony given in the trial then appeared in the press.[10]

That information prompted quite a variety of responses to the trial's outcome. The first reaffirmed the verdict. The *Cincinnati Enquirer* headlined "The Testimony Proves That He [Lt. Hetherington] Was Justified [in] Killing Robinson for His Dishonorable Conduct."[11] Doubt about the logic of the verdict came soon after. Looking back on the scandal, killing, and trial as a whole, one newsman found the verdict of innocence implausible. The letters between Robinson and Mrs. Hetherington revealed that "the affection between the pair had been anything but platonic." That, he reasoned, put James Hetherington "in a peculiar position." If Bessie was innocent, the shooting was murder. If his killing was retribution for Gower's "betrayal of a married woman" his reported reconciliation with her amounted to a "condonation of her offense." That was hardly in keeping with "the ideas of honor" that supposedly prompted Hetherington to kill Robinson.

When reporters in San Francisco interviewed Lieutenant Horace McIntosh, who had served aboard the *Marion* and was returning home in disgrace after running the *Alliance* aground, he suggested that the verdict was based on incomplete evidence. Facts that would "have vindicated Mrs. Hetherington ... [and shown] the sinister purpose of Robinson" were not presented at the trial. Discretion demanded otherwise. If he had cast it aside, Alexander Tison would have revealed "a number of grinning skeletons locked up in the closets of many residents in Yokohama." Nonetheless, McIntosh stated, the information presented in the trial had uncovered truth and produced a correct verdict.[12]

A *Los Angeles Times* columnist produced perhaps the most sweeping take on the verdict in the American press. People, he wrote, had rushed to judgment about it on the basis of incomplete information. They rejoiced at the verdict of acquittal without considering the larger moral and societal implications of the affair that led to the killing and the trial.

In his view, all three principals in the tragedy in Yokohama—Bessie, Gower Robinson, and James—were guilty. Mrs. Hetherington was not just a beautiful social butterfly but "a female animal, a little deer—[who] naturally takes up with the victorious stag." Robinson, the scoundrel, was dead and deserved his fate. And Lieutenant Hetherington? While many people commiserated with him, he was to be pitied for "having married such a fool of a woman." He also deserved blame for attempting to vindicate his wife's honor, for it was "a very uncertain quantity." In short, James the cuckhold was a far from innocent fool.

Judge Tillotson's verdict, then, was wrong. He found innocence where there was none. And those who welcomed his finding were wrong because they overlooked the larger significance of the case. Its principals were types. James and Gower were young, wealthy men whose "dilettante professions" allowed them to "come and go as fancy or pleasure dictates." Bessie was typical of the young woman who wants to be "in the swim," to dress as fashion dictates and dance in the social swirl. These people were rootless, far from home, and thus subject to the wiles of Satan himself. That was what had led to the tragedy in Yokohama. The verdict, then, stood more as admonition than revelation of truth. What the trial revealed about broader trends in society, at home in America, not just in some distant fragment of Western civilization in Japan, was more important than the particulars, legal or otherwise, of the verdict it produced.[13]

Such a sweeping, moralistic take on the verdict found scant agreement in the American legal community. When, months after these first reactions appeared, a full transcript of the trial proceedings became available to lawyers, some among them took strong objection to the verdict and the way it had been won. They complained that Tison had won the case emotionally rather than legally. By capturing the sympathy of judge and assessors, he won acquittal for Lieutenant Hetherington. But his reasoning ignored the facts. As one commentator in the prestigious *American Law Review*, founded and edited by Oliver Wendell Holmes Jr. and published by the Harvard Law School, put it: "If ever there was a case of manslaughter, this was it." Hetherington should never have gone free without punishment of some kind for having killed Robinson.

An expert on criminal law writing in the *Albany Law Journal* rendered an even harsher judgment on the verdict. Judge Tillotson and the associates ought to have shown "a better regard for law, justice, and public decency" than they did. The verdict was "a disgrace to the administration of Federal criminal justice." Tillotson had "earned the unenviable distinction of being the first [American] judicial officer to disregard the indisputable law of such cases," the critic argued, and "he ought to be removed from office." That did not happen.

Nor did the United States government concur in Oliver Wendell Holmes, Jr.'s, opinion about the significance of the case and its verdict. The extraterritoriality that had guaranteed Lieutenant Hetherington trial in an American rather than a Japanese court was the norm in relations between Christian and non–Christian nations and may have been "reasonable on its face." But the resulting circumstance was one "of which the government of Japan is justly restive." The implication of Holmes's words was clear: perhaps the time had come to end extraterritoriality for foreigners living in the Mikado's empire.[14]

That did not happen immediately. American officials in Yokohama and Washington believed instead that publishing the full transcript of the trial proceedings would lead readers and the public at large to conclude that the verdict in the Hetherington case was correct. Doing so would also serve larger purposes. Secretary of State James G. Blaine in Washington and acting Minister Edwin Dun in Tokyo sensed that publication would be diplomatically useful. Getting the whole story out might soothe frictions between Americans and Britons in Yokohama and elsewhere. It could also demonstrate the fairness and efficacy of trial under the provisions of extraterritoriality—immunity for foreigners from prosecution in Japanese courts—the process that the Japanese government was determined to end.

And what of the U.S. Navy? In the absence of any evidence to the contrary, one can only conclude its senior leaders in Washington agreed that publication of the full facts of the case as revealed in the transcript of the court proceedings was the best thing to do. The facts laid before the public would validate the verdict, end Lieutenant Hetherington's notoriety, and restore the reputation of naval officers and their wives in general.

In the end, many decades later, legal scholars acknowledged that there was no single correct verdict in the Hetherington case. They recognized, however, that the trial transcript, long buried in obscurity in university libraries, had great value as a law school textbook. Just as it had at the time of its publication, so too once again it could produce useful and instructive debate over how the prosecuting and defending attorneys had argued the case, the way the judge presided over it, and the verdict it produced. Thus they decided to include the transcript in the prestigious and widely available *Makers of Modern Law* series.[15] A disputed verdict from a long-ago murder case in a distant land could help educate fledgling lawyers, for any one of them might someday have to defend a client accused of killing his wife's lover.

The opinions about the Hetherington case remain many and contradictory for another, more significant reason. The trial was, after all, about the most basic of human emotions: love. Love that manifested itself in passion and adultery, jealousy and revenge, and death itself. Are we humans to be judged guilty or found innocent for following the path where love leads us?

23

Departures

On Tuesday, April 12, 1892, the USS *Marion* weighed anchor and headed down Tokyo Bay toward the open Pacific.[1] Captain Bartlett and his officers were glad to be leaving Yokohama. It was time to put an end to the traumatic events of the last two months—especially the trial of their onetime shipmate, Lieutenant Hetherington. The time had come to return to normal. That sentiment was widely felt in the Yokohama expatriate community. And it was felt with particular force by participants in the trial. They separated. Some returned to their lives and various pursuits as they had been before "the tragedy in Yokohama." Others, James and Bessie foremost among them, found that the scandal, killing, and trial had changed their lives forever. They left. But they could not escape the events that the trial had made known to the world. What happened to them all—the officers of the court, the attorneys, the most important witnesses they questioned, and, last but not least, the acquitted James Hetherington and his wife, Bessie?

The judge, Willard Tillotson, returned to the more routine duties of an American consul general in Yokohama. Despite the defeat in November 1892 of his Republican patron, President Benjamin Harrison, he stayed on until November 1894, when his Democratic replacement arrived. Then he and his family put Japan and all that had happened to them in Yokohama behind. Four years later, however, he looked back on his judgeship in the Hetherington case as a success. He was proud, he told a reporter, of having conducted the trial "in such a way as to best satisfy all parties." Tillotson returned first to Tacoma, Washington, and then moved to Redding, California, where he practiced law, dabbled in Republican politics, and eventually won election as district attorney for Shasta County. He lived there until death claimed him in 1952—60 years after he had presided over the Hetherington trial.[2]

All four assessors who concurred in Judge Tillotson's "not guilty" finding returned to their normal lives and professional pursuits in

Yokohama for a time. J.R. Simon was the first among them to leave—in 1894, two years after the trial, for his birthplace in France. The Rev. E.S. Booth stayed on in Yokohama the longest, serving as head of the Ferris School for Girls and officiating at Union Church services for 40 years. He retired and moved to New York City in 1922. Nine years later at the ripe age of 80, he died. Precisely when the other two assessors died or left Japan to return to their home countries remains unknown.[3]

The prosecuting and defending attorneys' subsequent lives followed different Japan-centric courses. Prosecutor Henry Litchfield returned to his previous duties with the British Court for Japan at the British Consulate in Yokohama. He married at Christ Church there in 1894 and took on a Japanese partner in his law firm when extraterritoriality came to an end five years later. Litchfield remained active in the social life of the Yokohama foreign community, serving as chairman of the board of directors of the United Club and president of the Amateur Rowing Club. Fifteen years after the Hetherington trial ended, in September 1907, he died and was buried in Yokohama.[4]

Alexander Tison went back to Tokyo filled, most likely, with feelings of triumph at having won acquittal for James Hetherington. His first murder case had been spectacularly successful. It had made him famous for a time and enhanced his reputation for legal prowess. But he never tried another murder case. His broader experience in Japan, rather than the Hetherington case in particular, determined the course of his later life. Enamored of Japan and the Japanese, he became a member of the elite Asiatic Society of Japan, a group devoted to scholarly study of the country, and served as its recording secretary. He requested and got an extension of his teaching contract at Tokyo Imperial University, which allowed him to remain in Japan until 1894. Then he sailed west around the world, bound for New York City, where he formed a law partnership, married, and sired three children.

Tison could not get Japan out of his system, however. He made four business trips back to Yokohama and Tokyo, where he renewed his friendship with former students who had gone on to become some of Japan's most prominent political and financial leaders. In 1907, Tison became a founding member of the Japan Society of New York, a group of business, professional, and academic leaders devoted to promoting good relations between the United States and Japan. He became one of its most active members, organizing many a banquet for visiting Japanese dignitaries over the years. In 1929, he was elected president of the society and served in that capacity for the next two years. By the time he died in 1938, Japanese emperors had repeatedly decorated him for his many activities in service of friendly relations between the United States and Japan.[5]

23. Departures

The two men who brought their influence to bear on the Hetherington trial unofficially both spent the rest of their lives in Yokohama. George Scidmore, who had counseled Willard Tillotson on the rules of procedure in a consular court, spent most of the rest of his diplomatic career there. Praised by a later American minister and ambassador to Japan as "a good lawyer and a gentleman ... who had been totally wasted at the Yokohama consulate," he served there as consul general for nearly eight years. Scidmore never married but enjoyed the social life of the foreign community. He was elected commodore of the Yokohama Yacht Club eight times. He lived in the shadow of his famous sister, Eliza, however. She published the first American guidebook for tourists in Japan and became a tireless promoter of planting the Japanese cherry trees that grace the Tidal Basin and Jefferson Memorial in Washington, D.C. By the time of his death in 1922, Scidmore was revered as one of Yokohama's most distinguished residents. He was laid to final rest in the Yokohama General Cemetery for Foreigners.[6]

John Frederick Lowder, Gower's lawyer who had tried to save his reputation and secure punishment for his killer, had no formal role in the trial but tried indirectly to influence its verdict. In 1897, he sparred with George Scidmore in another case of murder within the Yokohama expatriate community. That trial ended very differently from Lieutenant Hetherington's. Edith Carew, who poisoned her philandering husband, Walter, was found guilty in the British Consular Court; but her death sentence was commuted to 18 years imprisonment back in England. Outside of court, Lowder remained a leader in the Yokohama foreign community. He distinguished himself as one of the most outspoken opponents of the treaties that ended extraterritoriality for foreign nationals in Japan. The regime that had guaranteed Lieutenant Hetherington trial in an American consular court came to its end in 1899. Three years later, Lowder, who had practiced law under the extraterritoriality regime longer than anyone, died a wealthy man and was buried in Yokohama, the city that had been his home for nearly 40 years.[7]

What became of the key witnesses in the trial? The two most important naval officers among them continued their careers at sea and ashore until retirement. Commander Bartlett left the *Marion* in August 1892, commanded various cruisers thereafter, and headed the Office of Naval Intelligence during the Spanish-American War. He retired in 1902, was promoted to rear admiral a year later, and died in 1904. Allen Rogers, James Hetherington's best friend and ardent defender in court, stayed in the navy for another 13 years. Retiring as a commander in 1905, he returned to his hometown, Raleigh, North Carolina. Five years later, he married a beautiful woman 23 years his junior. Rogers sired three children by her. He died in 1932, 40 years after he had given such compelling testimony in the Hetherington trial.[8]

What is known about the later lives of Gower Robinson's friends and accomplices in the Hetherington affair remains uneven. Albert Read, his friend and neighbor, stayed on in Yokohama until some unknown point in the 20th century. So, too, did most of his circle of defenders, younger men all, who continued working for their respective firms. Only one of them, Brooke Hyde Pearson, is known to have married—later in 1892. He and his family left Japan for "home"—that is, England—in 1901. Robinson's American friend Chandler Gibbens worked his way up in the Jardine, Matheson, & Company firm but fell ill and left Japan in 1908. He died three years later in Belmont, Massachusetts, near his birthplace. Henry Blanchard, praised by Alexander Tison for telling the truth about carrying messages from Gower to Bessie, apparently left Yokohama shortly after the trial ended. Nothing is known of his subsequent life. The dead man's partner and executor, Waldemar Blad, found a succession of new partners for his bill and bullion firm that continued to exist until the eve of World War I. Blad left Japan for his homeland, Denmark, in 1910.[9]

The hotel staff and servants who provided such valuable information in the trial about Gower and Bessie's affair went on to live varied lives. The Grand Hotel manager, Louis Eppinger, who had detailed the Englishman's first encounters with Bessie Hetherington, stayed on in that capacity for another dozen years after the trial. He prided himself on providing the finest food and lodging in Yokohama for tourists and became a celebrity of sorts, appearing on the souvenir postcards they purchased. Eventually he married the Japanese woman who likely had been his mistress. By the end of his career, he had been elected a director of the Grand Hotel. He died in Yokohama 15 years after the trial ended.

Henry Clare, the Grand Hotel mail clerk who had testified about the correspondence between Bessie and Gower, left that position after the trial and went on to work in various positions for three major shipping companies in Yokohama. He prospered, found a wife in 1902, and four years later fathered a son. Cesare Pachini, the Grand Hotel night watchman, remained loyal to Robinson to the end. He had perjured himself rather than tell the truth about what he had done to facilitate Gower's trysts with Bessie. Never tried for his crime in either the American or the Italian consular court, he soon left Yokohama with his family.[10]

As for the key Japanese witnesses—Gower's *bettō* and his houseboy and the Hetheringtons' *amah*, Shiraishi Tome—very little is known about their lives after the trial. They served others in the expatriate enclave in much the same way they had done before Gower's death. Presumably they lived for years thereafter in Yokohama's Japan Town.[11]

23. Departures

Traumatized by what had happened to them in Yokohama, James and Bessie Hetherington knew that they must leave Japan as quickly as possible. Feelings within the expatriate community about the verdict in the trial, pro and con, ran too high. James could not just return to duty on the *Marion* and leave Bessie and Gladys at the Grand Hotel while he was at sea. His superiors in Washington recognized the strain he had been through and directed him to return to the United States as soon as possible. While awaiting the next passenger ship bound for San Francisco, he and his family should go stay in a Tokyo hotel. There they would be out of public view and less likely to stir controversy. Once back in America, James would have 60 days of leave to settle his personal affairs before being assigned to a new duty station.[12]

James welcomed those orders. But waiting in Tokyo for two weeks could not have been an easy time for the Hetheringtons. The scandal and killing had strained their marriage nearly to the breaking point, and pursuit of acquittal in the trial had forced reconciliation—at least in public—upon them. Their feelings toward one another understandably remained raw. Being cooped up in a hotel without the circle of friends and active social life they had known in Yokohama, and with little to do for weeks, must have been difficult for them.

Relief of a sort finally came on April 30. James had secured passage to San Francisco for the family on the SS *Oceanic*, which was scheduled to leave Yokohama the next day.[13] One can only guess at the emotions he and Bessie felt when their ship weighed anchor on Sunday, May 1, and headed east toward the open sea. Probably their thoughts and feelings were mixed as the familiar sights of the Yokohama shoreline sank below the horizon.[14] Regret at ever having come to Yokohama in the first place? A sense of loss at the damage their marriage and their reputations had suffered there? Relief at James's acquittal and vindication over the restoration of Bessie's reputation? Or perhaps just plain "Good riddance!" to Yokohama and what they had experienced there?

Perhaps the gentle rise and fall of the waves beneath the ship soothed their feelings about the past and enkindled hope for the future. Life at home in America was bound to be better than what they had experienced in Japan. The long sea voyage stretching before them might even give them the opportunity to repair their relations with one another and return to normal family life.

Whether and to what degree that happened remains unclear. The couple were rarely seen together during the voyage. Fellow women passengers reportedly "snubbed [Bessie] ... unmercifully," so after a few days she retreated to her cabin. When she came out for meals or concerts and lectures, she dressed soberly and treated her daughter, Gladys, with great care and tenderness. James, on the other hand, was seen frequently at the bar, where he socialized with other men. Despite the notoriety that still clung to him, they found him to be a hale-and-well-met sort of fellow. No one said anything to him about his having killed Gower Robinson, and no one asked him about how he had felt during the trial and at the moment of his acquittal.[15]

All of that changed dramatically, however, on Saturday, May 21, when the SS *Oceanic* tied up alongside the Occidental and Oriental Steamship Company wharf in San Francisco. When the Hetheringtons stepped ashore, a swarm of reporters besieged them. James, described by one of the journalists on that day as "a man nearly six feet [and] of massive build ... with the neck of a bull," brushed them off. He was "forcible in his refusal to discuss his recent troubles." Bessie at first "declined to be communicative" with the reporters, but then sought their indulgence. "There is nothing I can say that has not been told," she said. "I beg to be relieved from speaking further on the subject." James then hurried her and Gladys off to the luxurious Occidental Hotel.[16]

The next day, they took the ferry across the bay to Oakland, where in what is now Emeryville they boarded a train bound for Chicago.[17] Five more days of privacy and time for reflection passed as they headed east, crossing the Sierra Nevada and the Great Basin, traversing South Pass in Wyoming, and then descending across the high prairies and farmlands of Nebraska and Iowa until they crossed the Mississippi into Illinois.

When they alighted in Chicago, ravenous reporters followed them to the city's finest hotel, the Palmer House. James positively refused to speak to them and ordered the desk clerk to report that they were "not in." The newsmen had to settle for merely providing a physical description of the couple. James's full beard, "more akin to red than blonde," and Bessie's small size in comparison with his bulk caught their attention. Once the Hetheringtons settled into their room, a pleasant surprise awaited them. James's father, Henry, had come up from Dubuque to enjoy a brief visit with his son, daughter-in-law, and granddaughter.[18] Surely that lifted the whole family's spirits.

The next morning, the Hetheringtons boarded an eastbound train. A day and a half later they arrived in Wilmington, where her parents welcomed them warmly at the train station. Then they drove off in a carriage to the Hewes's home, where neighbors had gathered to greet them. Reporters were there, too; but just as he had earlier on their journey, James refused to speak to the journalists.[19] When the front door closed behind them, James and Bessie may well have heaved a sigh of relief. Their long journey was over, and in the quiet of her family's home, they could hope that their lives would return to normal.

But after all that had happened in Yokohama, would that be possible?

~ 24 ~

Reconciliation?

James and Bessie struggled for a decade to find the answers to that question. They returned to Wilmington hoping it would be their safe haven. They longed for privacy, peace, and healing from the wounds they and their marriage had suffered in Yokohama. The navy, perhaps at Admiral Belknap's behest, had recognized that the couple needed time to themselves and granted James six months' leave. But he and Bessie knew that they could not idle that time away, simply caring for their daughter and socializing with the Hewes family. They faced a challenge: achieving reconciliation between themselves and restoring their marriage to what it had been before "the tragedy in Yokohama" nearly destroyed it.

They knew that they had to try to reconcile, and that the world expected them to succeed. Alexander Tison had made their staying together as man and wife a precondition for taking on the Hetherington case. He won it by arguing that determination to save his family was the real reason James had killed Gower Robinson. Their families expected them to stay together. Henry Hetherington had told reporters even before the trial began that his son and daughter-in-law would never divorce. Never. Emlen Hewes, Bessie's father, felt the same way—as later events would reveal. But no one, least of all the couple themselves, had any idea of how difficult it would be to fully restore their union. Nor could they imagine having to confront yet another threat to it—one perhaps even more serious than what they had faced in Yokohama. They had no idea of how long it might take for them to recover their love, forgive what had happened in the past, and stand together in meeting the challenges that life put before them.

They tried. But could they succeed? Ten years passed before James and Bessie found an answer to that question.

For the last six months of 1892, Wilmington seemed like the best place to put their lives back together. The world beyond was headed toward economic disaster and political uncertainty. Drought, homelessness, and political unrest struck the American heartland. Homesteaders in the Dakotas, Kansas, and Nebraska, and even Colorado abandoned their farms and ranches. In the industrial East, banks, factories, and railroads failed, leaving hundreds of thousands of workers unemployed. Wall Street manipulators made enormous profits—until the stock market tanked and left them wondering what had happened. In November, voters responded by ousting the sitting Republican president and returning Grover Cleveland to the White House. A prolonged and painful recession followed.[1]

The navy shielded people in Wilmington from the worst of these conditions by continuing to pay the steelworkers, shipwrights, and dockyard support staff building ships of "the new navy" on the waterfront. It paid James, albeit only half his normal salary because he was on leave. That permitted him to buy the privacy that he and Bessie needed. He rented a small house at 1034 Seventh Street, not far from her parents' home, and for the first time since they had married the couple were able to live a "normal" life, not unlike that of their civilian neighbors. Their calm was interrupted but once, when Emlen Hewes's "spanking pair of bay horses" spooked and started to run, pulling the carriage with baby Gladys and her aunt Helen inside toward disaster. "Luckily, the family's black coachman managed to stop them."[2] For a time, at least, Bessie may have thought her husband's profession was not so bad after all. They were safe, and the navy paid, even in the worst of times.

The Hetheringtons knew, however, that this idyll must end. Someday, someday soon, the navy, James's mistress, would send him back to sea. That likely meant separation—before they could fully recover from all that had befallen them in Yokohama.

The bad news arrived on December 13, 1892, less than two weeks before Christmas. James was ordered to report for duty aboard the USS *Mohican* no later than January 6, 1893. The ship was then undergoing repairs and waiting further orders at Mare Island Naval Station, California. This time he did not make the mistake of demanding that Bessie and Gladys follow him there. After what had happened in Yokohama, both he and she probably felt it would be best for them to stay in Wilmington, where they could remain safe and happy living near the Hewes family home.[3]

Separation was quite normal for a navy family in the 1890s. With but one exception, that was the pattern of living—married but separated by the husband's naval duty for long periods of time—that the Hetheringtons followed for the next 10 years. That meant living different lives. He led the duty-bound life of the naval officer who missed but still provided for his family. She became a self-sacrificing single parent, managing with the help of her parents and sister. This was marriage maintained for reasons other

24. Reconciliation?

than satisfying the emotional needs of its partners. For the sake of their child. To meet society's expectations for an upper middle-class couple. As a naval officer's duty. But could such a marriage foster the healing James and Bessie needed and wanted? Their pursuit of reconciliation, of recovery from what they had suffered in Yokohama, would not be easy.

Living apart, married but separated by the breadth of a continent and more, proved less difficult for James than for Bessie. Over the next three years, from January 1893 until February 1896, he reverted to the familiar routines of shipboard life and enjoyed the camaraderie of fellow officers in much the same way as he had known before marriage. He served aboard two small vessels: first the USS *Mohican*, a 20-year-old hybrid sail-and-steam sloop of war, and then on the even older and smaller modified screw tug the USS *Pinta*. Neither ship was part of the "new navy" of larger, steam-powered, and heavily armed warships that was under construction in the 1890s. Both belonged to "the patchwork navy," having undergone extensive repairs and refitting since they had been laid down. The *Mohican* would have been familiar to James, for it was precisely the same size as the *Marion* and carried only a slightly larger crew. It would be more comfortable, however, having just gotten electric lights and a modern ventilating system. With less than a dozen officers on board, James quickly and easily found friendship in its wardroom.[4]

When he came aboard, the ship was about to depart for Hawaii, where Yankee conspirators had just overthrown the Hawaiian monarchy, deposing its famous Queen Liliuokalani. Its 90-day stay in Honolulu constituted an episode of "gunboat diplomacy" that is present with the threat but not the use of force. The *Mohican* never fired its guns at Honolulu, and its crew had frequent opportunities to go ashore.[5] One suspects, however, that his sojourn in Hawaii brought back bittersweet memories to James. After all, the *Marion*'s long stop for repairs there two years earlier had contributed to its delayed arrival in Yokohama and reunion with Bessie. That left her open to the wiles of Gower Robinson. A sad thought and reminder of the disastrous events that followed.

The *Mohican* returned to San Francisco in May 1893 but stayed barely a week before heading north to Sitka, Alaska. There it joined three other small navy ships and three coast guard revenue cutters to form the Bering Sea Squadron. Its duties were much the same as the *Marion*'s had been in 1891: patrolling the waters around the fur seals' breeding grounds on the Pribilof Islands. But the diplomatic environment had changed. Then the possibility of a clash between the United States and Great Britain had seemed real. Now that was less likely because the two sides had agreed to arbitrate their dispute and set up a multinational tribunal to decide what should be done. But its judgment left American officials dissatisfied. The judges rejected the United States' claim that the Bering Sea was its alone to patrol because it had inherited, through the purchase of Alaska from Russia, the tsar's 1821 ukase making it exclusive territorial waters. The United States must also pay Great Britain nearly a half-million dollars in compensation for the losses it had cost Canadian and British sealers. Diplomatic conflict between Washington and London continued, prompting the navy to order the *Mohican* to Sitka, which became its home port.

The ship stayed there for the next 15 months, spending winter and spring in port, then venturing out to the Pribilof Island sealing grounds for the summer.[6] That was a lonely time for James, for Bessie's letters took weeks to reach Alaska from Delaware. A chance for a family reunion came in the fall of 1894, when the *Mohican* finally headed south to San Francisco and across the bay to Mare Island for decommissioning. James took examinations for promotion there and did not report aboard on his next ship, the USS *Pinta*, until mid-November. Bessie and Gladys could have come west to see him, or he could have taken leave and gone to Wilmington. Neither of them made the journey. The *Pinta* was ordered north to its new homeport, Sitka.[7]

James knew he could not bring Bessie and Gladys there. While the town was beautiful, sprawling along an island-studded bay with snow-capped Mount Edgecumbe looming behind it, barely 1,200 souls, most of them indigenous people with faces and customs strange to white Americans, lived there. Summer was beautiful, but the long months of winter darkness brutalized one's spirits. Despite being the Alaska district's administrative capital, the town was pretty rough and tumble, even before the later gold rush made it more so. For James, reunion with Bessie remained a distant dream.[8]

Thirty-nine long months of separation cannot have fostered renewal of love between him and Bessie.

She, however, found her situation during that time less bearable than he did. Her independence of some form of male supervision vanished. During her journey to Japan and in Yokohama when James was at sea, she had been on her own, free to come and go as she pleased. Now she lived under her father's watchful eye, in or near his home. He and her mother and sisters surrounded her with familial love, but her wider social life shriveled. Although she joined the family on summer visits to Cape May, they were not what they had been before marriage. As a young matron, she was no longer the magnet for bachelors' eyes she had once been. She couldn't engage in playful conversation with men as she had as a maiden. Back home in Wilmington, her social life bordered on boring. Her calendar was not crowded with the balls, concerts, sporting events, and social calls that she had known in Yokohama.

24. Reconciliation?

What made her life most difficult, however, was the absence of sex. Having known its physical comfort with James and the passion it stirred with Gower, she missed the intimacy, the excitement, and the escape from everyday cares it provided. Bessie was still a young woman, only in her middle 20s, and it was natural for her to want sex. Going without it for more than three years must have been extraordinarily difficult for her. Then, suddenly, sometime early in October 1895, she gave in to her instincts and had intercourse with a third man.

Who was he? How did they meet? Where did their intimate encounter happen? We simply don't know. But what is beyond dispute is that he impregnated her. Nine months later, on July 11, 1896, Bessie gave birth to a baby boy. By the second week of November, she was waking up mornings feeling like she was about to vomit. She knew she was pregnant.

That realization threw Bessie into a tizzy—a state of nervous excitement. Facing a crisis situation, what was she to do? A young woman in America today, facing an unwanted pregnancy, can consider abortion. In the 1890s, that alternative would have been medically dangerous and illegal as well. For a woman of Bessie's social position living where she had been born and raised, that choice was unthinkable. Women "of the better sort" simply did not resort to abortion. In her anxious state, Bessie thought of another solution. She could try to get James back from Alaska and have sex with him immediately so as to make him think he had fathered the child growing in her womb.

That would be chancy and require a monstrous lie, but it was a plausible course of action. Even if James couldn't get home as quickly as she would like, she could still have sex with him when he did and tell him, less than nine months later, that the baby had arrived early. That would make him happy and smooth their way to full reconciliation. Bessie may have fantasized that she could make James the proverbial sailor—home from the sea, eager to make love, and 'ere long a father to be.

Not long after Bessie realized she was pregnant, a clerk in the Bureau of Navigation wrote out orders for Lieutenant Hetherington. Dated November 11, 1895, they read: "Det'[ache]d. home, on 3 months leave." That wording was extraordinary. No other U.S. Navy officer in 1895 or during the two years bracketing it was issued such orders. Normally an officer was detached from his duty station and directed either to report to his next one by a certain date or to revert to "waiting orders" status. Why was James simply directed to go home?[9]

Bessie may have had a hand in the writing of his orders. She may have remembered that back in 1890, James had gotten orders to the *Essex*, about to depart for two years in South American waters, changed on compassionate grounds. She had been suffering the complications of pregnancy then and certainly could not plead that now. But she could have concocted some emergency, medical or otherwise, that would have persuaded crusty old Rear Admiral Francis Munroe Ramsay, who still headed the Bureau of Navigation, to order her husband home.[10]

Or the navy may have come to her rescue on its own. James's service on the *Pinta* was due to end in January 1896. After more than three years' sea duty, it would be reasonable for him to have home leave before reporting to his next duty station—most likely one ashore. Washington may have issued the orders early knowing that Lieutenant Hetherington would need extra time to return from Alaska, go home to Delaware, and prepare to move with his family to his next assignment. The timing of the orders may have just been routine, even if their wording was not.

Their precise origin mattered less than the fact that it took so long for James to comply with them. In 1895, communication from Washington, D.C., to Sitka took weeks, for there was no overland telegraph or submarine cable to Alaska. James's orders had to be delivered by the monthly mail boat, which crawled up the Inside Passage, stopping at numerous small settlements along the way. The *City of Topeka* did not reach Sitka until January 11, 1896.

Early that morning the mailboat messenger came alongside the *Pinta*, handed a mailbag up to a sailor who grabbed it and took it to the officer of the deck, Ensign William Crose, who had served with James aboard the *Marion*.[11] Crose opened the bag and directed another sailor to distribute the mail. When James found the orders in his, he probably was shocked by how quickly he had to comply with them. Because the mailboat was due to depart Sitka that very morning, he had to scramble to pack his bags, pay his last formal call on the captain, and bid goodbye to his fellow officers. Fighting a nasty mix of snow and rain, he rushed to the *City of Topeka* and stepped aboard just before 10:00 a.m. that day. A few minutes later, the small steamer backed away from the wharf, headed into the harbor, and turned south toward the open sea.[12]

James faced a long journey home. It would take 10 days to 2 weeks, depending on the mailboat's stops along the way, to reach Port Townsend, Washington. Then he would have to take a ferry across Puget Sound to Seattle. Boarding a pullman car, he would travel east on the recently completed Great Northern Railroad for the better part of a week. After changing trains at Minneapolis–St. Paul, he had to go south to Chicago—another day's journey—where he would board a third train. A day and a half would pass before he reached Philadelphia and changed to a local train that carried him to Wilmington. He would not reach the city until the first week of February 1896 at the earliest—too late to have fathered the baby Bessie would deliver five months later.[13]

24. Reconciliation?

Hugs and kisses greeted James when he knocked on the Hewes family home door in Wilmington. Everyone was delighted to see him, and spirited conversation doubtless followed on through dinner. Later that evening, James and Bessie retired for the night. Sex, vigorous and passionate, likely followed. For James, that would have been only natural after so many long months apart from his wife. For Bessie, it was probably conflicted—tinged with guilt over her adultery in his absence, but purposeful nonetheless. She meant to make James believe, later, when her condition became obvious, that this was the night he had impregnated her. Lovemaking that night was Bessie's way of hiding her infidelity and concealing the paternity of the child she was carrying.

What the navy gave the navy could take away. Barely a month after he got home thinking he had 90 days' leave, James got orders to report to the Branch Navy Hydrographic Office at Port Townsend, Washington, as soon as possible. That brought the Hetheringtons' second idyll of reconciliation to an abrupt end. When he told Bessie the news, she probably shuddered at the prospect of going to some small town in the wilds of Washington. She likely thought the place was raw, in a state barely seven years old, with just fishermen and loggers living there. James knew better, for he had gone to Port Townsend for weeks on the *Marion* in 1891; twice on the *Mohican* in 1893 and 1894; and more recently on his way home from the *Pinta*.[14]

He tried to alleviate Bessie's concern by telling her that the town would be a lovely place to live. Perched on the northeastern tip of the Olympic Peninsula, it jutted out into the water where Puget Sound opened up into the Strait of Juan de Fuca and the Pacific beyond. The port was busy, servicing as many ships a year as New York Harbor did because vessels arriving from Canada or Asia had to check in at the U.S. Customs House there before proceeding south into the sound or down the coast. That requirement brought all kinds of interesting people to town, and she could make new friends with them and people already living there.[15] Best of all, they could live together with Gladys like an ordinary civilian family. He would come home every night, and their reconciliation could continue. Their love would grow deeper in such a place.

What James said may or may not have lessened Bessie's fears about moving to Port Townsend, but his words really didn't matter. She knew she had to go. She had no choice. She had to be a dutiful navy wife and mother, following her husband to wherever his mistress the navy sent him.

James had to leave almost immediately so as to report for duty in Port Townsend on March 18, 1896. That left Bessie, pregnant and with lively five-year-old Gladys to keep occupied, on her own to negotiate another long transcontinental train trip. When they arrived, she found herself in a small town, less than a tenth the size of Wilmington with only about a sixth of Dubuque's population. Like them, it was really two towns. Downtown was where City Hall, banks, the customs house, and James's office were located. It had a typical waterfront population: shipyard and itinerant lumber mill workers, as well as sailors and loggers. Bars and brothels clustered along the streets to meet their needs off work. A bit farther back from the waterfront right next to City Hall, an upscale bordello catered to gentlemen merchants and local officials. The streets were so rough, however, that downtown was "not considered safe for a decent woman."

Uptown sat on a bluff, and just as in Wilmington, Dubuque, and Yokohama, that was where "the better sort" lived. James and Bessie rented a handsome newly built home and soon acquired two cats. Life was easy. A commercial avenue, with markets, restaurants, dry goods stores, and even a horse-drawn trolley, was nearby. The Hetheringtons found a church and readily joined in community social life. It was not as elegant as Yokohama's had been, but there was plenty to do—baseball games and band concerts, art exhibitions, concerts, and picnics. James walked to and from work, and, starting that fall, Bessie took Gladys to school. The Hetheringtons made "many friends," became "well known" in the community, and seemed to be living just like their neighbors.[16]

Of course, they were not. The navy could disrupt their lives at any moment. It did so only 10 days after the Hetheringtons reunited in Port Townsend. James was ordered to serve as president of a general court-martial set to convene in Sitka on April 20. Follow-up orders directed him to "take first steamer and convene court as soon as possible." He did, but

Lieutenant James Henry Hetherington at Port Townsend, Washington, 1896 (NH 49125, Naval History and Heritage Command).

24. Reconciliation?

organizing an investigation, finding fellow officers to serve on it, and the proceedings themselves took a long time. He had to stay in Sitka until the verdict was made final in Washington. Orders to return to his regular duties in Port Townsend were not sent until the second week of July. He did not get home until August 4, 1896.[17]

There a pleasant surprise awaited him. He had a son—or so Bessie made him believe. Three weeks earlier, on July 11, she had given birth and named the child Emlen Hewes after her father. She could have told James the truth about the baby's paternity and begged for his forgiveness and mercy. That would have been difficult, to say the least. More likely, she lied, telling him that the baby had arrived early. Given his minimal knowledge of human biology (none was taught at the Naval Academy in his cadet midshipman days), James probably believed her. The baby also looked like him, already showing his sturdy frame as well as her yellow hair and bright blue eyes. Bessie had reason to hope that baby Emlen might help heal the scars that Yokohama had left on her marriage. After all, what man would not be delighted to have fathered a son?

James was. But Emlen, even as he grew more active, cute, and lovable, cast a dark shadow over the Hetheringtons' marriage. Could Bessie look at the child or give herself fully to James in their marriage bed without suffering twinges of guilt over the adultery that had produced him? Living a lie may well have made Bessie more susceptible to misunderstandings with James. Smooth on the outside but pitted and rough-edged on the inside, James and Bessie's married life grew more strained over the year following Emlen's birth.

Just how troubled it was became obvious in August 1897, when once again unusually early orders came for James. He was to report by September 1 to the USS *Marietta*, a new schooner-rigged gunboat being built in San Francisco. The ship was to be placed in commission that day and then join the new battleship *Oregon* in the Pacific Squadron. The squadron's patrolling responsibilities stretched from Alaska to Chile and out to Hawaii. San Francisco would be its home port. When not at sea, James's new ship would spend long periods of time at Mare Island Naval Station, 25 miles northeast of the city and across a narrow strait from the town of Vallejo. Could Bessie and the children join him there?[18]

James likely tried to persuade Bessie that they should. Life in Northern California offered pleasing prospects. The area had a Mediterranean climate, warm in summer but cooled daily by fog blowing in from San Francisco Bay. Rain came mainly in the winter months. Mare Island was the largest naval station on the West Coast, and it had handsome houses for officers and their families to live in. Residents could play on the first golf course west of the Mississippi and pray in a chapel soon to get Tiffany glass windows and electric lighting fixtures. There was a good elementary school for Gladys, and Bessie could participate in such officers' wives' activities as high teas, a sketch club, and quarterly art exhibitions. Ships' bands would provide music to enjoy at dances and concerts.

If the family couldn't or didn't choose to live on the naval station, they could find housing in Vallejo, which was half again as big as Port Townsend. Beautiful homes and commercial buildings lined its upper streets. Although lower Georgia Street was rough, lined with bars, gambling joints, and brothels, one could ride past them to the ferry and reach San Francisco in a matter of minutes. Bessie and James knew from their earlier stays there that the city, then California's largest and most ethnically and racially diverse, boasted fine hotels, elegant shopping, excellent restaurants, and good music and theater. They could celebrate birthdays or anniversaries there and never be bored.[19]

James really wanted his family to accompany him to California. He likely argued that even though he would be away at sea for long periods, doing so would be better than living apart. They would have more time to repair their marriage. The children would be better off. Caring for them would be easier for her if both parents were present as much as possible. And he himself was likely to be happier, more even-tempered, and a better father by keeping his family together and intact. After all, it was his duty to do so.

If James made those arguments, Bessie did not find them convincing. She had her own reasons not to. In civilian Port Townsend, she had been herself; at Mare Island naval station, she would once more become Mrs. Lieutenant Hetherington. Her social life would be as constrained as it had been in Yokohama by the navy's traditions. James would be with her some of the time, but there were likely to be long stretches when she would be living among strangers, left alone to manage the children. Would they really be living more together than apart? Wouldn't she be better off back home in Wilmington, where her father could watch over her and her mother and sisters help with the children?

Bessie's preference confronted James with a Hobson's choice. He still loved her and wanted her and the children to be at his side. But he was not about to force her to do anything. At the same time, he likely remembered how disastrous leaving Bessie alone in Yokohama had been. Having her and their children live in her hometown with her family might be the lesser evil. He gave in to Bessie's wishes.

One day late in August 1897, the Hetheringtons left Port Townsend and took the ferry bound for Seattle. After staying overnight in a hotel there, they boarded different trains the next day. James saw Bessie, Gladys, and Emlen safely aboard the Great Northern, headed east. Then he took

24. Reconciliation?

the Southern Pacific south. That must have been a difficult day for everyone. Was that the day James or Bessie or both of them abandoned all hope of full reconciliation? Was this the moment their marriage came to its end?

No. They simply went their separate ways.

Bessie returned to life with her family in Wilmington, albeit this time with two children to care for. James slipped back into the life of a married bachelor naval officer, aboard a brand-new ship for the first time in his career. His duty? For the next six months, the *Marietta* operated routinely along the coast of North America from Alaska to Guatemala. Things were calm in the Pacific, but war was brewing in the Caribbean. Revolution had broken out in Cuba and then stalemated. Americans, their emotions fanned by press reports of savage Spanish attempts to crush the rebels, sympathized with the Cubans, and some even volunteered to fight alongside them. Firms that owned or controlled Cuba's sugar plantations grew worried about the safety of their investments. That was enough to convince President William McKinley to order the navy to send the USS *Maine* to Havana Harbor, ostensibly to protect American lives and property in Cuba.

Barely two weeks later, in January 1898, a tremendous explosion rocked the battleship, killing 260 officers and men aboard. Spain was blamed for the attack, even though later examination of the wreckage suggested that a fire in the ship's coal bunkers rather than a mine or shelling from shore batteries was responsible for the disaster. Cries of "Remember the *Maine*" fanned public demands for war. On April 11, 1898, President McKinley finally sent his war message to Congress, and eight days later the legislators declared war against Spain.

Anticipating just that, the secretary of the navy on March 6 had ordered the battleship *Oregon*, then at Bremerton, Washington, to head south to San Francisco and prepare for a voyage around Cape Horn to the Caribbean. Two weeks later, on March 22, the tiny *Marietta*, then at Panama, was ordered to proceed to ports along the South American coast to arrange for coaling of the huge battleship that would follow. James suddenly found himself headed to war for the first time in his career.

A voyage of epic proportions—more than 13,000 miles for the *Marietta* and nearly 3,000 more for the *Oregon*—followed. The two ships met just south of Valparaiso, Chile, and then raced down around southern tip of South America and through the Strait of Magellan until they stopped for refueling and reprovisioning at Punta Arenas. Gliding into the strait again, they burst out into the Atlantic. Tensions mounted as they headed north toward Rio de Janeiro on "strictly war footing": no lights on, guns loaded, and crews sleeping at their battle stations. When the two ships reached Rio and their men learned that war against Spain had been declared, their fighting spirits soared. Fearing they might encounter a large Spanish squadron, the *Marietta* and the *Oregon* continued north under wartime conditions. But no clash with the enemy occurred.

Later, when the ships reached Bahia in northern Brazil, the *Oregon's* captain decided that the battleship must race ahead to war in the Caribbean. He ordered the slower *Marietta* to follow as quickly as it could or, if necessary, to beach itself to avoid capture. Then the *Oregon* rushed on to Key West, Florida, the forward staging base for war. The *Marietta* steamed slowly along for 3,800 nautical miles, arriving there nine days later. The two ships then headed south to Cuba—the *Oregon* to fight in the decisive battle of Santiago de Cuba, the *Marietta* for more prosaic duty—blockading Havana Harbor. There James Hetherington got his first and only taste of war.[20]

It proved brief. After the Spanish agreed to peace terms in mid-August, the *Marietta* headed north, bound for Key West and then Hampton Roads (greater Norfolk), Virginia. When James and the crew disembarked there on August 21, 1898, they were welcomed as war heroes. Everyone was thrilled and delighted that the war had been won in barely 90 days. Three days later, James got a surprise. Orders arrived detaching him from the *Marietta* effective immediately and directing him to report to the USS *Independence* at Mare Island Naval Station, California, by September 15.[21]

That gave James time enough to visit Bessie, Gladys, and Emlen at Wilmington on his way west. He was eager to see them and received a war hero's welcome. In all likelihood, he begged Bessie to follow him to California. All of the good things he had said about living on or near Mare Island a year ago remained true. This time, however, life together there could be even better. His new ship, the *Independence*, the receiving ship for new seaman recruits, remained dockside most of the time, venturing only once or twice a year on brief training cruises within San Francisco and San Pablo Bays. In effect, he would have shore duty. The family would reunite, and he and she could live and love together once more.

Bessie turned a deaf ear to those arguments. She was not about to leave Wilmington. She was neither ready to live with James again nor willing to divorce him. The Hetheringtons would continue to live an untruth—married in the eyes of the world, but living apart. James left for California alone.

His duties there over the next four years were dull in comparison with the excitement he had known during the 90-day war. The *Independence* was the navy's oldest vessel, its first ship of the line, and a veteran of the War of 1812 and the Mexican War of 1846–1847. The huge old wooden hulk lay mired in the mud at Mare Island. As a senior lieutenant, James

24. Reconciliation?

would be more administrator and instructor than a regular seagoing officer. His one chance to escape came during the Samoan crisis of 1899, when he was ordered to replace one of the two lieutenants aboard the USS *Philadelphia* who had been killed there. The fighting ended before he could do so. He returned to training duties, this time aboard the screw steamer USS *Adams*.

That training vessel at Mare Island only occasionally ventured beyond San Francisco Bay on voyages to Hawaii. In June 1900, he became the ship's second-in-command, the executive officer burdened with all the administrative work its captain did not do. After serving briefly in the same capacity aboard the USS *Alert*, a decommissioned screw steamer also at Mare Island, in August 1901, he was promoted to lieutenant commander and ordered back to the *Independence*.[22]

James likely spent hours feeling bored and lonely during his service on these ships. While he still enjoyed the camaraderie of his fellow officers, it was not the same as it had been in his younger days. He was older, married, and too senior to go out drinking or in search of female company with more junior officers. Relations with his fellow officers during what was essentially shore duty did not become as close as they would have been at sea. As a de facto bachelor, he didn't fit in easily at dinner parties or other social occasions with his married peers or seniors. Occasionally he even saw the *Marion*—a painful reminder of all that had befallen him in Yokohama. "Cradled snugly" in a berth on San Francisco's waterfront, it had been transferred in 1898 to California's naval militia.[23]

One day late in October 1901, the arrival of a letter interrupted his routine. It brought important but not surprising news. Bessie had decided to end their marriage once and for all. The letter contained a copy of the petition for divorce she had filed in Wilmington Superior Court. In it she alleged that James had deserted her on October 2, 1898, shortly after his last visit.[24] That, of course, was not true. He had simply followed orders and gone to Mare Island to report for duty aboard the *Independence*. She was the one who had decided to stay in Wilmington, living apart from him.

Reading the letter and petition must have saddened James. But doing so may also have been liberating for him. His marriage, despite attempts at reconciliation, despite its secrets, and despite its deceptions to hide its true condition from others, had finally failed. There would be no reconciliation. His marriage was over. When he responded to Bessie's divorce petition, James made no attempt to contest it.

Four months later, on February 27, 1902, the superior court granted Bessie the divorce she sought. The Hetheringtons' marriage came to its end, once and for all. But the divorce decree contained a highly unusual provision about the children. Bessie and James each retained legal responsibility for a child. The judge assigned custody of Emlen, the son James had not fathered, to Bessie. James retained legal custody of his natural daughter, Gladys.[25]

Why?

James was willing to let his wife go. Bessie had in fact long ago left his bed, in effect deserting him. He would not, however, let her destroy his family—at least in the eyes of the law. He retained legal custody of Gladys because he was determined to preserve his family. That determination, as he had testified at his trial, was why he had shot and killed Gower Robinson in 1892. Now, 10 years later, that same determination to save his family, even if it lacked a wife, remained as strong as ever.

Gladys would be his daughter, his family, until the day he died—and beyond.

25

Afterlives

Divorce freed James and Bessie to begin life anew. They chose very different paths that ended at graves far apart: his in Washington, D.C., hers in Dayton, Ohio. What each of them did along the way following the divorce provides valuable clues to who they were, why the tragedy in Yokohama occurred, and how it was resolved. The Hetheringtons' story cannot be understood in full until those separate life paths are followed to their end.

The tale of Bessie's life after divorce begins with a question raised by her petition for dissolution of her marriage. If, as she alleged, the reason for permanent legal separation was desertion by James in October 1898, why didn't she file that request with the court immediately? What caused her to do so three years later, in October 1901? The answer to those questions is twofold. First, Delaware law required an abandoned spouse to wait three years before filing for divorce on grounds of desertion. Second, she wanted to be free to remarry. And she did so on Friday, April 18, 1902, barely six weeks after the divorce. On that evening, clad in blue silk trimmed with white lace and white chiffon, she wed John Walter (J.W.) McConnaughey in New York City. Her new husband was the treasurer of King County, Washington. Seattle is its county seat. The newspapers described him as a millionaire real estate broker and paint manufacturer. They also seized the opportunity to recount the details of the scandal, murder, and trial in Yokohama 10 years earlier.[1]

The news stories exaggerated Bessie's new husband's wealth and social status. McConnaughey was born 42 years earlier in Dayton, Ohio, and had come to Seattle by way of Kansas City, where he sold life insurance, and Portland, Oregon, where he was a bookkeeper. In 1892, he and his brother started what became a successful paint and varnish manufacturing firm, but he worked at the same time as a mortgage and loan broker. Two years before the wedding, he was living as a roomer in a boardinghouse—hardly appropriate quarters for a millionaire.[2]

How had the newlyweds met, living a continent apart? Bessie herself answered that question for a reporter on her second wedding day. She explained that they came to know one another while she and James were living in Port Townsend, Washington. J.W., as he preferred to be called, could have traveled there from Seattle on paint or mortgage loan business and been introduced to her there. Their acquaintance likely blossomed into something more over the years. The two could have met in Seattle if she took the ferry across Puget Sound for a day or more of shopping. That could have happened while James was away on temporary duty for extended periods. His absence could have provided the opportunity for repeated visits in 1896 and 1897. After refusing to follow James to Mare Island, California, Bessie early in 1898 reportedly traveled to Seattle. Why might she have done so, if not to see J.W.? Their connection over the following years likely continued, even if only through correspondence. That would have reprised the way Bessie and Gower Robinson had communicated back in Yokohama.[3]

Bessie and her new husband-to-be may also have met in Philadelphia in 1901. He might, after his election that year as county treasurer, have traveled east in search of funds from New York or Philadelphia banks to fund infrastructure projects and promote economic growth in Seattle. The city had been the "jumping-off place" for the Alaska gold rush of 1898, which in turn had flooded it with newcomers demanding better housing, goods, and public services. Sometime during 1901, Bessie left the small cottage outside Wilmington, once her maid's mother's home, where she had been living, and moved to Overbrook, Pennsylvania—a developing suburb-to-be of the City of Brotherly Love. That would have made it easy for Bessie and J.W. to seek one another out in greater Philadelphia.[4]

In any event, Bessie was unlikely to have married J. Walter McConnaughey barely two months after her divorce became final if the couple had not known and been in contact with each other for some time.

Bessie's New York City wedding took place under a cloud of sorts. Her older sister, Mary, had recently died, and her mother and younger sister, Helen, had moved to Overbrook, leaving her father behind in Wilmington. They came up from Philadelphia to witness the ceremony, but Emlen Hewes reportedly refused to attend. Perhaps his Quaker legacy kept him from doing so. In the Friends tradition, marriage required prior counseling of the man and woman by a committee from the local Meeting before it could be sanctioned and take place. None of that bothered Bessie, however. On this wedding day she told a reporter that her round-faced husband-to-be was "awful nice-looking and awful nice." The journalist said she was "evidently very happy."[5]

After the wedding, the couple traveled to Philadelphia, where they honeymooned for a week at the luxurious Hotel Stenton. Then Bessie (now Bessie Hewes Hetherington McConnaughey) and J.W. departed for Seattle. Her son, Emlen, was not with them. The boy, just five years old, had manifested mental and behavioral problems that made it impossible for him go to a regular school. Following the move to Overbrook, he was enrolled in the Training School for Feeble-Minded Children in Elwyn, Pennsylvania. He was later certified as feeble-minded and insane and transferred to Norristown State Hospital for the Insane, where he spent the rest of his life.[6]

Bessie's life in Washington State played out placidly for another 33 years. Her new husband, Walter, gave her the untroubled love, sexual fulfillment, and sense of normality that James had been unable to provide after what transpired in Yokohama. He provided economic stability, upper-middle-class respectability, and rootedness in place. With the exception of brief periods when he took up farming in Yakima County in central Washington and two years when his work took them to Tacoma and Bremerton, the McConnaugheys lived in Seattle for the rest of their lives. They never owned their own home but moved infrequently to residences all located in a few block area.[7]

Bessie suffered the loss of her parents at a distance—her mother in 1903 and her father four years later. But she saw her daughter, Gladys, grow up at her side, graduate from high school, blossom into a beautiful young woman, and marry a college graduate. Gladys and her husband, Julian, soon gave her a granddaughter. Sadly, the girl died before reaching her teens, bringing an end to Bessie's biological line. She died on March 15, 1935, in her 64th year. Five days later, with J.W. looking on, she was laid to rest in the McConnaughey family plot in Dayton.[8]

While Bessie's path pointed her in a new direction, James's life after divorce continued much the same as it had been before. With no wife, and Gladys far from him, it was lonely. He never remarried. But he had his mistress, the navy, and he returned gladly to her embrace. The navy treated him well, guiding his steps for the rest of his life. On October 25, 1902, he reported aboard the protected cruiser USS *Newark* as its executive officer. Second in command only to the captain, he carried out duties that were largely administrative. The ship was attached to the North Atlantic squadron and spent the better part of the next three years cruising in Caribbean and South American waters. His life then was much as it had been for most of the 1890s as a senior bachelor officer.[9]

From March through September of 1905, he served as executive officer of the USS *Minneapolis*, another protected cruiser slightly newer than the *Newark*. He supervised preparations for taking a Naval Observatory expedition to the western Mediterranean to observe a total solar eclipse. It would occur on August 30 of that year. The voyage across the Atlantic was unusual, for the ship was crowded with distinguished scientists from all over the United States and loaded with their complex astronomical equipment. James knew this would be his last sea voyage as a naval officer, for he had been placed on the retired list effective June 30, 1905. That happened to him—and several of his Naval Academy classmates who had not yet attained the rank of full commander—because the navy officer corps was limited in size by congressional fiat. The navy needed to be able to promote and retain more officers junior to those who had entered the service in the 1870s. Those younger officers had more of the technical engineering skills needed in the "new navy" of bigger, iron-clad, and more heavily armed warships than older men like James who had spent most of their careers on sailing or hybrid sail-and-steam vessels.[10]

Lieutenant Commander Hetherington's last days of active duty may have brought back memories of his first trans–Atlantic voyage nearly 30 years earlier. Then the *Richmond* had hurried past Gibraltar in an effort to catch up with former President Grant on the French Riviera. This time the *Minneapolis* paused at the legendary rock after firing the first American salute to the Spanish flag since the war that had ended six years earlier. The Americans then headed farther east in the Mediterranean until their ship dropped anchor in a small harbor near Valencia, Spain. There they experienced the wonder of an eclipse that afforded spectacular views of the sun's corona.[11]

The next day, September 1, 1905, the *Minneapolis* sailed for home. James Hetherington was not aboard. He stayed in Europe, on leave from active duty on the retired list, for the next three years. He traveled from one country to another, visiting famous sites and enjoying a pleasant life that most Americans could only dream of. When he returned to the United States, the navy recalled him to active duty as superintendent of lighthouse districts, first very briefly in Detroit, Michigan, and then at Charleston, South Carolina. His work was not onerous and he lived comfortably in a handsome old boardinghouse on Meeting Street, at the historic heart of the city, until 1911. Promoted retroactively to commander, he took leave and sailed for Italy, where he spent the spring and summer of that year. James returned to Charleston, staying there for the next two years, with interruptions only for medical treatment at naval hospitals in Washington, D.C., and Philadelphia.[12]

In May 1913, Commander Hetherington was named governor of the Naval Home in the City of Brotherly Love. He lived in quarters that dated back to the 1830s and ranked as a masterpiece of Greek Revival architecture. Officially he was responsible for the care of retired and wounded sailors, but his duties were light and he had ample time to stroll the beautifully groomed acres surrounding the home. He stayed there for the rest of his

25. Afterlives

life, save for visits with his daughter, Gladys, now Mrs. Julian H. Thomson. He spent Christmas 1916, his last, with her, her husband, and his granddaughter. In his later years, James suffered from heart disease, and on September 16, 1917, his heart stopped. He was 61 years old. Three days later, Commander James Henry Hetherington, U.S. Navy, was laid to rest, with full military honors and his daughter, Gladys, in attendance, at Arlington National Cemetery.[13]

A navy man and a family man to the end.

1892, 1917, 1935. Three lives ended. Three deaths separated by decades in time. Three graves a continent and an ocean apart. Three people whose lives came together in Yokohama in an explosive relationship. Love. Love that led to murder. Murder that ended one life and changed the life course of the other two. Love that did not find its fulfillment until life's end for all three. Love that finally let them be who they really were.

Love came late to George Gower Robinson. As a young man, he knew physical love with a woman many times over. But he never experienced emotional love, a feeling so deep that he knew he had to have it until his dying day. Then he met Bessie Hetherington. From that moment on, he was possessed by that love, one so powerful that he had to defy propriety,

Commander James Henry Hetherington, USN, grave, Arlington National Cemetery (https://www.findagrave.com/memorial/49203140/john-h-herthington).

break his word, and risk his reputation and his business to pursue it. He did so, even though his actions were inappropriate and morally wrong in the eyes of society. In the trial, Alexander Tison painted him as a ruthless, defiant, and provocative lecher. But something more than lust—love itself—drove the behavior that led to his death. John Frederick Lowder tried to get him to deny the love he felt, to give it up, and to seek his lover's husband's forgiveness. But even on his deathbed, Gower Robinson could not let go of the love he had found at last. He made Bessie Hetherington the ultimate beneficiary of his will. They buried him, and he carried his love for her to the grave.

James Henry Hetherington was no less possessed by love than the man he killed. But it was a conflicted love. He loved his profession, the naval service, to the extent that it functioned as a mistress in his life. He loved Bessie Hewes as a bridegroom should on the day of their wedding, and he intended their love to blossom in a proper, conventional way. They would love in private, give life to their children, and deepen their affection for one another as the years went by. They would behave properly and command respect as a happily married naval family.

But James's marriage was never normal. It was always a threesome, made so first by the presence of his mistress, the navy, and then by the intrusion of Gower Robinson. The seducer ignited a passion in James stronger than any he had ever known. It was protective love, yes, protective of his wife, Bessie; of his daughter, Gladys; and of his family—just as his defender, Alexander Tison, had argued in court. But it was also every bit as possessive and commanding as prosecutor Henry Litchfield had claimed. James's attack on Gower Robinson may have started with warning shots, but the final fatal shot was deliberate at the moment he fired it. That was the only way James could redeem his honor, restore his confidence as a lover, and rid his marriage of the succubus that was sucking away its life's blood.

That shot and his trial that followed wounded James's love for Bessie beyond repair. It remained, but it was never the same as it had been before they went to Yokohama. He clung to its remnants long after they left Japan, but in the end his mistress triumphed. Before and after the divorce, she directed his movements, commanded his affections, and sustained his livelihood. James Hetherington carried that professional love and paternal love—especially love for his daughter—to his grave.

What finally can be said of Bessie Hewes Hetherington McConnaughey? Over the course of her life, the longest of the three, she had known more love than either her husband James or her lover Gower. But hers was restless and troubled love. Propriety and passion warred within her. As a young woman, a Delaware belle, her physical beauty commanded

25. Afterlives

the attention of men of all sorts. Flirting gave her a flicker of sexual release. Marriage to James gave her more sexual satisfaction but demanded that she assent to the directing presence of his mistress, the U.S. Navy, in their lives. Bessie found something more in her liaisons with Gower Robinson, sexual fulfillment perhaps, glamour, wealth, and the prospect of greater freedom certainly.

Once she experienced that, she was forever torn between her marital and maternal obligations and her natural sexual needs and desires. She tried but failed to become a proper, conventional navy officer's wife in Yokohama. She struggled to be a loving single parent thereafter. But virtual celibacy? Bessie found life without sex during the long separations from her husband impossible. That led her to the relationship, however brief, that produced her son, Emlen. He hovered over her relationship with James like a dark cloud. He became a maternal burden she could not bear. Eventually she realized she had to divorce—to put an end to marriage without the kind of love she needed.

Her life with James Hetherington, their life together, had been anything but normal. At its end, ironically, she longed for the conventional. She found it—sexually satisfying in private, respectable in public, and unremarkable in every other way—with John Walter McConnaughey. His love unending she carried to her grave.

What happened in Yokohama in 1891–1892 was a tragedy. Not just a sad or unfortunate sequence of events, but tragedy as the ancient Greeks understood the word: a series of events with fatal consequences brought about by the very nature of the persons involved. And the cause of the tragedy in Yokohama was love—love in various forms and combinations that came together in an explosive mixture.

In the end, it all came down to love.

Chapter Notes

Preface

1. *Seattle Post-Intelligencer*, September 1, 1923; *Seattle Star*, September 5, 1923.

Chapter 1

1. Hetherington, Henry S., entry in *Encyclopedia Dubuque* at http://www.encyclopediadubuque.org; https://iowagravestones.org/gs-pfview.php?id=1017611; 1850 U.S .Federal Census, accessed via ancestry.com.
2. Robert F. Klein, ed., *Dubuque: Frontier River City: Thirty-Five Historical Sketches by Chandler C. Childs* (Dubuque: Research Center for Dubuque Area History, Loras College, 1984), 118, 130, 152–153.
3. Hetherington, Henry S., entry in *Encyclopedia Dubuque*; Panic of 1857, https://en.wikipedia.org/wiki/Panic_of_1857.
4. Hetherington, Henry S., entry in *Encyclopedia Dubuque*; Mohammad A. Chaichian, *White Racism on the Western Urban Frontier: Dynamics of Race and Class in Dubuque, Iowa (1800–2000)* (Trenton, NJ: Africa World Press, 2006), 1; Iowa in the American Civil War entry, https://en.wikipedia.org/wiki/Iowa-in-the-American-Civil-War; 1870 United States Census, accessed via ancestry.com.
5. Dubuque High School in *Encyclopedia Dubuque*; Dubuque Senior High School at https://en.wikipedia.org/Dubuque_Senior_High_School.
6. George S. Hetherington marker, Iowagravestones.org; Sarah Hill gravestone image at Iowa Gravestone Photo Project, https://Iowagravestones.org/gs_view.php?id=1017613; Maria Soule gravestone image at https://iowagravestones.org/gs_view.php?id+1017609; Henry Hetherington-Maria A. Soule entry, February 17, 1869, Iowa Select Marriage Index, 1758–1996, accessed via ancestry.com.
7. Craig L. Symonds, *The U.S. Navy: A Concise History* (New York: Oxford University Press, 2016), 55; United States Naval Academy Alumni Association, Inc., *Register of Alumni Graduates and Former Naval Cadets and Midshipmen, 1845–1981* (Annapolis: U.S. Naval Academy Alumni Association, 1981), 164–171. This source will hereinafter be cited as *USNAR*.
8. Panic of 1873 at https://en.wikipedia.org/wiki/Panic_of_1873; Caroline Fraser, *Prairie Fires: The American Dreams of Laura Ingalls Wilder* (New York: Henry Holt and Company, 2017), 64, 70–71, 85; Henry Samuel Hetherington entry, *Encyclopedia Dubuque*.
9. *USNAR 1845–1981*, 161–172.
10. Ballotopedia.org/United_States_congressional_delegations_from_Iowa, William G. Donnan entry; William B. Allison entry, https//:en.wikipedia.org/William_B.Allison; A.P.C., "Glimpse of Annapolis and the Naval Academy," *Oliver Optic's Magazine: Our Boys and Girls* 17 (April 1875), 210–211.
11. *USNAR*, 172.
12. United States Naval Academy and David Dixon Porter entries at https://en.wikipedia.org/wiki/, https://en.wikipedia.org/wiki/United_States_Naval_Academy; A.P.C., "The Naval Academy Again. Getting In and Staying There," *Oliver Optic's*

Magazine: Our Boys and Girls 17 (May 1875), 262–266.

13. *USNAR*, 172.

14. Peter Karsten, *The Naval Aristocracy: The Golden Age of Annapolis and the Emergence of Modern American Nationalism* (Annapolis: Naval Institute Press, 1972), 37–40.

15. United States Naval Academy Yearbook 1879, U.S. School Catalogs, 1765–1935 for James Henry Hetherington, accessed via ancestrylibrary.com.

16. United States Naval Academy Yearbooks 1974–1878, accessed in U.S School Catalogs, 1765–1935 entry for James Henry Hetherington, at ancestry.com.

17. United States Naval Academy and David Dixon Porter entries at https:en.wikipedia.org/wiki/.

18. A.P.C., "Glimpses of Annapolis and the Naval Academy," *Oliver Optic's Magazine: Our Boys and Girls* 18 (July 1875) 213–214; Karsten, *The Golden Age of Annapolis*, 31. Before the Civil War, the summer cruise had been "the single most important aspect of the Naval Academy program." It remained an essential element of midshipmen's learning in postwar years. Charles Todorich, *The Spirited Years: A History of the Antebellum Naval Academy* (Annapolis: Naval Institute Press, 1984), 179.

19. *USNAR*, 172; Less than half of those appointed to the Naval Academy in the last half of the 19th century graduated. William P. Leeman, *The Long Road to Annapolis: The Founding of the Naval Academy and the Emerging American Republic* (Chapel Hill: University of North Carolina Press, 2010), 235.

Chapter 2

1. Hetherington Record of Service, September 20, 1878.

2. USS *Richmond* (1860) entry, http://Wikipedia.org/wiki/USS Richmond_(1860).

3. *New York Times*, November 9; 1878; *Boston Daily Globe*, November 9, 15, and 24, 1878.

4. USS *Richmond* (1860) entry at http://wikipedia.org/wiki/USS_Richmond_(1860).

5. Frank Emory Bunts, *Letters from the Asiatic Station 1881–1883* (Cleveland: The Caxton Press, 1938), 24–26.

6. Edwina S. Campbell, *Citizen of a Wider Commonwealth: Ulysses S. Grant's Postpresidential Diplomacy* (Carbondale: Southern Illinois University Press, 2016), 3, 92–144.

7. Campbell, 98–100.

8. *Boston Daily Globe*, April 1, 1906; *Richmond II* (1860) entry, *Dictionary of American Naval Fighting Ships* at http:www/history.navy.mil/content/history/nhhc/research/histories/ship-histories/danfs/r/Richmond II.html; *Annual Report of the Secretary of the Navy on the Operations of the Department for the Year 1879* (Washington, D.C.: Government Printing Office, 1880), 34. Material from this source and its subsequent volumes will be cited as *Secretary of the Navy, Annual Report* with appropriate date following; *Boston Daily Globe*, April 1, 1906.

9. Richard T. Chang, "General Grant's 1879 Visit to Japan," *Monumenta Nipponica* 24 (1969), 376; N.B. Dennys, ed., *The Treaty Ports of China and Japan* (London: Trubner and Company, 1867), 563–566.

10. Chang, 377; USS *Richmond* deck log, July 3, 1879; USS *Monongahela* deck log, Record Group 24, U.S. National Archives, Washington, D.C.

11. USS *Monongahela* deck log, July 4, 1879, Record Group 24, NAID167215167, United States National Archives, Washington, D.C.

12. *The Japan Weekly Mail and Times*, July 5, 1879, reprinted in Edition Synapse in Association with Yokohama Archives of History (Tokyo: Edition Synapse, 2009), 360–363; Chang, 378; Stephen Mansfield, *Tokyo: A Biography* (Tokyo: Tuttle, 2016), 87.

13. U.S. Naval Hospital and Case papers, 1825–1889, for J.H. Hetherington, Yokohama, Japan, 1877–1881, Roll 168, U.S. National Archives, accessed via ancestry.com.

14. Yasuhiro Makimura, *Yokohama and the Silk Trade: How Eastern Japan Became the Primary Economic Region of Japan, 1843–1893* (New York: Columbia University Press, 2017), 73–115, passim.

15. *The Directory & Chronicle for China, Japan, Corea, Indo-China, Straits Settlements, Malay States, Siam, Netherlands, India, Borneo, the Philippines, & c*

(Hong Kong: The *Hong Kong Daily Press* Office, 1877), 340–352. Material from subsequent volumes of this source will be cited as *Directory and Chronicle* with appropriate date.

16. *Secretary of the Navy Annual Report, 1879* (Washington, D.C.: Government Printing Office, 1880), 34–35; Bunts, 64–65; Daniel Pidgeon, *An Engineer's Holiday, or, Notes of a Round Trip from Longitude 0 to 0* (London, 1882) in Hugh Cortazzi, ed., *Victorians in Japan: In and Around the Treaty Ports* (London: The Athlone Press, 1987), 296.

17. *Secretary of the Navy Annual Report, 1878*, 447; Frederick G. Notehelfer, ed., *Japan through American Eyes: The Journal of Francis Hall Kanagawa and Yokohama 1859–1866* (Princeton: Princeton University Press, 1992), 46, 394–395; Elinor and James A. Barnes, eds., *Naval Surgeon: Revolt in Japan 1868–1869* (Bloomington: Indiana University Press, 1963), 30–31; http://www.oldphotosjapan.com/photos/284/nectarine-no-9brothel#.WsWbw4jwaUk; Neil Pedlar, *The Imported Pioneers: Westerners Who Helped Build Modern Japan* (New York: St. Martin's Press, 1990), 63; Ronald Gower Sutherland, Lord, *My Reminiscences* (3rd. ed., New York: Charles Scribner's Sons, 1884),190.

18. Robert Seager, II, *Alfred Thayer Mahan: The Man and His Letters* (Annapolis: Naval Institute Press, 1977), 72–77; Bunts, *Letters from the Asian Station*, 106.

19. *The Trial of Lieutenant Hetherington, U.S.N., for Shooting George Gower Robinson, Esq.* (Yokohama: Box of Curios Printing Office, 1892), 229. This source will hereinafter be cited as *Trial Transcript*.

20. Bunts, *Letters from the Asiatic Station 1881–1883*, 11–12, described this journey in reverse a year after James Hetherington made it.

21. Hetherington Record of Service, May 13, 31, June 4, 1880.

Chapter 3

1. Proverbs 30:18–19.
2. Hetherington Record of Service, April 4, 1881, March 3, June 14, 1883, June 26, 1884; *Annual Report of the Secretary of the Navy* (Washington, D.C.: Government Printing Office, 1880–1884) *1880–1881*, 2:413; *1882–1883*, 92–93; *1884*, 19–20, 106–107, 256, 392.
3. Hetherington Record of Service, June 14, 1883.
4. Jason W. Smith, *To Master the Boundless Sea: The U.S. Navy, the Marine Environment, and the Cartography of Empire* (Chapel Hill: University of North Carolina Press, 2018), 22, 75–77, 96, 102–103, 127–133.
5. Smith, 8; *Report of the Superintendent of the U.S. Coast and Geodetic Survey Showing the Progress of the Work during the Fiscal Year Ending With June 1886* (Washington, D.C.: Government Printing Office, 1886), 47. Hereinafter *USC&GS Annual Report*.
6. *USC&GS Annual Report, 1883–1887* (Washington, D.C.: Government Printing Office, 1884–1889), passim.
7. *USC&GS Annual Report, 1886* (Washington, D.C.: Government Printing Office, 1886), 55.
8. Emil R. Salvini, *The Summer City by the Sea: Cape May, New Jersey: An Illustrated History* (Belleville, NJ: Wheal-Grace Publications, 1995), 29, 32, 69; Cape May Point, New Jersey, at https://en.wiipedia.org/wiki/Cape_May_Point,New_Jersey.
9. *USCG Annual Report, 1885* (Washington, D.C.: Government Printing Office, 1886), 47.
10. *Trial Transcript*, 225.
11. *Trial Transcript*, 225.
12. Emlen Hewes entry, U.S. Quaker Meeting Records, 1681–1935, and Delaware Marriage Records, 1744–1912, both accessed via ancestry.com; https://www.geni.com/people/Bessie-Hewes/6000000000091666650865.
13. History of Delaware at https://en.wikipedia.org/w iki/History_of_Delaware; Carol E. Hoffecker, *Wilmington, Delaware: Portrait of an Industrial City, 1830–1910* (Charlottesville: University Press of Virginia, 1974), 117.
14. Hoffecker, *Wilmington*, 17–22, 37; https://en.wikipedia.org/wiki/Wilmington_Delaware; *Secretary of the Navy Annual Report, 1884–1885* (Washington, D.C.: Government Printing Office, 1885), 165, 206.
15. Hoffecker, *Wilmington*, 47, 68, 112–113; Emlen and Mary Augusta Hewes property indentures, January 7 and April

17, 1885, in Delaware, Land Records, 1677–1947, accessed at ancestry.com; *Wilmington Evening Journal*, March 8, 1902 accessed via Library of Congress>Chronicling America.

16. Hoffecker, xv, 37; History of Delaware at https://en.wikipedia.org/wiki/History_of_Delaware.

17. *Twentieth Annual Catalog of the Officers and Students of Vassar College* (Poughkeepsie, NY: Haight & Dudley Printers, 1885), 15–35, accessed at https://catalog.haithitrust.org/Record/002133289.

18. Preparatory School entry, Vassar Encyclopedia, accessed at http://vcencyclopedia.vassar.edu/curriculum/preparatory-schoo.html.

19. *Dubuque Daily Herald*, March 9, 1892, at https://newspaperarchive.com/dubuque-daily-herald-mar-09-1892-p-4/; Hetherington service record, December 6, 1886; August 25, 1887.

20. https://en.wikipedia.org/wiki/USS_Michigan<(1843); James Dykstra, "The USS *Michigan*," *Military History of the Upper Great Lakes*, October 11, 2015, at ss.sites.mtu.edu/mhugl/2015/10/11/the-uss-michigan/; *Secretary of the Navy Annual Report, 1886–1887* (Washington, D.C.: Government Printing Office 1887), 25, 130; *Trial Transcript*, 225.

21. Minnie Rebecca Carpenter entry, 1880 U.S. census, accessed at ancestry.com; *Dubuque Daily Herald*, March 9, 1892.

22. Wedding description adapted from *The Book of Common Prayer of the Church of England with Daily Prayers* (Glasgow: William Collins and Co., 1845), 203; *Wilmington Evening Journal*, December 10, 1889; Wilmington, Delaware, dispatch in *Boston Globe*, March 7, 1892.

23. J. Harold Ellens, *Sex in the Bible: A New Consideration* (Westport, CT: Praeger, 2006), 85–87.

Chapter 4

1. en.wikipedia.org/wiki/Erie, Pennsylvania.
2. Hetherington Record of Service, January 1, 6, 1890.
3. Hetherington Record of Service, April 1, 1890.
4. *Trial Transcript*, 226.

5. *Trial Transcript*, 226–227; *Secretary of the Navy Annual Report, 1890* (Washington, D.C.: Government Printing Office, 1890), 130.

6. *Trial transcript*, 227–228; 1900 United States Federal Census for Gladis (Gladys) Hetherington, accessed via ancestry.com.

7. David Dixon Porter, "Naval Education and Organization," *United Services: A Quarterly Review of Military and Naval Affairs* 1 (July 1879), 470–471.

8. *Trial Transcript*, 228–229; Hetherington Record of Service, April 24, 1891.

9. *Trial Transcript*, 229–230.

Chapter 5

1. *Trial Transcript*, 230.
2. *Secretary of the Navy Annual Report, 1891* (Washington, D.C.: Government Printing Office, 1892), 161.

3. Bering Sea Arbitration at https://en.wikpedia.org/wiki/Bering_Sea_Arbitration; Charles S. Campbell, Jr., "The Anglo-American Crisis in the Bering Sea, 1890–1891," *Mississippi Valley Historical Review* 48 (December 1961), 393–398–406; Paul Gibb, "Selling Out Canada? The Role of Sir Julian Pauncefote in the Bering Sea Dispute, 1899–1902," *International History Review* 24 (December 2002), 817, 820–829, 844.

4. *Trial Transcript*, 230; Jefferson County Historical Society, *Images of America: Port Townsend* (Charleston, SC: Arcadia, 2008), 19; Esquimalt Royal Naval Dockyard entry at https://en.wikipedia.ogr/Esquimalt_Royal_Navy-Dockyard.

5. *Secretary of the Navy Annual Report, 1892* (Washington, D.C.: Government Printing Office, 1892), 854: *Marion* (Sloop of War) entry at https://www.history.navy.mil./research/histories/danfs/m/marion-sloop-of-war.html; *Trial Transcript*, 121, 187, 199, 229.

6. *Trial Transcript*, 230–231.
7. *Boston Daily Globe* and *New York Tribune*, both March 7, 1892.
8. Central Pacific and Union Pacific Railroad advertisements and schedules at http://cprr.org/Museum/Ephemera/CP-UP_Timetable_1881/index.html.
9. Excerpts from Helen Hunt Jackson, *Bits of Travel at Home* (Boston:

Roberts Brothers, 1887) at http://cprr.org/Museum/Bits_of_Travel_at_Home.html.
   10. Pacific Mail Steamship China at http://timetableimages.com/maritime/images/pm100.html.
   11. *San Francisco Chronicle*, September 27, 1891.
   12. Basil Hall Chamberlain and W.B. Mason, *A Handbook for Travelers in Japan, Third Edition* (London: John Muray and Yokohama: Kelly & Walsh Limited, 1891), 12; *Trial Transcript*, 76, 213.
   13. *China Directory and Chronicle, 1890*, 284. Hereinafter *China Directory* with appropriate date.
   14. Hughes Krafft comment quoted in Christopher Reed, *Bachelor Japanists: Japanese Aesthetics and Western Masculinities* (New York: Columbia University Press, 2016), 101.
   15. John Frank Lowder entry in Bernd Lepach, *Meiji Portraits*. This source is an online biographical compilation of persons and business firms of influence in Japan in the Meiji period (1868–1912). Dr. Lepach resides in Leipzig, Germany. meiji-portraits.de/welcome.html; Saitō Takio, *Yokohama gaikokujin bochi ni iru hitobito (People in the Yokohama Foreign General Cemetery)* (Yokohama: Yūrindo, 2012), 29–32.
   16. Anatoli Grigorievitch Lobanov-Rostovsky entry in Lepach, *Meiji Portraits*; Prince Anatoly Lobanov de Rostoff at https://www.geni.com/people/Prince-Anatoly-Lobanov-de-Rostoff/600000000 8731745136.
   17. *Trial Transcript*, 76; https://www.pekintimes.com/article/20120525/NEWS/305259966.
   18. George Gower Robinson entry, in Lepach, *Meiji Portraits*.
   19. John S. Robinson entry in Lepach, *Meiji Portraits*; *China Directory and Chronicle, 1877*, 220.
   20. Meg Vivers, *An Irish Engineer: The Extraordinary Achievements of Thomas J. Waters and Family in Early Meiji Japan and Beyond* (Brisbane: Copyright Publishing, 2013), 183.
   21. *Arizona Republic*, March 18, 1892; *San Francisco Call*, April 4, 1892; *Trial Transcript*, 80, 132, 160; Herman Jackson Warner, George Edward Woodberry, ed., *New Letters of an Idle Man* (London: Constable, 1913), 148.
   22. *Trial Transcript*, 141, 208, 210; *Boston Daily Globe*, March 7, 1892; *Washington Post*, March 12, 1892.
   23. *Trial transcript*, 76–786–78; Columbus R. Cummings, Mayor of Pekin, Illinois, at https://www.pekintimes.com/article/20120525/NEWS/305259966; *Boston Globe*, March 9, 1892.
   24. A trap was a two-wheeled vehicle pulled by horses. It could accommodate up to three people: driver, passenger, and bettō.
   25. *Trial Transcript*, 208–209.
   26. *Trial Transcript*, 213.

Chapter 6

1. *Trial Transcript*, 87.
2. *Trial Transcript*, 231–232.
3. Rudyard Kipling, *From Sea to Sea* (Leipzig: B. Tauschnitz, 1900), 56. The book described Kipling's experiences in Yokohama in 1889 and was first published two years later.
4. *China Directory, 1890*, 284, 288–290; Kipling, *From Sea to Sea*, 69.
5. Naoko Abe, *The Sakura Obsession* (New York: Vintage Books, 2019), 129; Tokyo descriptions from Basil Hall Chamberlain and W.B. Mason, *A Handbook for Travelers in Japan* (3rd ed., London: John Murray, and Yokohama: Kelly and Walsh Ltd., 1891), 63, 75–87.
6. Karsten, *The Naval Aristocracy*, 132–133.
7. *Trial Transcript*, 233–237.
8. *Trial Transcript*, 249–250.
9. *Trial Transcript*, 234–37, 242–243.
10. Bartlett held the rank of commander. But as a ship's commanding officer, he was, by custom, always addressed as "Captain." Hereinafter he will bear that title.
11. *Trial Transcript*, 238–241.
12. Adolfo Farsari, in Lepach, *Meiji Portraits*; https://en.wikipedia.org/wiki/Adolfo_Farsarl. Born Italian, he emigrated to America, fought in the Union Army during the Civil War, and came to Japan in 1873. His studio, formed with a Japanese partner, became the preeminent purveyor of photographs of Japan to tourists and Yokohama residents alike.
13. *Trial Transcript*, 241–246.

Chapter 7

1. Chandler Gibbens entry, Massachusetts, Town and Vital Records, 1620–1988; Albert Carter Read entry, UK, Foreign and Overseas Registers of British Subjects, 1628–1969; Caspar Andreas Valdemar Blad entry, Denmark Church Records, 1812–1918, all at ancestry.com; *Trial Transcript*, 141.
2. *Trial Transcript*, 124–126, 141–147, 160–162, 246; After a short but distinguished career as an architect in Japan, the brother-in-law had gone into mining in New Zealand and then into partnership with his brothers. They had just added the Tomboy gold mine near Telluride, Colorado, to their already huge mining syndicate. Vivers, *An Irish Engineer*, 84–134, 191–220.
3. *Trial Transcript*, 148.
4. *Trial Transcript*, 132–135; Brooke Hyde Pearson entry, UK, Foreign and Overseas Registers of British Subjects, 1628–1969, at ancestry.com.
5. *Trial Transcript*, 136–137, 247.
6. *Trial Transcript*, 238–249.
7. *Trial Transcript*, 248–253.
8. *Trial Transcript*, 256.
9. *Trial Transcript*, 97–100.
10. *Trial Transcript*, 176–177.
11. *Trial Transcript*, 181–184.
12. *Trial Transcript*, 89–90, 153–154, 177–178.
13. *Trial Transcript*, 101, 168, 219.
14. *Trial Transcript*, 260.
15. *Trial Transcript*, 103–104, 261–262.

Chapter 8

1. *Trial Transcript*, 118–119, 128, 157.
2. *Trial Transcript*, 120.
3. *Trial Transcript*, 268.
4. *Trial Transcript*, 197.
5. Martin Pors, Heinemann & Company, Otto Reimers, and Otto Reimers & Company entries, in Lepach, *Meiji Portraits*. By 1892, the Heinemann firm had become Otto Reimers & Co.
6. *Trial Transcript*, 203.
7. The phrase comes from Romans 12:19, which, in turn, is paraphrased from Deuteronomy 32:35.
8. *Trial Transcript*, 269–270.
9. *Trial Transcript*, 270–273.
10. *Trial Transcript*, 48–49.
11. *Trial Transcript*, 50–51; Pietro Beretta, Beretta & Co., and Pietro Sacconi entries, in Lepach, *Meiji Portraits*.
12. *Trial Transcript*, 40–44; Stuart Eldridge, Edwin Wheeler, Harry V. Henson, and E.H. Andreis entries, in Lepach, *Meiji Portraits*; Thomas Hall Tripler entry, England, United Grand Lodge of England Freemason Membership Registers, 1751–1921, at ancestry.com.

Chapter 9

1. Richard Fritz Theodor Kleffel in Lepach, *Meiji Portraits*; Maurice Eden Paul 1865–1944 entry in *Oxford Dictionary of National Biography* at https://doi.org/10.1093/odnb/9780198614128.013.5631.
2. *Trial Transcript*, 40–41.
3. https://en.wikipedia.org/wiki/Inquest.
4. Image Y291-6, Yokohama Archives of History. The British Consulate at Yokohama from W.H. Morton-Cameron, comp., W. Feldwick, ed., *Present Day Impressions of Japan: the History, People, Commerce, Industries, and Resources of Japan and Japan's Colonial Empire* (London: The Globe Encyclopedia, 1919); Yokohama entry Room for Diplomacy catalog of British embassy and consulate buildings, 1800–2010, at https://roomfordiplomacy.com/Japanese-consulates incorrectly asserts that no photographs of the pre-1923 consulate exist; *Japan Mail*, February 20, 1892, reprinted as Tokyo: Edition Synapse, 2009. Unless otherwise indicated, all information about the inquest in this and following paragraphs is taken from this source.
5. Troup, Allcock, Box, and Prevost entries, *Meiji Portraits*; Hugh Cortazzi, *British Envoys in Japan*, 308; Grace Fox, *Britain and Japan 1858–1883* (Oxford: The Clarendon Press, 1969), 361; Richard T. Chang, *The Justice of the Western Consular Courts in Nineteenth-Century Japan* (Westport, CT: Greenwood Press, 1984), 127; Allcock, Box, and Prevost entries, in *China Directory and Chronicle, 1892*, 29, 42, 627.
6. Allcock, Box, and Prevost entries, in *China Directory and Chronicle, 1892*, 549.

7. *USNAR*, 168.
8. Henry Charles Litchfield entry, in Lepach, *Meiji Portraits*.
9. *Wilmington Evening Journal*, April 11, 1892. Bessie's father showed the letter to a journalist and allowed its publication in paraphrased form.
10. Admiral Belknap comments as reported in *New York Tribune*, March 15, 1892.
11. *North China Herald*, April 8, 1892.
12. *China Directory 1892*, 31.

Chapter 10

1. George M. Brooke, Jr., ed, *John M. Brooke's Pacific Cruise and Japanese Adventure, 1858–1860* (Honolulu: University of Hawaii Press, 1976), 166–168.
2. *China Chronicle, 1892*, 42, 549; Peter St. John Hellendale entry, *Meiji Portraits*.
3. Eric Casson, *The Church on Colonel's Corner* (Yokohama: Christ Church, 1962), 6–8: en.wikipedia.org-Christ _Church_Yokohama; http://www.yokohamachristchurch.org/archive_material.html. The account of the funeral service that follows is based on its description in *North China Herald*, February 26, 1892.
4. Casson, 6–8.
5. Vivers, *An Irish Engineer*, 63, 75, 84, 98, 147. The uncles' endeavors included design and construction of a Nagasaki coal mine, the Osaka Mint, an extension to the emperor's palace, and a famous Tokyo bridge.
6. Richardson Affair entry, *Japan: An Illustrated Encyclopedia* (Tokyo: Kodansha, 1993), 1263.
7. *China Chronicle, 1892*, 22, 437.
8. John 11: 25 and 26.
9. *The Book of Common Prayer of the Church of England* (1662 edition) (Glasgow: William Collins and Company, n.d.). I am indebted to the Rev. Marjorie Suedekum of Saint Matthew's Episcopal Church, Grand Junction, Colorado, for informing me that the Anglican Church in Japan used this edition of the prayer book for its services in the 1890s.

Chapter 11

1. *China Chronicle, 1892*, 36, 44; *Tokyo Mainichi Shimbun*, February 15, 1892, ff; *Encyclopedia of Japan*, 1079.
2. *North China Herald and Supreme Court & Consular Gazette*, February 26, 1892; Robert Young at https://www.findagrave.com/memorial/80036086/rober-young; Robert Young in Lepach, *Meiji Portraits*.
3. *North China Herald and Supreme Court & Consular Gazette*, February 26, 1892; *The Straits Times Weekly Issue*, March 9, 1892; *The Advertiser* (Adelaide, South Australia), April 11, 1892; *Manchester Guardian*, March 7, 1892.
4. SS City of Peking at en.wikipedia.org/SS_City_of_Peking; *San Francisco Call*, March 6, 1892.
5. The regional wire services were not combined to form the Associated Press until December 1892, https://en.wikipedia.org/wiki/Associated_Press.
6. *Boston Daily Globe*, March 7, 1892.
7. *Boston Daily Globe*, March 7, 1892, incorporating wire reports from Dubuque and Wilmington newspapers; *Washington Post*, March 7, 1892.
8. A masher was variously defined as "any foppish overdressed fellow who parades more than he postures" or "a moral spittoon." Kerry Seagrave, *Beware the Masher: Sexual Harassment in American Public Places, 1880-1930* (Jefferson, NC: McFarland, 2014), 12.
9. *Washington Post*, March 12, 1892; *San Francisco Call*, April 5, 1892.
10. *Boston Daily Globe*, March 7, 1892, drawing on wire reports from San Francisco, New York City, and Washington, D.C.
11. *Wilmington Evening Journal*, March 7, 1892, accessed via Library of Congress, *Chronicling America: Historic American Newspapers*.
12. *Washington Post* and *Boston Daily Globe*, March 7, 1892.
13. *New York Tribune*, March 9, 1892; *Saint Louis Post-Dispatch*, March 9 and 13, 1892; *China Chronicle, 1890*, 72. Dr. Norfleet's story about Bessie likely was third-hand. The *Monocacy* had left Yokohama before Bessie arrived there, so he could not have gotten the information firsthand. *Secretary of the Navy Annual Report, 1891*, 162.

14. February 22 Yokohama report, printed in *Arizona Daily Republican*, March 18, 1892.
15. The RMS *Oceanic* was the first modern passenger liner in the famed British White Star Line. It was chartered to the Occidental and Oriental Steamship Company. https://en.wikipedia.org/wiki/RMS_Oceanic_(1870).
16. *San Francisco Call*, February 28, March 15; *New York Times, Los Angeles Times*, March 15, 1892.
17. *Los Angeles Times*, April 1, 1892; *San Francisco Call*, April 4 and 5, 1892.
18. *Baltimore Sun*, February 19, 21, May 20, 1892; *Chicago Tribune*, February 22, 1892; *Washington Post*, August 9, September 23, 1892, July 17, 1901. The case gained particular notoriety because Mrs. Deacon was the daughter of Rear Admiral Charles H. Baldwin, reportedly the wealthiest man in the United States Navy. Edward Deacon commanded widespread public sympathy but was convicted of manslaughter, then pardoned by the president of France.
19. *Los Angeles Times*, March 11, 1892, based on March 10 report from Dubuque; *Washington Post*, March 12, 1892; Hammersmith, *Spoilsmen in a "Flowery Fairyland,"* 121, 132.
20. *Saint Louis Post-Dispatch*, March 13, 1892; *New York Tribune*, March 15, 1892.
21. *Washington Post* and *San Francisco Chronicle*, March 12, 1892; *Saint Louis Post-Dispatch*, March 13, 1892. The only man hanged was a Confederate sympathizer who shot a Union man in Nagasaki. The consul there wrongly sent him to Shanghai, where the consul, the son of Secretary of State William Seward, convicted him.

Chapter 12

1. Unless otherwise indicated, all material in this chapter comes from *Trial Transcript*, 1–9. U.S. Social Security Applications and Claims Index, 1936–2007, accessed via findagrave.com; United States Census, 1870, 1880, and 1900, Washington, birth records, 1870–1935, all accessed via ancestry.com; *Los Angeles Times*, March 3, 1891; *Tacoma City Directory, 1896*, 593, accessed via ancestry.com; W.D. Tillotson entry, U.S. Register of Civil, Military, and Naval Service 1863–1959, volume 1, 1891, 40 accessed via ancestry.com; *Seattle Post-Intelligencer*, September 24, 1890.
2. Saitō Takio, *Yokohama Gaikokujin bochi ni iru hitobito (People in the Yokohama Foreign General Cemetery)* (Yokohama: Yūrindo, 2012), 38–39; George H. Scidmore entry, Encyclopedia Dubuque, at http://www.encyclopediadubuque.org/index.php?title+SCIDMORE%2D_George_H; *Washington Post* and *South China Morning Post*, November 28, 1922; Eliza Ruhamah Scidmore at https://www.britannica.com/print/article/528753; http://www.elizascidmore.com; Eliza's Japan at elizascidmore.coom/eliza-s-japan.
3. The book incorporated as an appendix his 1882 *A Digest of Leading Cases Decided in the United States Consular Court at Kanagawa, Japan, of Decisions and Opinions of the United States Minister in Japan, of Decisions of the United States Cirtcuit Court for the District of California, of Opinions of the Attorney General of the United States, and of Instructions from the Department of State of the United States, Relating to Consular Court Jurisdiction in Japan* (Yokohama: R. Meikeljohn and Co., 1882).
4. *New York Times*, July 17, 1938; Tison entry in Lepach, *Meiji Portraits*; Alexander Tison entry, *History of Eaton County, Michigan*, at https://www.zoominfo.com/p/Alexander-Tison/1349979740.
5. *Chicago Tribune*, May 29, 1892.
6. *San Francisco Chronicle*, April 10, 1892.
7. *Los Angeles Herald*, March 15, 1892; *New York Tribune*, April 30, 1892; James's March 10, 1892, letter to Emlen Hewes, paraphrased and published in *Wilmington Evening Journal*, April 11, 1892.
8. *Trial Transcript*, 1–2.
9. T.B. Van Buren to Editor, June 1, 1882, in *New York Tribune*, July 5, 1882.
10. Richard T. Chang, *The Justice of the Western Consular Courts in Nineteenth-Century Japan*, 11–12; Scidmore, *Outline Lectures on the History, Organization, Jurisdiction, and Practice of the Ministerial and Consular Courts of the United States of America in Japan* (Yokohama: Kelly & Walsh, 1887), 15–16.

11. It is unclear which of the six men surnamed Rice listed in Lepach, *Meiji Portraits*, Tison was referring to.
12. *Trial Transcript*, 3; A. Gilmore Smith in Lepach, *Meiji Portraits*.
13. A. Gilmore Smith, Edmund Samuel Booth, J.R. Simon, and Nathaniel Ferdinand Smith entries, Lepach, *Meiji Portraits*; Biography of Rev. Eugene Samuel Booth D.D. by Ralph Monclar at https://www.booksie.com.
14. Chang, *The Justice of the Western Consular Courts in Nineteenth-Century Japan*, 9–11.
15. *Trial Transcript*, 55.

Chapter 13

1. *Trial Transcript*, 8–10.
2. Hammersmith, *Spoilsmen in a "Flowery Fairyland,"* 81, 86–87.
3. *Trial Transcript*, 10–12.
4. *Trial Transcript*, 13.
5. *Trial Transcript*, 13–14.
6. The transliteration of Japanese names in the text of the trial transcript is anachronistic. I have rendered them in accordance with today's usage.
7. Miura substituted for John McLean, the consulate general's regular interpreter, who was absent for reasons that remain unknown. McLean entry in Lepach, *Meiji Portraits*; *China Chronicle and Directory, 1892*, 628.
8. *Trial Transcript*, 15–21.
9. The personal name Akira is incorrectly romanized as Achirais in the trial transcript.
10. *Trial Transcript*, 21–31.
11. *Trial Transcript*, 30–31; *Japan Weekly Mail*, April 2, 1892.
12. *Trial Transcript*, 31–39, 46–47.
13. *Trial Transcript*, 39–49.
14. *Trial Transcript*, 49–50.

Chapter 14

1. *New York Tribune*, March 15, 1892; *Daily American* (Nashville, Tennessee), March 15, 1892.
2. Thomas Keneally, *American Scoundrel: The Life of the Notorious Civil War General Dan Sickles* (New York: Anchor Books, 200)], 150–197; Daniel Sickles at https://en.wikipedia.org/wiki/Daniel_Sickles; Daniel Sickles Trial 1859 at https//www.encyclopedia.com/law/law-magazines/Daniel-Sickles-trial-1859.
3. Unless otherwise indicated, *Trial Transcript*, 53–87 is the source for material in this chapter.
4. Over the next seven court days, Tison called 30 individuals to testify. They substantiated the story of how "the tragedy in Yokohama" had come about as previously presented in chapters six, seven, and eight and as he had outlined in his opening remarks. I have edited it so as to emphasize portions containing "new" information and material meant to strike judge and assessors with particular force.
5. Louis Eppinger entry in Lepach, *Meiji Portraits*.
6. Herbert Maurice Bevis entry in Lepach, *Meiji Portraits*; *China Directory*, *1877*, 207; *1888*, 41; *1892*, 35.
7. Norman Ashleigh Walter and David Sheard Brearly entries in Lepach, *Meiji Portraits*. Walter started and then partnered in a bill and brokerage firm. He died in Yokohama in 1902.

Chapter 15

1. *Trial Transcript*, 87–123 is the principal source for this chapter.
2. *China Directory, 1892*, 440.
3. *Trial Transcript*, 199–202.

Chapter 16

1. *Trial Transcript*, 124–187.

Chapter 17

1. Unless otherwise indicated, *Trial Transcript*, 209–233, is the source for this chapter.
2. Kiyomizu Isao, *Bigō ga mita Meiji shokugyō jijō (Working Conditions in the Meiji Era as Seen by Bigot)* (Tokyo: Kodansha gakujutsu bunko, 2009), 14, 32, 36–37.
3. Wiki.en.wikipedia.org/Cabinet_card.
4. Nembrini de Gonzaga, Carlo, in Lepach, *Meiji Portraits*, Saitō, *Yokohama gaikokujin bochi ni iru hitobito*, 45–47. Nembrini de Gonzaga was a superb l

inguist. Born in what was then Austria-Hungary, he had mastered five languages.

Chapter 18

1. *Trial Transcript*, 221–238.

Chapter 19

1. Unless otherwise indicated, *Trial Transcript*, 237–258 is the source for this chapter.
2. The letter appears here with italics and punctuation as in the original.
3. Mr. and Mrs. Walter S. Stone. He had come to Yokohama in 1890 as an agent for the American Trading Company and lived near Gower on the bluff. *Trial Transcript*, 191–192.

Chapter 20

1. *Trial Transcript*, 258–274.

Chapter 21

1. *Trial Transcript*, 275–299.
2. Tison was referring here not to Sir Hugh Fraser, the British minister in Tokyo, but to John Frederick Lowder, who had claimed he had the minister's backing to serve as co-counsel for the prosecution.
3. Malachi 2:14–15.

Chapter 22

1. *Trial Transcript*, 299–302, plus printed addendum, 302–303.
2. The phrase comes from the title of Joseph M. Henning's *Outposts of Civilization: Race, Religion, and the Formative Years of American-Japanese Relations* (New York: New York University Press, 2000).
3. *Washington Post*, April 10, 1892.
4. *Boston Globe, San Francisco Call*, and *San Francisco Chronicle*, April 10, 1892.
5. *Japan Herald* and *Japan Gazette* editorials as reported in *San Francisco Chronicle*, May 22, 1892, https://en.wikipedia.org/wiki/Francis_Brinkley; *Japan Mail*, quoted in *Los Angeles Times*, May 22, 1892.

6. *North China Herald*, April 22, 1892.
7. *San Francisco Call*, April 30, 1892; *San Francisco Chronicle*, May 22, 1892.
8. *Manchester Guardian* and *London Times*, April 10, 1892; *The Advertiser* (Adelaide, South Australia), April 11, 1892; *London Times*, May 20, 1892; *Manchester Guardian*, May 21, 1892.
9. *New York Tribune, San Francisco Call*, and *Washington Post*, April 10, 1892.
10. *Saint Louis Post-Dispatch, Atlanta Constitution, New York Tribune, Paris Herald Tribune*, April 10, 1892; *Hartford Courant*, April 11, 1892.
11. *Cincinnati Enquirer*, April 22, 1892.
12. McIntosh was an 1871 graduate of the Naval Academy. *USNA*, 169; *New York Times, San Francisco Call*, and *New York Tribune*, April 30,1892.
13. *Los Angeles Times*, March 15 and April 22, 1892.
14. *American Law Review* 26 (1892), 894, reprinting excerpt from *Albany Law Review*.
15. *The Making of the Modern Law, Trials, 1600–1926* and Gale MOML print and online editions.

Chapter 23

1. *Annual Report of the Secretary of the Navy for the Year 1892*, 159. The *Marion* underwent repairs at the Imperial Japanese Navy base at nearby Yokosuka before returning briefly to Yokohama, calling at Kobe, and departing Japan on May 9, 1892.
2. *China Chronicle*, 1894; *San Francisco Call*, February 23, 1897; Tacoma, Washington, City Directory 1895 and 1896, 593; 1900–1930 U.S. census records; California Death Records 1940–1997, all accessed via ancestry.com.
3. Reverend Eugene Samuel Booth, at https://www.findagrave.com/memorial/158436093/eugene-samuel-booth; J.R. Simon, Nathaniel F. Smith, and Samuel Sondheim entries, Lepach, *Meiji Portraits*.
4. United Kingdom Foreign and Overseas Register of British Subjects, 1628–1969, Subsection Miscellaneous Foreign Marriages 1826–1921, accessed via ancestry.com; Henry Charles Litchfield (abt. 1843–abt. 1907) at https://www.wikitree.com/wiki/Litchfield-914; *China*

Chronicle and Directory, 1899, 28, 38, 51; *1905*, 46, 54, 61.

5. *New York Times*, July 17, 1938; *New York Tribune*, July 17, 1938 https://www.zoominfo/p/Alexander-Tison/1349979740; *China Chronicle, 1892*, 21; Michael Auslin, ed., *Japan Society Celebrating a Century, 1907-2007* (New York: Japan Society, 2007), 14-28. This is a revised and updated edition of Edwin O. Reischauer's *Japan Society 1907-1982: 75 Years of Partnership across the Pacific* (New York: Japan Society of New York, 1982).

6. *South China Morning Post*, November 28, 1922; *Washington Post*, November 28, 1922; George H. Scidmore entry, *Encyclopedia Dubuque*; Hammersmith, *Spoilsmen in a "Flowery Fairyland,"* 240, 243; Saitō Takio, *Yokohama Gaikokujin bochi...*, 38-39; Eliza Ruhamah Scidmore at https://www.britannica.com/print/article/528753; http://www.elizascidemore.com/eliza-s-japan; Diana P. Parsell, *Eliza Scidmore: The Trailblazing Journalist Behind Washington's Cherry Trees* (New York: Oxford University Press, 2023), 259-318, 328.

7. Saitō, 31; Walter Raymond H. Carew entry in Lepach, *Meiji Portraits*; Lowder left his wife, Julia, very well off. He willed her all his personal effects plus 14,834 pounds. England and Wales National Probate Calendar, January 27, 1903, entry (files of wills and administrations) at ancestry.com.

8. Cogar, *Dictionary of Admirals of the U.S. Navy* 2:18; *USNAR*, 172; Jeanie Bartlett died in 1907, three years after her husband, in Nice, France. Jeanie Rosalie Jenckes Bartlett entry, ancestry.com; Allen Grey Rogers entries, 1920 and 1930 United States Federal Census; Allen Grey Rogers entry, North Carolina Death Certificates, 1909–1976.

9. Blanchard, Blad, Gibbens, Pearson, and Read entries in Lepach, *Meiji Portraits*; Valdemar Blad and Chandler Gibbens in *Chronicle and Directory, 1899*, 45; *1903*, 791, 805; *1905*, 908, 959; *1910*, 615; *1912*, 612; *1914*, 654; Chandler Gibbens death certificate in Massachusetts, Death Records, 1841-1915, accessed via ancestry.com.

10. Eppinger and Clare entries in Lepach, *Meiji Portraits*; Pachini had disappeared from the list of foreign residents in *China Chronicle* by 1895.

11. The houseboy Nakatani Masanosuke stayed on at bluff #172 working for Brooke Pearson, who occupied Gower Robinson's former home for a time. Trial Transcript, 212.

12. Hetherington record of service, May 6, 1892.

13. The *Oceanic*, laid down in 1870, was dubbed "the mother of the modern liner." Originally owned by the White Star Line, it flew the British red ensign. But in 1892, it was operated by the Occidental and Oriental Steamship Company, which in turn was owned by the American Union Pacific and Central Pacific Railroads. En.wikipedia.org/wiki/List_of_White_Star_Line_Ships; www.theshipslist.com/ships/lines/occidental.shtml.

14. *Los Angeles Times*, May 22, 1892.

15. *Saint Louis Post-Dispatch*, May 22, 1892.

16. *Los Angeles Times* and *Saint Louis Post-Dispatch*, May 22, 1892; https://en.wikipedia.org/wiki/Occidental_Hotel.

17. The city of Emeryville was not incorporated until 1897. http: en.wikipedia.org/wiki/Emeryville,_California.

18. *Chicago Tribune*, May 29, 1892.

19. *New York Times* and Baltimore *Sun*, May 31, 1892.

Chapter 24

1. Fraser, *Prairie Fires*, 168-169, 179; https://en.wikipedia/wiki/Panic_of_1893.

2. *Wilmington City Directory, 1893*, 314 at U.S. City Directories 1822-1995 for James Henry Hetherington, accessed via ancestry.com; *Wilmington Evening Journal*, July 14, 1892.

3. Hetherington Record of Service, December 13, 1892.

4. USS *Mohican* entry, in Dictionary of American Naval Fighting Ships at https://www.history.navy.mil/research/histories/ship-histories/danfs/m/-mohican-ii.html.

5. https://en.wikipedia.org/wiki/USS_Mohican_(1883).

6. *Secretary of the Navy Annual Report, 1893-1894* (Washington, D.C.: Government Printing Office, 1894), 44, 182, 186; https://en.wikipedia.of/wiki/

Bering_Sea_Arbitration; brittanica.com/event/Bering-Sea-Dispute.

7. USS *Pinta* entry at www.history.navy.mil/research/histories/sip-histories/danfs/pinta.html; *Annual Report of the Secretary of the Navy for 1894–1895* (Washington, D.C.: Government Printing Office, 1895), 131, 145; *Annual Report of the Secretary of the Navy for 1895–1896* (Washington, D.C.: Government Printing Office, 1896), 224, 242–243.

8. Hetherington Record of Service, October 8, 16, and 31, November 16, 1894; https:en.wikipedia.org/wiki/Sitka,_Alaska.

9. Hetherington record of service, November 11, 1895.

10. *USNAR*, 161; *Secretary of the Navy, Annual Report 1895* (Washington, D.C.: Government Printing Office, 1895), 132.

11. https://en.wikipedia.org/wiki/William_Michael_Crose. Crose later served as governor of American Samoa; *Trial Transcript*, 230.

12. USS *Pinta* deck log, January 11, 1896, Record group 24, United States National Archives.

13. Thanks to advances in neonatology and technology for the care of premature infants, babies born at five months and even earlier survive today. That was not true in 1896. Doctors doubted that incubators could replace, even temporarily, the warmth and nourishment that nursing mothers gave a newborn. Incubators did not exist in the United States, and Bessie Hetherington likely had never even heard of them. She would have to rely on James's obstetrical ignorance and his credulity, not some new medical device, for him to believe that he had fathered the child she would deliver "prematurely." Jeffrey W.P. Baker, MD, PhD, "Historical Perspective: The Incubator and the Medical Discovery of the Premature Infant," *Journal of Perinatology* 5 (2000), 321–324.

14. Hetherington Record of Service, March 11, 1896; *Trial Transcript*, 230; *Secretary of the Navy, Annual Report, 1893–1894*, 186.

15. Hetherington Record of Service, March 18, 1896; Jefferson County Historical Society, comp., *Images of America: Port Townsend* (Charleston, SC: Arcadia, 2008), 7.

16. Elaine Naylor, *Frontier Boosters: Port Townsend and the Culture of Development in the American West 1850–1890* (Montreal: McGill-Queens University Press, 2014), 114, 118, 128; Jefferson County Historical Society, *Images of America: Port Townsend*, 19 ff.; *Port Townsend Leader*, October 22, 1901, March 1, 1902.

17. Hetherington Record of Service, March 11, 18, 28; April 11; July 8; August 4, 1896.

18. *Marietta III (PG-15)* at https://www.history.navy.mil/research/histories/ship-histories/danfs/marietta-iii.html.

19. https:/en Wikipedia.org/wiki/Mare_Island_Naval_Shipyard; Arnold S. Lott, *A Long Line of Ships: Mare Island's Century of Naval Activity in California* (Annapolis: United States Naval Institute, 1954), 123–124; https://en.wikipedia.org/wiki/Vallejo,_California; *San Francisco Call*, November 18, 1895; Brendan Riley, *Lower Georgia Street: California's Forgotten Barbary Coast* (Charleston, SC: Arcadia, 2017), 5–6, 23–24.

20. *Annual Report of the Navy Department. Report of the Secretary of the Navy. Miscellaneous Reports, 1897–98* (Washington, D.C.: Government Printing Office, 1898), 40, 139, 343–344, 645–646. This chronology of the two ships' voyage in this source is more accurate than that in the semi-official *Dictionary of American Fighting Ships*, Wikipedia, and other online sources. Stanford Sternlicht, *McKinley's Bulldog: The Battleship* Oregon (Chicago: Nelson-Hall, 1977), 71–82.

21. Hetherington Record of Service, August 24, 1898.

22. Hetherington Record of Service, January 28, 1899, to July 20, 1901; *Philadelphia IV (C-4), DANFS*; https://en.wikipedia.org/wiki/Second_Samoan_Civil_War.

23. *San Francisco Call*, January 31, 1898.

24. *Los Angeles Herald*, October 19, 1901.

25. *Smyrna* (Delaware) *Times*, October 23, 1901, March 5, 1902, accessed via Library of Congress, *Chronicling America: Historic American Newspapers*; *New York Times*, February 28, 1902.

Chapter 25

1. *Smyrna* (Delaware) *Times*, October 23, 1901; *Cincinnati Enquirer*, April 24, 1902.

2. *San Francisco Chronicle*, April 27, 1902; Portland, Oregon, City Directory, 1890–1891; Seattle City Directories, 1892–1902; 1900 United States Federal Census, all accessed vis ancestry.com.

3. *The Evening Republican* (Wilmington, Delaware), April 19, 1902; *Wilmington Evening Journal*, February 7, 1898.

4. *The Evening Republican*, April 19, 1902; *San Francisco Chronicle*, April 24, 1902.

5. *The Evening Republican*, April 19, 1902.

6. *Cincinnati Enquirer*, April 24, 1902; Emlen Hewes Hetherington Draft Registration Card and Registrar's Report, September 5, 1918, in World War I Draft Registration Cards, 1917–1918, accessed via ancestry.com.

7. *Seattle Republican*, January 19, 1906; Seattle city directories, 1902–1931; Port Orchard 1923 City Directory; Tacoma City Directory, 1924, all accessed via ancestry.com; John W. McConnaughey entries, 1920 and 1930 United States Federal Census.

8. *Wilmington Evening Journal*, August 26, 1907; Emlen Hewes and Mary Augusta Hewes entries at myheritage.com; Bessie Hewes McConnaughey death certificate, Washington Select Death Certificates, 1907–1960, accessed via ancestry.com; Gladys Hewes Thomson and Bessie McConnaughey entries on geni.com.

9. https://en.wikipedia.org/wiki/USS_Newark_(C-1).

10. USS *Minneapolis* at history.navy.mil/research/histories/ship-histories/danfs/m/minneapolis-i/html; Hetherington Record of Service, May 5, July 6, 1905.

11. *Boston Globe*, July 22, 1905; *Los Angeles Times*, August 27, 1905; *Chicago Tribune*, August 29, 1905.

12. Hetherington Record of Service, September 1, 1905–April 12, 1912.

13. https://en.wikipedia.org/wiki/Philadelphia_Naval_Asylum; Hetherington Record of Service, May 16, 1913–September 19, 1917; *Boston Transcript*, September 18, 1917, U.S. Navy Casualties Books, 1776–1941, accessed via ancestry.com.

Bibliography

Unpublished Sources

Record Group 24, United States National Archives.
USS *Monongahela* deck log, July 1879.
USS *Pinta* deck log, 1896.
USS *Richmond* deck log, July 1879.

Published Sources

Government Documents

California Death Records, 1940–1997.
Delaware Land Records, 1677–1947.
Delaware Marriage Records, 1774–1912.
England and Wales National Probate Calendar (Files of Wills and Administrations).
Iowa Marriage Records, 1880–1940.
Iowa Select Marriage Index, 1758–1996.
Massachusetts Death Records, 1841–1915.
Massachusetts Town and Vital Records, 1620–1988.
North Carolina Death Certificates, 1909–1976.
Register of Commissioned and Warrant Officers of the United States Navy, Including Officers of the Marine Corps. Washington, D.C.: Department of the Navy, 1814–1905.
Secretary of the Navy, *Annual Report of the Secretary of the Navy on the Operations of the Department for the Year 1879* (Washington, D.C.: Government Printing Office, 1880). Title varies, 1878–1905.
Superintendent of the U.S. Coast and Geodetic Survey, *Report of the Superintendent of the U.S. Coast and Geodetic Survey Showing the Progress of the Work during the Fiscal Year(s) Ending with June (1884–1889)*. (Washington, D.C.: Government Printing Office, 1884–1889.)
United Kingdom Foreign and Overseas Register of British Subjects, 1628–1969, Subsection Miscellaneous Foreign Marriages, 1826–1921.
U.S. Naval Hospital and Case Papers, 1825–1889 for J.H. Hetherington, Yokohama, Japan, 1877–1881, Roll 168.
U.S. Navy Casualties Books, 1776–1941.
U.S Register of Civil, Military, and Naval Ser4vice 1863–1959, Volume 1, 1891.
U.S. Social Security Applications and Claims Index, 1936–2007.
Washington, Select Death Certificates, 1907–1960.
World War I Draft Registration Cards, 1917–1918.

Bibliography

Books

Abe, Naoko, *The Sakura Obsession*. New York: Vintage Books, 2019.
Appignanesi, Lisa, *Trials of Passion: Crimes Committed in the Name of Love and Madness*. New York: Pegasus Crime, 2015.
Auslin, Michael, ed., *Japan Society Celebrating a Century, 1907-2007*. New York: Japan Society, 2007.
Barnes, Elinor, and James A., eds., *Naval Surgeon: Revolt in Japan 1868-1869*. Bloomington: Indiana University Press, 1963.
The Book of Common Prayer of the Church of England with Daily Prayers. Glasgow: William Collins and Co., 1845.
Brooke, George M., Jr., ed., *John M. Brooke's Pacific Cruise and Japanese Adventure, 1858-1860*. Honolulu: University of Hawaii Press, 1976.
Bunts, Frank Emory, *Letters from the Asiatic Station 1881-1883*. Cleveland: The Caxton Press, 1938.
Campbell, Edwina S., *Citizen of a Wider Commonwealth: Ulysses S. Grant's Postpresidential Diplomacy*. Carbondale: Southern Illinois University Press, 2016.
Carroll, John, *Trails of Two Cities: A Walker's Guide to Yokohama, Kamakura, and Vicinity*. Tokyo: Kodansha International, 1994.
Casson, Eric, *The Church on Colonel's Corner*. Yokohama: Christ Church, 1962.
Cep, Casey, *Furious Hours: Murder, Fraud, and the Last Trial of Harper Lee*. New York: Knopf, 2019.
Chaichian, Mohammad A., *White Racism on the Western Urban Frontier: Dynamics of Race and Class in Dubuque, Iowa 1800-2000*. Trenton, NJ: Africa World Press, 2006.
Chamberlain, Basil Hall, and Mason, W.B., *A Handbook for Travelers in Japan*. 3rd ed. London: John Murray, and Yokohama, Japan: Kelly and Walsh Ltd., 1891.
Chang, Richard T., *The Justice of the Western Consular Courts in Nineteenth-Century Japan*. Westport, CT: Greenwood Press, 1984.
Chisholm, Donald, *Waiting for Dead Men's Shoes: Origins and Development of the U.S. Navy's Officer Personnel System, 1793-1941*. Stanford: Stanford University Press, 2001.
Cogar, William B., *Dictionary of Admirals of the U.S. Navy, Volume 1: 1862-1900*. Annapolis: Naval Institute Press, 1989.
_____, *Dictionary of Admirals of the U.S. Navy, Volume 2: 1900—1918*. Annapolis: Naval Institute Press, 1991.
Cortazzi, Hugh, *Victorians in Japan: In and Around the Treaty Ports*. London: The Athlone Press, 1987.
Cortazzi, Hugh, et al., eds., *British Envoys in Japan 1859-1972*. Kent: Folkestone, 2004.
Dennys, N.B., ed., *The Treaty Ports of China and Japan*. London: Trubner and Company, 1867.
Ellens, J. Harold, *Sex in the Bible: A New Consideration*. Westport, CT: Praeger, 2005.
Ericson, J., *The Sound of the Whistle: Railroads and the State in Meiji Japan*. Cambridge: Harvard University Press, 1996.
Fox, Grace, *Britain and Japan 1858-1883*. Oxford: The Clarendon Press, 1969.
Fraser, Caroline, *Prairie Fires: The American Dreams of Laura Ingalls Wilder*. New York: Henry Holt and Company, 2017.
Hammer, Joshua, *Yokohama Burning: The Deadly 1923 Earthquake and Fire That Helped Forge the Path to World War II*. New York: The Free Press, 2006.
Hammersley, Lewis Randolph, *The Records of Living Officers of the U.S. Navy and Marine Corps*. 5th ed. Philadelphia: L.R. Hammersley and Company, 1894.
Hammersmith, Jack L., *Spoilsmen in a "Flowery Fairyland."* Kent: Kent State University Press, 1998.
Helm, Leslie, *Yokohama Yankee: My Family's Five Generations as Outsiders in Japan*. Seattle: Chin Music Press, 2013.
Henning, Joseph M., *Outposts of Civilization: Race, Religion, and the Formative Years of American-Japanese Relations*. New York: New York University Press, 2000.

Bibliography

Hoffecker, Carol E., *Wilmington, Delaware: Portrait of an Industrial City, 1830–1910*. Charlottesville: University Press of Virginia, 1974.
Japan: An Illustrated Encyclopedia. Tokyo: Kodansha, 1993.
Jefferson County Historical Society, *Images of America: Port Townsend*. Charleston, SC: Arcadia, 2008.
Karsten, Peter, *The Naval Aristocracy: The Golden Age of Annapolis and the Emergence of Modern American Nationalism*. Annapolis: Naval Institute Press, 1972.
Keneally, Thomas, *American Scoundrel: The Life of the Notorious Civil War General Dan Sickles*. New York: Anchor Books, 2003.
Kipen, David, ed., *Dear Los Angeles*. New York: The Modern Library, 2019.
Kipling, Rudyard, *From Sea to Sea*. Leipzig: B. Tauschnitz, 1900.
Kiyomizu Isao, *Bigō ga mita Meiji shokugyō jijō (Working Conditions in the Meiji Era as Seen by Bigot)*. Tokyo: Kodansha gakujutsu bunko, 2009.
Klein, Robert F., ed., *Dubuque: Frontier River City: Thirty-five Historical Sketches by Chandler C. Childs*. Dubuque: Research Center for Dubuque Area History, Loras College, 1984.
Knox, Clement, *Seduction: A History from the Enlightenment to the Present*. New York: Pegasus Books, 2020.
Labaree, Benjamin W., William M. Fowler, Jr., John B. Hattendorf, Jeffrey J. Safford, Edward W. Sloan, and Andrew W. German, *America and the Sea: A Maritime History*. Mystic, CT: Mystic Seaport, 1998.
Leeman, William P. *The Long Road to Annapolis: The Founding of the Naval Academy and the Emerging American Republic*. Chapel Hill: University of North Carolina Press, 2010.
Lott, Arnold S., *A Long Line of Ships: Mare Island's Century of Naval Activity in California*. Annapolis: United States Naval Institute, 1954.
Lyon, Randolph W., comp., *Encyclopedia Dubuque*. Dubuque: First National Bank of Dubuque, 1991. (www.encyclopediadubuque.org).
Makimura, Yasuhiro, *Yokohama and the Silk Trade: How Eastern Japan Became the Primary Economic Region of Japan, 1843–1893*. New York: Columbia University Press, 2017.
McBride, William M., *Technological Change and the United States Navy, 1865–1945*. Baltimore: Johns Hopkins University Press, 2000.
Morton-Cameron, W.H., comp., W. Feldwick, ed., *Present Day Impressions of Japan: The History, People, Commerce, Industries and Resources of Japan and Japan's Colonial Empire*. London: The Globe Encyclopedia, 1919.
Naval History and Heritage Command, *Dictionary of American Naval Fighting Ships*. (https://www.history.navy.mil/research/histories/).
Naylor, Elaine, *Frontier Boosters: Port Townsend and the Culture of Development in the American West 1850–1890*. Montreal: McGill-Queens University Press, 2014.
Notehelfer, Frederick G., ed., *Japan Through American Eyes: The Journal of Francis Hall Kanagawa and Yokohama 1859–1866*. Princeton: Princeton University Press, 1992.
Parsell, Diana P., *Eliza Scidmore: The Trailblazing Journalist Behind Washington's Cherry Trees*. New York: Oxford University Press, 2023.
Pedlar, Neil, *The Imported Pioneers: Westerners Who Helped Build Modern Japan*. New York: St. Martin's Press, 1990.
Reed, Christopher, *Bachelor Japanists: Japanese Aesthetics and Western Masculinities*. New York: Columbia University Press, 2016.
Reischauer, Edwin O., *Japan Society 1907–1982: 75 Years of Partnership across the Pacific*. New York: Japan Society of New York, 1982.
Riley, Brendan, *Lower Georgia Street: California's Forgotten Barbary Coast*. Charleston, SC: Arcadia, 2017.
Saitō Takio, *Yokohama gaikokujin bochi ni iru hitobito (People in the Yokohama Foreign General Cemetery)*. Yokohama: Yūrindo, 2012.
Salvini, Emil R., *The Summer City by the Sea: Cape May, New Jersey: An Illustrated History*. Belleville, NJ: Wheal Grace Publications, 1995.
Scidmore, George H., *Outline Lectures on the History, Organization, Jurisdiction, and*

Practice of the Ministerial and Consular Courts of the United States of America in Japan. Yokohama: Kelly & Walsh, 1887.
Seager, Robert, II, *Alfred Thayer Mahan: The Man and His Letters.* Annapolis: Naval Institute Press, 1977.
Segrave, Karen, *Beware the Masher: Sexual Harassment in American Public Places, 1880–1920.* Jefferson, NC: McFarland, 2014.
Smith, Jason W., *To Master the Boundless Sea: The U.S. Navy, the Marine Environment, and the Cartography of Empire.* Chapel Hill: University of North Carolina Press, 2018.
Sternlicht, Stanford, *McKinley's Bulldog: The Battleship Oregon.* Chicago: Nelson-Hall, 1977.
Still, William N., Jr., *American Sea Power in the Old World: The United States Navy in European and Near Eastern Waters, 1865–1917.* Westport, CT: Greenwood Press, 1980.
Strange, Daniel, comp., *Pioneer History of Eaton County Michigan, 1833–1866.* (http://name.umdl.umich.edu/BAD0917.001.00.)
Sutherland, Lord Ronald Gower, *My Reminiscences.* 3rd ed. New York: Charles Scribner's Sons, 1884.
Symonds, Craig L., *The U.S. Navy: A Concise History.* New York: Oxford University Press, 2016.
Todorich, Charles, *The Spirited Years: A History of the Antebellum Naval Academy.* Annapolis: Naval Institute Press, 1984.
The Trial of Lieutenant Hetherington, U.S.N., for Shooting George Gower Robinson, Esq. Yokohama: Box of Curios Printing Office, 1892.
Twentieth Annual Catalog of the Officers and Students of Vassar College. Poughkeepsie, NY: Haight and Dudley Printers, 1885.
United States Naval Academy Alumni Association, Inc., *Register of Alumni Graduates and Former Naval Cadets and Midshipmen, 1845–1981.* Annapolis: United States Naval Academy Alumni Association, Inc., 1981.
Vivers, Meg, *An Irish Engineer: The Extraordinary Achievements of Thomas J. Waters and Family in Early Meiji Japan and Beyond.* Brisbane: Copyright Publishing, 2013.
Warner, Herman Jackson, and Woodberry, George Edward, eds., *New Letters of an Idle Man.* London: Constable, 1913.
Wenzlhuemer, *Connecting the Nineteenth-Century World: The Telegraph and Globalization.* New York: Cambridge University Press, 2013.
Yokohama kaikō shiryōkan and Yokohama rekishi hakubutsukan, *Yokohama monogatari (The Story of Yokohama).* Yokohama: Yokohama kaikō shiryōkan and Yokohama rekishi hakubutsukan, 1999.
Zwonitzer, Mark, *John Hay, Mark Twain, and the Rise of American Imperialism.* Chapel Hill: Algonquin Books, 2016.

Articles

A.P.C. "The Cruise," *Oliver Optic's Magazine: Our Boys and Girls* 18 (July 1875), 264–266.
_____, "Glimpses of Annapolis and the Naval Academy," *Oliver Optic's Magazine: Our Boys and Girls* 17 (April 1875), 210–214.
_____, "The Naval Academy Again. Getting In and Staying There," *Oliver Optic's Magazine: Our Boys and Girls* 17 (May 1875), 262–265.
Baker, Jeffrey W.P., MD, PhD, "Historical Perspective: The Incubator and the Medical Discovery of the Premature Infant," *Journal of Perinatology* 5 (2000), 321–324.
Campbell, Charles S., Jr., "The Anglo-American Crisis in the Bering Sea, 1890–1891," *Mississippi Valley Historical Review* 48 (December 1961), 393–406.
Chang, Richard T., "General Grant's 1879 Visit to Japan," *Monumenta Nipponica* 24 (1969), 373–392.
Crawford, Michael J., "Whose Flag Has Displayed in Distant Climes, 1816–1860," in W.J. Holland, Jr., ed., *The Navy* (Washington, D.C.: Naval Historical Foundation, 2012), 28–43.

Bibliography

Dykstra, James, "The USS Michigan," *Military History of the Upper Great Lakes* (October 15, 2015). (ss.sites.mtu.edu.mhugl/2015/10/11/the-uss-michigan/.)
Gibb, Paul, "Selling Out Canada? The Role of Sir Julian Pauncefote in the Bering Sea Dispute, 1899-1902," *International History Review*, 24 (December 2002), 817–844.
"Law Reporting in Japan," *The Stenographer* 3 (1893), 350.
Porter, David Dixon, "Naval Education and Organization," *United Services: A Quarterly Review of Military and Naval Affairs* 1 (July 1879), 470–487.
Vivers, Meg, "The Role of British Agents and Engineers in the Early Westernization of Japan with a Focus on the Robinson and Waters Brothers," *The International Journal for the History of Engineering & Technology* 85 (2015) 115–139.
Wakita, Mio, "Sites of 'Disconnectedness: The Port City of Yokohama, Souvenir Photography, and its Audience," hhttps://helup.uni-heidelberg.de/journals/index/php/transcultural/article/view/11067/5640).

Directories

The Directory & Chronicle for China, Japan, Corea, Indo-China, Straits Settlements, Malay States, Siam, Netherlands India, Borneo, the Philippines, & c. Hong Kong: The *Hong Kong Daily Press* Office, 1874–1895.
Lepach, Bernd, *Meiji Portraits* (www.Meiji-Portraits.de).
Port Orchard Washington City Directory, 1923.
Portland, Oregon City Directory, 1890–1891.
Seattle City Directory, 1892–1902.
Tacoma City Directory, 1896.
Wilmington City Directory, 1889–1902 in *U.S. City Directories, 1882–1995*.

Periodicals

The Advertiser (Adelaide, South Australia)
American Law Review, 26 (1892)
Arizona Daily Republic
Atlanta Constitution
Baltimore Sun
Boston Daily Globe
Bridgewater (NJ) *Courier-News*
Chicago Tribune
Cincinnati Enquirer
Dubuque Daily Herald
Hartford Courant
The Japan Weekly Mail and Times reprinted in Edition Synapse in Association with Yokohama Archives of History Tokyo, Japan: Edition Synapse, 2009.
London Times
Los Angeles Herald
Los Angeles Times
Manchester Guardian
New York Times
New York Tribune
Newburgh (NY) *Telegram*
North China Herald and Supreme Court & Consular Gazette
Paris Herald Tribune
Philadelphia Record
Saint Louis Post-Dispatch
San Francisco Call
San Francisco Chronicle
Seattle Evening Republican
Seattle Post-Intelligencer

Smyrna (DE) *Times*
South China Morning Post
The Straits Times
Tokyo Mainichi Shimbun
(Vinita, OK) *Indian Chieftain*
Washington Post
Wilmington Evening Journal

Miscellaneous

Denmark Church Records, 1812–1918.
England, United Grand Lodge of England Freemason Membership Registers, 1751–1921.
U.S. Quaker Meeting Records, 1681–1935.

Index

Numbers in **_bold italics_** indicate pages with illustrations

USS *Adams* (II) 231
Agassiz, Louis 25
Aizawa 76, 190
CSS *Alabama* 24
Alaska 41, 223–224, 229
USS *Alert* (II) 231
Aleutian Islands 40
akibare (clear autumn weather) 45
Albany Law Journal 211
Allcock, George Henry 82, 88, 91, 94
USS *Alliance* (II screw gunboat) 33, 160, 162, 185, 210
Allison, Senator William B. 8
amah (nanny) 45; *see also* Shiraishi Tome
American Law Review 211
Andreis, E.H. 79
Annapolis, Maryland 9, 11, 22, 25
Arlington National Cemetery 237
Arthur, Charles S. 164
USS *Ashuelot* (sidewheel gunboat) 16–18, 21
Asiatic Society of Japan 114, 214
Asiatic Station 15
Aspinwall, Columbia 22
assessors 116–117, 131, 198, 202–203, 206
autopsy 81–82

Baldwin, Rear Adm. Charles H., USN 248*ch*1*n*18
Balfour, Captain Charles J., RN 95, 174–175
Baretta, Pietro 78, 84
Bartlett, Jeanie 5, 68, 155, 251*ch*23*n*8, testimony, 138–140
Bartlett, Cmdr. John Russell, USN 43, 57, 60, 65–66, 69, 71–72, 115, **_140_**, 207–209, 213, 215, 245*ch*6*n*10; testimony 140–146
Bayard Thomas F. 158–159

SS *Belgic* 210
Belknap, Frances 55, 105
Belknap, Rear Adm. George Eugene, USN 86, 105–107, **_106_**, 197
Benham, Capt. Andrew Ellicott Kennedy 16–17
Bering Sea dispute 40–42, 221–222
bettō, 50, 76, 78, 184
Bevis, Herbert Maurice 58, 64; testimony 135–136
Bill and Bullion Brokers 48
Blad, Caspar Andreas Valdemar 63–64, 79, 93, 118–119, 152, 169, 216; testimony 158–160
Blaine, Sec. of State James G. 212
Blanchard, Henry 67–68, 194, 216, 161–163
Bluff foreign residential quarter 20, 49, 56, 81, 96
Book of Common Prayer 95–96
Booth, the Rev. Eugene Samuel 117, **_118_**, 214
Boston, Massachusetts 13
Box, Thomas Holyoake 82, 86, 88–89, 91
Brazil 35, 228
Bremerton, Washington 229
Brinkley, Capt. Francis 207
British consulate 82
Brooke, John Henry 207
Brooklyn Navy Yard 34
Bund (harborside boardwalk) 47, 66, 76, 82

Caledonien 84
Call Me Back 56, 153
Camp Hill Road 50, 75–76, 87
Cape May, New Jersey 26–27, 43, 45–47, 104, 222
Carew, Edith 215

261

262 Index

Caribbean Sea 24
Carpenter, Minnie 30
Central Pacific/Union Pacific Railroad 43
USS *Charleston* (C-2) 56, 160
Charleston, South Carolina 236
Charleston Navy Yard 14
Chefoo (Yantai) 17
Chesapeake Bay 9
Chicago IL 43, 218, 224
Chile 229
SS *China* 40, 43–45, 47, 49, 54, 105
Christ Church, Yokohama 49, 56, 59, 93, 177, 214
Churchill, Ensign Creighton, USN 189; testimony 160–161
Chūzō, Kaneko 165–166
Cincinnati Enquirer 210
SS *City of Topeka* 224
Clare, Henry 215
Cleveland, Pres. Grover 220
Colby, Paymaster Henry, USN 42
Conroy, George Leroy 30
Consulate General in Yokohama, American 77, *111*
Coroner's inquest 82–85
Crose, Ens. William Michael, USN 71, 224, 252*ch*24*n*11
Cummins, Columbus R. 49, 105, 134

daimyō 94
USS *Dale* (I) 11
Dayton, Ohio 233, 235
Deacon, Edward case 248*ch*11*n*18
Delaware 27
Delaware Bay 26, 44
De Long, Charles 121
Denver, Colorado 63, 136
Deshima 18
Detroit, Michigan 236
Diamond Head 43
Dubuque Iowa 5–7, 38, 43, 47, 102–103, 111, 175, 207, 218, 226
Dun, Edwin 212
Dupont Corporation 28

Eldridge Dr. Stuart 78, 81, 83, 85–86, 95, 125
Elwyn, Pennsylvania 235
Emeryville, California 218, 251*ch*23*n*17
RMS *Empress of Japan* 210
England 108
English Hatoba (English pier) 76, 82, 141
Episcopal Church in America 31
Eppinger, Louis 64, 78, 216, 134–135
Erie, Pennsylvania 30, 32, 38
Esquimalt harbor 42

USS *Essex* (III) 33–35, 223
extraterritoriality 81, 109, 211–212, 214–215

Farsari's Photo Studio 58, 245*ch*6 *n*12
Finletter, Thomas D. 30
Fortress Monroe, Virginia 37
France 108
Franklin, Pennsylvania 27
Fraser, Sir Hugh 118, 195, 250*ch*21*n*2
Friedenthal, Herr 49
Fuji, Mount 45, 48

SS *Gaelic* 107
Gamble, Captain 49
Gankiro 21
USCGS *George S Blake* 25–26, 141
German Naval Hospital 81
Gibbens, Chandler 62, 64, 66, 68–69, 74, 93, 144–145, 152, 216; testimony 155–159
Golden Gate 40, 44
Gonzaga, Consul Marquis Nembrini de *see* Nembrini, Marquis Gonzaga de
Grand Hotel 21, 45, **46**, 47–50, 52, 56, 58, 60, 64, 68, 75–76, 103, 107, 130, 142, 144, 148–149, 206, 216
Grant, Ulysses S. 16–19
Great Northern Railroad 224
Great Wall of China 17
Gulf Stream 25

Hail Columbia 19
Halifax, Nova Scotia 11
Hampton Roads, Virginia 37, 236
Harmony, Rear Admiral David B., USN 96
Harrison, President Benjamin 111, 213
harusame (spring rain) 110
Havana 229
Hawaii 42, 227
Hayes, Pres. Rutherford B. 16
Hellendale, Peter St. John 93, 96
Henson, Harry 78
Her British Majesty's Royal Naval Hospital 81
Hessler, Dr. Frederick A., USN 150, 189
Hetherington, Bessie Hewes 1, 26–27, 234–235; correspondence with Gower Robinson 59, 151, 156–157, 187–188; divorce 231–232; early family life 27–28; infidelities 50–51, 68–69, 224; journey to Japan 43–45, 50–51; marital relations 52, 138, 141; marriage 1, 30–31; as navy wife 55–56; photograph 166, 180; pregnancies 33, 224; reputation 103–105; seduction 50; Vassar education 28–29
Hetherington, Clara 7

Index   263

Hetherington, Emlen Hewes 227, 230, 232, 235
Hetherington, Gladys 115, 138–139, 230, 232, 235, 237; *see also* Thomson, Mrs. Julian
Hetherington, Henry Samuel 5–7, 102, 209, 218–219
Hetherington, Lt. James Henry, USN 1, **12**, **226**, **237**; birth 5; death 237; divorce 231–232; education 8, 10–11, 15–16; graduation 11; grave 237; marriage 30–31, 118; murder by 76–77; reputation 102–103; sea duty 24–26, 30, 40, 42–44, 220–222, 229–230, 235–236; trial testimony 175–183, 187–193
Hetherington, Maria Soule 7
Hetherington, Sarah Hill 5
Hetherington family home **6**
Hewes, Bessie *see* Hetherington, Bessie Hewes Hetherington
Hewes, Emlen 27, 207, 219, 234
Hewes, Helen 30, 230, 234
Hewes, Mary 234
Hewes, Mary Augusta 27, 102
Holmes, Oliver Wendell, Jr. 211
Hong Kong 16, 48; and Shanghai Banking Corporation 48, 58, 64, 103, 135
Honolulu, Hawaii 42, 221
Honshu 62
Hunker, Lt. John Jacob, USN 42

Illinois Central Railroad 6
Imperial Hotel, Tokyo 164, 190
Incubator 252*ch*24*n*13
USS *Independence* (II) 230–231
Inland Sea (Seto naikai) 18
Iowa 8, 38
Irwine, Chap. Edward Champneys 94–96
Isaac Ferris Anglo-Japanese Girls School 157, **158**, 214

Japan 37–38, 40, anti-foreign violence in, 20, 38, 40, 43, 45, 94, 99, judicial system, 108–109, 211, 214
Japan Gazette 119
Japan Herald 207
Japan Mail 207–208
Japan Society of New York 214
Jardine, Matheson & Company 155, 216
Jigokudani (Hell Valley) 48
Jujiya Bookstore 75

Kanagawa Prefectural Office 82
Kaneko, Chūzō 84, 122; testimony 165–166
Kaufmann, Max 170–171
USS *Kearsarge* (I) 24

Key, Phillip Barton 130
Key West, Florida 230
Kipling, Rudyard 22, 245*ch*6*n*3
Kleffel, Dr. Richard Fritz Theodor 81, 95
Kobe 86, 120, 145, 208
Kondo Motokichi 125

Lake Erie 30
LePrevost, A. 22, 88–89, 91
Litchfield, Henry Charles 83, 119–125, 127–128, 131, 140, 198–201; absence 202; post-trial activities 214
Lobanov, Princess Charikalia 47
Lobanov-Rostovsky, Prince Anatoli Grigorievitch 47, 70, 76, 95, 188
London 207
Los Angeles Times 210
Low, C.P. & Co. 161
Lowder, John Frederick 47, **79**; early life and social standing 47, 58, 65; Gower's attorney 83–90, 118–119, 126, 183, 195–196, 238; post-trial career 215, 245*ch*5*n*15, 250*ch*21*n*2, 251, 23*ch*23*n*7
Lowder, Julia 47, 65, 183, 251*ch*23*n*7

USS *Maine* (BB-1) 229
Makers of Modern Law Trials, 1600–1926 2, 212
Manchester Guardian 101, 209
Manslaughter 90, 196, 203
Mare Island Naval Station 137, 220, 227–228, 230
USS *Marietta* (III) 227, 229–230
Marine Villa, Cape May 43
USS *Marion* (I) 37–38, 40, **41**, 67, 71, 75–77, 138, 141, 146, 149–150, 164, 176–177, 179, 183, 187–189, 192, 205–208, 210, 213, 217; Bering Sea patrol 42–43; crew 42, 208; decommissioning and disposal 231; Yokohama arrival 52–53
Massachusetts Bay 14
Masuda Akira 124
McCance, Richard 78, 114, 127, 205
McConnaughey, Bessie Hewes Hetherington *see* Hetherington, Bessie Hewes
McConnaughey, John Walter (J.W.) 1, 233–235, 239
McCurley, Capt. Felix, USN 185
McIntosh, Lt. Horace, USN 210, 250*ch*22*n*13
McKinley, Pres. William 229
McLean, John 249*ch*13*n*7
Mediterranean Sea 38
HMS *Mercury* 174
Mexican War 230

USS *Michigan* (I) 30, 32–33
USS *Minneapolis* (C-13) 235–236
Mississippi River 5
Miura Rikitaro 122
Miyanoshita, Japan 48
Mobile Bay, battle of 14
Modus vivendi 41
USS *Mohican* (II) 220–221
USS *Monocacy* (I) 105
USS *Monongahela* (I) 21
Morocco 24
Morse, F.S. 69
murder, legal definition 90, 203

Nagasaki 18
Nakatani Masanosuke 170, 195, 199, 251*ch*23*n*11; testimony 166–169
Naval Academy 11, 22
Nectarine # 9 Junpuro 21
Nembrini, Marquis Gonzaga de 84, 94, 172–173, 249*ch*17*n*4
New Jersey 26
New Orleans, Louisiana 14, 24
New York City 26, 32, 35
USS *Newark* (C1) 235
Nikko 49
Norfleet, Surgeon Edwin, USN 105, 247*ch*11*n*13
Norfolk, Virginia 15, 22, 230
North China Herald and Supreme Court & Consular Gazette 101, 208

SS *Oceanic* 103, 217–218, 248*ch*11*n*15, 251*ch*23*n*13
Odawara Street 76
Okada Kantarō 124, 167
USS *Oregon* (BB-3) 227, 229–230
Overbrook, Pennsylvania 234–235

P & O (Peninsular and Oriental) Steamship Company 125
Pachini, Cesare 171, 195, 199, 216; testimony 171–173
Pacific Mail Steamship Company 45
Panama, Isthmus of 22
Panama City 22
Panic of 1857 6
Panic of 1873 8
Paris 108, 207
Patterson, Rear Adm. Thomas Harwood, USN 18
Paul, Maurice Eden 81
Paul Heinemann & Company 75
Pearson, Brooke 64, 69, 78, 93, 144, 159, 161, 182, 216; testimony 153–155
Peking (Beijing) 16

Perkins, Lt. C. Marrast, USMC 42, 150
Perry, Commodore Matthew Calbraith 93
Perry Square, Erie, Pennsylvania 33
Philadelphia 26, 29, 224, 234, 236
USS *Philadelphia* (C-4) 231
Philadelphia Branch Hydrographic Office 103
Philadelphia Naval Home 236
USS *Pinta* (Screw Tug) 221–222, 224
Pors, Martin 75, 77, 83–84, 101, 190–192, deposition 120–123; inquest testimony 86–90, 101
Port Townsend, Washington 42, 224–228, 234
Portland, Maine 34
Poughkeepsie, New York 28–29
Pribiloff Islands 40
Puget Sound 42, 225

Queen Liliuokalani 221

Ramsay, Commodore Francis Munroe, USN 33, 224
Ray, Paymaster Charles, USN 72, 75
Read, Albert Carter 63–64, 79, 93, 127, 156, 159, 169, 216, testimony 151–153
Reamey, Lt. Lazarus, USN 82–83, 185
Redding, California 213
Rice, George Edwin 117
Richardson, Charles J. 94
USS *Richmond* (II) 13–19, **14**, 22, 103, 146, 236
Robinson, Adaliza Letitia Gower 48, 101, 20
Robinson, George Gower 1, **97**; business 48, death 79, family 48; grave 97; letters to Bessie 63–64, 133, 181–182; reputation 48–49, 103–104, 107–108, 139, 141; seduction of Bessie 50–51, 67–68, 162, 165–166, 168–172; will 152–153, 155–157, 159
Robinson, Gwendoline 48, 63
Robinson, John S. 48
Rodgers, Rear Adm. Christopher Raymond Perry, USN 10
Rogers, Lt. Alan P., USN 11, 42, 65–66, 73, 160, 162, 178, 190, 216; testimony 126–127, 146–150
Rogers, Surgeon Franklin, USN 62
Rokkaku, Police Surgeon 82
rōnin 92
Rosina 48

Saint Andrew's Day ball 56, 141, 146
San Francisco 40, 43–44, 104–105, 107, 177, 209, 218, 227–228
San Francisco Call 102

San Francisco Chronicle 102
Santiago de Cuba, battle of 230
Satsuma 94
Schmidt-Leda, Consul Dr. Otto 95
Scidmore, Eliza Ruhamah 112–113, 215, 251*ch*23*n*6
Scidmore, Vice-Consul George H. 112–113, 116, 215
Seattle, Washington 228, 233–235
Seiyo-kan restaurant 19
Severn River 9, 11
Seward, Sec. of State William H. 248*ch*11*n*21
Shanghai 101
Shanhaiguan 17
Shasta County, California 213
Shimada Tsunekichi 170
Shiraishi Tome 45, 50, 52, 64, 76, 115, 154, 167–168, 190, 216; testimony 169–170
Siberia 37
Sickles, Daniel 130
Simon, J.R. 117, 214, 223
Simon & Evers Co. 170
Singapore 16, 37, 101
Sisters of Saint Maur 59
Sitka, Alaska 224, 226–227
Slocum, Ensign George Ralph, USN 147
Smith, A. Gilmore 117
Smith, Gertrude 207
Smith, Nathanel Ferdinand 117
Sondheim, Samuel 117
Stanton, Edwin 130
Stephenson, Dr. Frank Bates, USN 42, 68
Stevens, Durham 109
Stibolt & Company 83, 93
Stone, Walter S. 250*ch*19*n*3
Strait of Juan de Fuca 42
Sudekum, the Rev. Marjorie 247*ch*10*n*9
Suzuki Mito 84, 123–124

Tacoma, Washington 110–111, 213, 235
Taku Bar 16
USCGS *Thomas R. Gedney* 25
Thompson, Secretary of the Navy Richard 16
Thomson, Mrs. Julian 235, 237; *see also* Hetherington, Gladys
Tientsin 16–17
Tillotson, Consul Gen. Willard D. 85, 94, *112*; criticism 207, 210–211; early life 110–111; political career 112, 211–213; presiding judge 117–120, 137, 144, 158–159, 164, 169, 171–180, 184, 187–192, 194, 198; verdict 203–206
Tison, Alexander 83; as defense attorney 116, 118–120, 127–134, 137–138, 144, 194–199, 202–206, 219, 238; early life 113–114; post-trial career 214
Tokyo 49, 53–54, 135, 217
Tokyo Asahi Shimbun 207
Tokyo Mainichi Shimbun 100
"tragedy in Yokohama" 99, 102, 239
trap 50, 76, 165, 171; defined 245*ch*5*n*24
Treaty port 100, 109
Trinity Episcopal Church 30
Tripler, Dr. Thomas Hall 79
Troup, James P. 82, 84, 88–91, 94

Uchimura Rosetsu 125
United Club 49, 53, 66, 73, 75–78, 83–84, 87, 147–149, 207, 214
United States Naval Academy 9
U.S. Naval Hospital, Yokohama 19, 62
United States Navy 7; condition 7; social customs 62, 65; traditions 18, 35

Vallejo, California 228
Van Buren, Consul Gen. Thomas B. 116
Varnum, R.M. 107
Vassar Female College 27–29
Vicksburg, siege of 14
Victoria, British Columbia 42

Walter, Norman Ashleigh 136–137, 249*ch*14*n*7
War of 1812 230
Washington, DC 26, 140
Water Street 78
Waters, Gwendoline *see* Robinson, Gwendoline
Waters, Tom 63, 246*ch*7*n*2
West Point, New York 31
West Point Military Academy 29
Wheeler, Dr. Edwin 78–79, 81–83, 85, 125–126
Wilmington, Delaware 27–29, 33, 39, 43, 56, 102–104, 109, 207, 209, 218, 222, 224–226, 228–230

Yokohama 1–4, 216–217, 219, 221–222, 237; Amateur Rowing Club 214; appearance in 1879 20–22; appearance in 1891–92 53; foreign community 2, 47, 132; port opening 20; Racing Club 49; Yacht Club 215
Yokohama General Cemetery for Foreigners (*Gaikokujin bochi*) 96–97
Yokohama National University 2
Yokohama station 50, 135
Yokohama United Club 53; *see also* United Club